The Art of Raising a Puppy

The bell tower at New Skete.

THE MONKS OF NEW SKETE

THE ART OF
Raising a Puppy

Little, Brown and Company

Boston   New York   London

FIRST EDITION

Photographs by the Monks of New Skete

Excerpts from "East Coker" and "Little Gidding" in *Four Quartets,* copyright 1943 by T. S. Eliot and renewed 1971 by Esme Valerie Eliot. Reprinted by permission of Harcourt, Brace, and Jovanovich, Inc.

LIBRARY OF CONGRESS CATALOGING-IN-PUBLICATION DATA

Monks of New Skete.
    The art of raising a puppy / The Monks of New Skete. — 1st ed.
      p. cm.
    Includes bibliographical references and index.
    ISBN 0-316-57839-8
    1. Puppies. 2. Puppies — Training. 3. Dog breeds. I. Title.
SF426.M65 1991
636.7'07 — dc20   90-46685

20

Q-FF

Designed by Barbara Werden
PRINTED IN THE UNITED STATES OF AMERICA

The loneliness and solitude of man can be dispersed by spiritual intercourse, but man is of the earth too, and Nature lives in him and holds him fast. She is his mother, and just as in all young things that stray from home there is a yearning after associations which recall the color and the atmosphere of the old home now lost, so does the solitary man seek Nature, a life in Nature, Nature's answer, the animal that understands his voice and can respond to it.

— F. J. J. Buytendijk, *The Mind of the Dog*

There is a word from the time of the cathedrals: *agape,* an expression of intense spiritual affinity with the mystery that is "to be sharing life with another life." *Agape* is love, and it can mean "the love of another for the sake of God." More broadly and essentially it is a humble, impassioned embrace of something outside the self, in the name of that which we refer to as *God,* but which also includes the self and *is* God. We are clearly indebted as a species to the play of our intelligence; we trust our future to it; but we do not know whether intelligence is reason or whether intelligence is this desire to embrace and be embraced in the pattern that both theologians and physicists call God. Whether intelligence, in other words, is love.

— Barry Lopez, *Arctic Dreams: Imagination and Desire in a Northern Landscape*

Abba Xanthias said, "A dog is better than I am, for he has love and does not judge."

— *The Sayings of the Desert Fathers*

Contents

Acknowledgments

No one ever learns in a vacuum. The ideas and insights that make up this book are not only the fruit of our own experiences with dogs here at New Skete. They also reflect the constant interaction we have had with many different breeders, veterinarians, and trainers over the past twenty years, people who have graciously offered their time and knowledge to help us grow. In particular, we would like to thank Helen (Scootie) Sherlock, whose guidance, support, and understanding have helped us in incalculable ways, and Ruth Anderson, Roby Kaman, Wanda Rohloff, and Pat Rosson, whose friendship over the years has afforded us the opportunity to refine and analyze our ideas about breeding and puppy rearing.

We are grateful to Wendy Volhard, who graciously allowed us to use her puppy test for this book; to Peter Borchelt, Ph.D., who offered us important advice on socializing puppies in urban areas; to Thomas Wolski, D.V.M., who encouraged us in this project and who provided valuable suggestions at several key points; to Donald Lein, D.V.M., Ph.D., director of the diagnostic laboratory at Cornell University Veterinary School, who has generously given us his time and advice in matters pertaining to our breeding program; to Jeanne Carlson, whose ideas on puppy handling were especially helpful; and to Evelyn Mancuso, who for many years has unfailingly sent us valuable information from a wide range of periodicals.

Several people read early portions of the manuscript and provided important feedback and encouragement: Frank and Marcella Savage, William Congdon, William MacBain, and Robert Savage.

Finally, Kit Ward, Kelly Aherne, and Betty Power, our editors at Little, Brown, were especially helpful and encouraging throughout the writing of this book, and their careful handling of the text has made it clearer and more direct.

The Art of Raising a Puppy

Introduction

Monasteries are not as otherworldly as you might imagine. If they appear secluded and removed from the mainstream of society's activity, it is only because they attempt to create a climate that fosters an authentic engagement with life at its most profound and human level, something often lost amid the noise and distraction of today's world. When we are quiet enough, freed from all our inner noise and chatter, we can see with new respect the natural beauty and wisdom of the world around us and appreciate our ties to it. Such perceptive silence opens up our lives to healthy reverence and awe for all things; it creates a capacity for openness that is both humanizing and life-giving.

So what does all of this have to do with raising a puppy? A great deal, we believe. Our monastery is set in a quiet, rural area in upper New York State. For more than twenty years, as part of an effort to support ourselves, we have been actively involved in the breeding and raising of German shepherd dogs. We have also operated a training and consultation program that is open to dogs of all breeds. During this time we have worked closely with numerous professionals — breeders, trainers, and veterinarians — to deepen our understanding of all facets of canine care.

We have learned that our monastic environment offers us a unique perspective. Here we are forced to reexamine our attitudes about everything, including dogs. We are constantly challenged to become more open to the *language* dogs use to communicate with us. This experience confirms our deepest intuitions about the relationship of human beings not only with their dogs but with every aspect of their lives.

In our book *How to Be Your Dog's Best Friend*, we made

what we had learned about dog behavior and training available for other people and their dogs in the varied and diverse environments where they live. We hoped to foster in our readers a more realistic understanding of their dogs and an increased awareness of the benefits of their companionship. Drawing on our own experience here at New Skete, we described how dog training actually goes far beyond the elementary instruction of basic obedience commands; it must encompass a whole new attitude and lifestyle with your dog. It must touch on the levels of a dog's own life that have often been ignored. This is why we explored the broader issue of companionship itself.

We still firmly believe in this approach, and the years since the publication of our book have deepened our understanding and commitment to the principles we discussed there. We have been energetically involved in the breeding of healthier, sounder German shepherds, as well as in working with owners of many breeds on a counseling/training basis. These are demanding tasks, and the fact that we are a close-knit community permits us to pay careful attention to each of these concerns and learn from them.

But we still see that, elsewhere, ignorance on a vast scale continues to make dogs the victims of human thoughtlessness and abuse. As anyone seriously involved in the field knows, working with dogs and their owners is a bittersweet experience. It regularly forces us to witness the collision of philosophy with reality. The remarkable little puppy so filled with the capacity for life and companionship one week can easily become an incontinent, destructive, and hyperactive annoyance the next. We have seen this happen repeatedly. Poor management all too often leads to irritating or even dangerous behavior problems that quickly sever the human/dog bond before it ever has the chance to develop. While many of the dogs we deal with are intelligent, happy, and well adjusted, many are not. Every day we encounter dogs who have serious behavior problems, for whom obedience training has been described as the "last chance." Usually they clearly manifest signs of a bad start in life: poor breeding, limited handling and socialization as puppies, lack of owner understanding concerning the importance of proper diet, exercise, discipline, and obedience training. As we work with these cases, we cannot help but be convinced that most of these dogs, had they been treated more carefully and intelligently as puppies, would never have developed the problems that now beset them and their owners.

If we look honestly at the way many people today manage

their dogs, we are faced with a staggering reflection of irresponsibility and lack of compassion. It is difficult to speak of a dog as "man's best friend" when more than five million unwanted adult dogs and puppies are euthanized every year. We are not speaking here of the humane killing of animals done out of a sense of responsible stewardship. What we are pointing to is the massive human negligence that leads to euthanasia.

If anyone doubts the serious implications of this situation, a trip to the local animal shelter can be a real eye-opener. We recall one client who dismissed our advice about spaying her female shepherd, explaining she felt it was important for her children to have the experience of seeing puppies born. When we asked her how she intended to care for and give homes to the puppies, she responded that she really had not thought about it at all and that probably she would simply leave them at the local humane society when it was time for them to be weaned. We asked her what value such an experience would have if the principal lesson her children would learn is that puppies are cute little playthings which, when sufficiently used, may then be conveniently disposed of. Fortunately, our questioning convinced her of her mistaken thinking, and she left with a new respect for the implications of bringing puppies into the world.

In our view, the dog is not a possession, a personal commodity to be used solely for our own amusement or ego-gratification. Rather, it is a living, autonomous, yet highly social, pack-oriented creature that has an amazing capacity for companionship and love. Your role in determining whether this will be the case for your own dog is a vital one. Capacity is precisely that, a natural potential. A good relationship with your dog can be established only if there is an enlightened commitment to working with its proven needs, instincts, behavior patterns, and, yes, capacities.

We know numerous trainers and animal behaviorists whose talent and dedication have helped many a problem dog change its behavior, enabling it to live a happy and safe life with its owner. Often in such cases, owners find themselves changed as well. Nevertheless, it makes sense to avert behavior problems before they have the chance to begin. We have found that untangling behavior problems is a long and difficult process, requiring lots of time and energy and often a substantial financial investment. When faced with this prospect, many owners choose simply to give up their dog or else take the risk of trying to control the problem without precise and intensive retraining. Fortunate indeed is the problem dog whose owner goes the extra mile in trying to solve its particular problems.

The key to developing a healthy, rewarding relationship with your dog lies in getting off to a good start with him as a puppy. There is an art to raising a puppy that is not solely the domain of the naturally gifted. It can be acquired by any responsible owner; what is needed is a desire for true companionship, an openness to learning, and a willingness to invest time and energy in caring for and training the puppy. The more informed you are on the background, development, and training of your pup, the more you will approach him with the patience and understanding necessary for an enjoyable and rewarding relationship.

This is why we have written this book. Our hope is to provide a responsible guide to raising a puppy that will sensitize and educate owners to the many possibilities present with their new or expected companion. Our experience has been that when owners purchase their new puppy, they are rarely aware of just how much development and growth has already taken place in his life. They have only the most general idea of where he came from and lack a context from which to appreciate his true uniqueness. When this knowledge is acquired, it provokes a sense of responsibility that is more clearly in keeping with the nature of a human/dog relationship. Relating in a healthy way with their pup, they will change as their puppy changes, they will grow as their puppy grows. The bond becomes enriching and genuinely transforming.

In this book we will bring you into our world here at New Skete, using our experience as the lens through which you may broaden your understanding of your pup. By taking you through the birthing process and the critical early stages of a puppy's early development, we will show you how scientific knowledge underlies the practical world of breeding and caring for a puppy. This background will help you understand the experiences your pup has had before arriving in your home. Later we will look at the practical aspects of adopting a puppy, including how to evaluate your own needs, choose the right breed, and prepare and train your pup. The stage will then be set for a balanced, lasting relationship between you and your best friend.

CHAPTER ONE

Monk as Midwife

We are going on a walk with one of the brothers and his monastery shepherd, a daily, routine occurrence here that now has special significance. It is the fifty-ninth day of Anka's pregnancy. On this crystal-clear March afternoon, the sun lights up the ordinarily dark woods surrounding the monastery. Anka has been restless all day. Taking her into the woods for a brief walk quickly provides a promise of marvels to come, the first link in an intricate chain of events leading up to her labor. Now nature firmly yet silently displays signs hinting that gestation is nearing full term. It is important for the brother to notice these, for although the average span of gestation is sixty-three days, it is not unusual for a shepherd to begin labor as early as the fifty-eighth day after her first breeding. Throughout this time, Anka's body has been talking to her in new and different ways, and on this walk, its natural eloquence becomes an open invitation for us to witness the first promptings of new life.

As she runs along the trail, her swollen abdomen gently sways from side to side, and her wagging tail allows us a glimpse of an overly enlarged vulva. From a few feet ahead of us on the trail, she repeatedly looks back as if for reassurance, carefully avoiding the remnant patches of snow that have not yet thawed. The woods are as restless as Anka. The wind sweeps through the trees, gently ushering her back and forth along the path. Her quick, clipped panting is absorbed in the quiet commotion. Even the trees sense something is up.

Usually on such walks, Anka is beside herself with curiosity. From the time she leaves with her monk-master, she immerses herself in a feast of scents, darting from moss-covered tree stumps to low-lying wild junipers to old stone

hedgerows through which heaven knows how many animals of the woods have passed. Stopping frequently to listen, then quietly moving forward and gliding over the leaves that cover the path, she will occasionally startle a group of pheasants or wild turkeys, who then take to the air in a blaze of chaos. With intense delight she pursues, leaping in short bursts of energy.

Nevertheless, she quickly gives up the chase, responding to the voice of her master. This comes from steady training and a quality of bonding that overrides her prey instinct. A simple utterance of her name draws her back to the trail and she is soon preoccupied with wrestling a stick from a dead tree, eagerly providing herself with something to play with for the remainder of the walk.

Today, however, is different.

Anka seems to be lost in herself, in a very unusual way. Today, she lacks any of the casual playfulness so naturally manifest on ordinary walks. Now she displays impatience, constant circular pacing, rounded eyes, and nervous, panting tongue. She stops only to mark, a frequent need now that

there is constant uterine pressure on her bladder. As she reaches a spring-fed pond, she pauses momentarily to drink and then is off again, glancing quickly at the small shrubs that line the path.

Anka pausing momentarily along the trail.

Something clicks.

Suddenly bolting ahead, she disappears around a group of large pines. As we near the trees, we hear frantic pawing beneath a large, low-hanging evergreen. The branches move slightly, and dead leaves, pine needles, and dirt come flying out from beneath the tree, where Anka is improvising a nest. In her instinctively maternal way, she is preparing a natural den, a kind of cave. What makes this behavior remarkable is that none of it has been taught. Anka is a maiden bitch, only two years of age the week before. She is simply responding to a deep, instinctual knowing.

Were this den in the wild, it would have been more carefully planned. In research done on wolves, excavated dens have often been found in elevated areas such as cut banks or vacated caves, sites that provide a clear frontal view of the surrounding area. In fact, it is not uncommon for wolves to remodel vacant fox dens or even abandoned beaver lodges. The preferred soil is dry and sandy. Most dens are located

Anka nesting underneath a pine tree.

near rivers, lakes, springs, or other sources of water, owing to the mother's constant need for drinking water. Usually the entrance hole is one to two feet in diameter and linked to an inner chamber by an upwardly sloping tunnel up to ten feet in length. Often the female wolf will stay close to the site a full three weeks before she is due.

All of this is evoked by Anka's digging.

As we pause to observe her for some time, she finally settles comfortably on her side in what is now a smooth, slightly depressed circle. Barely visible from the outside, her face peeks out from beneath the branches. Her look, alert and expectant, indicates that she is rather pleased with herself. It is clear, however, that all of this is merely preliminary, for as of yet there have been no uterine contractions, no intense licking of the vaginal folds, no rapid lowering of her body temperature — the sure signs of the onset of labor. Nonetheless, it is obvious that the process is moving irrevocably toward the final stages of gestation and birth. Just before the walk, her temperature had fallen to 100.5° Fahrenheit, a sign that labor is still a little while away. At the beginning of labor, her body temperature will drop at least another full degree, to between 98.0° and 99.5°. We can see that Anka is aware of the mystery that is occurring within her. Responding to all sorts of natural cues, she is consenting to it, allowing it to culminate in its own time. Now she is ready to go back to the puppy kennel.

Here at New Skete, we have reserved a separate building for the whelping and raising of litters. There are six individual whelping rooms, which helps us to maintain a controlled environment that is clean, dry, and protected. Over the past week, Anka has been left for short periods each day in her whelping room, a ten-foot-square space, allowing her to become familiar and relaxed with it. It is important that she feel at ease and secure in the room, enabling her to focus entirely on the whelping. At New Skete, we use a plastic wading pool for the nest because it is durable, easy to clean, and has high sides that keep the pups safely confined.

Returning from the walk, Anka drinks more water and then climbs into the whelping nest and relaxes atop several layers of newspaper. Stretching out so that her abdomen is exposed, and panting heavily, she manages to rest for a time. Then we offer her a bowl of food.

Ordinarily, dogs are not inclined to eat from twelve to twenty-four hours prior to whelping: Anka, however, has never been known to spurn a meal, even early on in pregnancy when this would have been expected. She still has a voracious appetite and gulps down the meal without hesitation.

It is now late at night. As is our practice here in the monastery, Anka spends the evening in the room of the brother responsible for her. Before lights out, her temperature was 99.4°, and her panting was becoming increasingly labored. We spread old bedsheets on the bedroom floor in case she begins to whelp while her master is still asleep.

When a brother is expecting the whelping to begin in the middle of the night, he sets his alarm at regular intervals to check for the beginning of labor. This time it is hard to sleep anyway because of Anka's increased restlessness. By 1:30 A.M. her breathing has become a wildfire panting, her body tied rhythmically to her breathing and quivering incessantly as if she were chilled. Now, she licks her vulva ever more frequently, methodically preparing the birth canal by cleansing it. Getting up, she paws at the sheets she is lying on and pulls them into a nest. Then, quite suddenly, her face becomes rigid and her breathing stops. She announces her first contraction with a slight moan, her tail arching out behind her. As her breathing continues, a second contraction follows momentarily, and then a third. Panting then resumes with its previous intensity as Anka takes a slight rest.

Over the years, we have not found it unusual for whelping to develop like this, in the middle of the night, so when it is obvious that labor has finally begun, the brother simply takes it in stride as he goes about the last-minute preparations. Anka is understandably restless during this brief wait, pacing around as if she has to use the kennel run. This behavior is quite common, for the sensation of a puppy entering the birth canal seems very similar to that of a bowel movement. When offered the chance to use the run, however, it is immediately clear that this is not what Anka wants. All she wants is to have her puppies. She has no sympathy for the fact that it is 1:30 in the morning.

On the short walk from the monastery to the puppy kennel the only light comes from the stars, but Anka leads the way. Once in her room she makes a beeline for the whelping box and begins pawing at the papers in short, reflexive spasms of energy, the beginning of the birth ritual. Holding the newspaper on the floor of the nest with her paws, she starts to shred it violently with her mouth and then to moan and circle in the box. Finally settling down, she once again begins to lick her vulva. Four sustained contractions quickly follow. As she pushes, her lips purse and her ears are erect and held back ever so slightly, as if listening to her body. She then turns her head down to her tail and begins licking the paper. There beneath her tail is the final sign: a puddle of liquid. She has broken her water, that is, discharged her uterine liquid. Now the vigil begins in earnest, and the first pup can be expected within the hour. Anka is still lying against the side of the whelping box but pants more gently and almost fully closes her eyes. It is as if she were gearing herself up for the final thrust.

Here at the monastery it is our practice usually to have the mother's master be the attending brother, a presence

Anka giving
birth to a puppy.

intended to quietly reassure and assist her during the whelping. His responsibility is to be on hand, to watch as the whelping takes place, assisting where needed, and to see that things run as smoothly as possible. Should complications develop, his ability to respond immediately may be very important in determining whether a puppy will live.

After resting a half hour, Anka finally stirs and starts scratching at the newsprint abruptly; her back humps and her tail arches, causing her to squat low in the box, as if she were pressing herself together. There follows a long-drawn-out contraction, and suddenly the amniotic sac begins to push through the vulva. As the sac emerges gradually, like a gigantic blob of ink, the light from the heat lamp above the whelping box allows a glimpse of two silhouetted front paws reaching forward within the sac. As she pushes courageously, Anka lets out a scream that can only be described as primordial, her eyes like saucers as she is initiated mercilessly into motherhood.

She quickly begins to lick her vulva as if to help the rest of the sac out. As she does so, the amniotic membrane surrounding the pup is ruptured, and with it, a stream of fluid and blood drains to the floor. In the midst of it is a dark, wiggling puppy. Anka immediately consumes the placenta and begins to lick the puppy, tentatively at first, but then quickly and vigorously. While she is doing this, the attending brother cuts the umbilical cord and then uses a rubber-bulb syringe to draw fluid from the puppy's throat. A few quick squeezes clear the breathing passage, and the pup lets out its first gasps and wails, struggling as if annoyed by the gentle toweling that removes the amniotic fluid from its warm body. The scene reveals a natural harmony and coordination: Anka fully trusting her helper, and the brother respectful of her duties as well.

As soon as the pup is dried off, he is weighed on the scale, writhing back and forth on the cool surface. Anka's first puppy is a large male by our standards, a pound and a half, and when he is placed on the floor of the whelping box, he lifts his head up, waving it back and forth from side to side, and immediately crawls toward Anka, who is lying on the opposite side of the box. Anka encourages him by licking him and nudges him forward. There is no hesitation in the pup's movement as he stubbornly and insistently heads for the middle of Anka's body, somehow unmistakably aware of where the nipples are. To watch this is to witness the remarkable determination of this first pup to reach the teat. Puppies are born blind and deaf; the fact that their only working senses are smell and touch makes the movement all the more remarkable.

Moving forward, the pup forges straight to the rear teats, those with the most ample supply of milk, and he fastens himself onto one of them. The head bobs back and forth rhythmically as the pup pushes his paws against the teat in harmony with his suckling, a kneading motion that stimulates the flow of milk. Simultaneously his rear legs thrust against the floor as if to propel himself deeper into the breast. Anka continues to periodically clean the pup, then relaxes with a deep sigh, grateful that the ordeal is over.

She soon learns that it has only begun.

Some forty minutes after the birth of the first male, a resting Anka is suddenly roused and begins turning in the box and scratching the floor again. Her pup, now with a bright orange rickrack collar around his neck, is a sheen of black as he sleeps quietly in the box. To avoid injury during the next delivery, he is placed in a small cardboard box over a heating pad that is wrapped with a towel. It is necessary to keep the puppy very warm, for apart from the mother he has no capacity to regulate his own body temperature. The heating pad will keep him warm and content while Anka delivers her next pup.

As she passes through a similar chain of events for this second puppy, there is already a marked difference in Anka. It is clear that she now understands what is happening. There is very little moaning, only at the end of contractions,

Anka licking off the newly born pup.

and as her face sets, her look of determination is sober and resolute. Proper exercise during her pregnancy has left her with good muscle tone, and the steady contractions are strong and sure. Quickly, with a final quivering that ripples through the length of her body, she passes the second puppy while lying down. This one comes out gently with the placenta attached to the umbilical cord. As the amniotic sac containing the puppy lies momentarily on the floor, we clearly see the pup floating inside and moving its paws in a vigorous, thrashing motion. Anka quickly bursts the sac and cleans the pup off while he squirms around on the newspapers. After biting down on the umbilicus until it is only about an inch and a half long, Anka picks up the puppy in her mouth and begins to parade around the box in a circular motion. This precipitates a loud, high wail from the puppy that seems to satisfy Anka, and as she places him gently back on the floor, he twists and turns as she continues to lick him off. Though a bit smaller than the first, the puppy instinctively knows where to go, but his movement is slower than the first puppy's, and it takes Anka more licking and nuzzling to encourage him to move along. The first pup is now placed back in the whelping box to join his newborn brother, and both nurse contentedly on a fatigued mother. For several moments Anka scrupulously cleans the puppies off, then finally takes a long sigh and relaxes for the next episode.

Night passes into dawn. In the ensuing deliveries, Anka follows the same pattern, with one exception. It is the exception that brings an edge to the night of wonder. Anka has a difficult time in passing the fourth pup; for a long time, her numerous contractions yield nothing. Finally, when the pup does come out, all attempts to revive her are without effect. She is stillborn, fully developed, but her lungs are full of fluid. As seconds pass, we try not to lose hope; it is not unknown for a pup to begin breathing after several minutes. We repeatedly aspirate fluid from the pup's lungs and manipulate her back and forth in our hands. Dopram, a stimulant helpful in reviving slow-starting puppies, is then given under the tongue. Finally air is blown down the lungs, but in vain. The pup does not move. Anka looks on at the attempts with grave concern, clearly aware that something is wrong. Whimpering as the pup is kept away from her, she paces back and forth impatiently in the box, demanding something that cannot be given. Quickly the pup is taken from the room, and Anka retreats back to the remaining three pups, burying her disappointment in scrupulous attention to their needs. We hope that this reaction is linked to a quick forgetting.

Meanwhile, outside the room, holding a cold and lifeless pup vividly confronts us with the radical difference between life and death. The body is inert and limp. A white tongue sticks out of the side of its mouth. There is no potential, no vibrancy, nothing. It is a sad note amid a joyful chorus of life.

As the hours slide by, Anka takes her time delivering the final pups. There will be two more, alive, happily. The long pauses between pups invariably become valuable moments of reflection, important if we seek to appreciate the beauty of what is happening. In the moments of actual birth, events take place so quickly that we cannot take time to fully fathom the mystery that is occurring. Too much is going on at once.

An in-depth understanding of what has been happening this night is more the cumulative fruit of the entire whelping. Unlike human birth, which usually provides us with only a single delivery, here we watch birth occur again and again, giving us the opportunity to absorb the incredible marvel of it. Similarly, in equal measure, we become aware of the drastic change that has taken place in Anka, one that is as real as the pups that nurse at her side. It, too, is a birth of sorts, a birth into motherhood, and the event is inscribed all over her. As the puppies nurse, Anka is radiant; her clear eyes glow, and she grins in quiet fulfillment. Mother and pups bring to each other a completion beyond shallow sentimentality.

Anka and her litter at the end of the whelping.

By 10:30 A.M. Anka is resting quietly in her box with five healthy puppies close by her side. Each pup has a different colored rickrack collar for identification purposes. By using wide rickrack for male puppies and narrow for females, we can efficiently recognize pups at a glance. This will be particularly important later on when we begin making behavioral and structural notes about the litter. As they sleep, we can see quite clearly that there are three males and two females. Huddled close together, they sleep very restlessly; they twitch and jerk about continually. This entirely normal phe-

Monk as Midwife | 17

nomenon is known as activated sleep, which is linked to the development of the pups' neuromuscular systems. Healthy pups are never still for an extended time while they sleep. They shift and twitch repeatedly.

After her sixth puppy arrived, at 8:30 A.M., it was clear that Anka had finished. Her abdomen had shrunk, and a thorough palpation of her uterus indicated that there were no more puppies to come. Her breathing was relaxed as she stretched out on her side, exhausted, to allow the pups to nurse. When we see that whelping is finished, we usually give the mother an injection of oxytocin, a hormone that stimulates passage of any retained afterbirth or placenta. We then make sure that the whelping area is disinfected and fresh papers are placed in the box, after which the mother is cleaned by being rinsed off in a tub of warm water and then thoroughly dried. We then offer her a bowl of food, which, in this case, Anka devoured.

The conclusion of the whelping is quiet, a peaceful aftermath to the whole process of birth. The only sound heard is the occasional mewing of the pups. After all the concluding chores have been taken care of, Anka is left alone with her litter, and the monk, a tired midwife, retires for some much-needed sleep. Other brothers will check in on Anka periodically throughout the morning and afternoon to make sure that everything is well.

CHAPTER TWO

The Mystery of Development

A puppy's life clearly displays what characterizes the whole of life: the mystery of development. The entire universe, it seems, is in a continuous process of growth that extends from before the first moments of each individual existence to the end of life and beyond. Nothing is excluded from this movement, though our own consciousness of its breadth can be dulled by the chaotic pace of modern living. Too often we take it for granted, carelessly letting it pass unacknowledged. Our busy lives can easily grow insensitive to the basic wonder of life, leaving us spiritually impoverished and unhappy. This is perhaps why animals (particularly our dogs) are so important to us and why we benefit from their companionship: they root us in life.

Part of the joy in raising a puppy is the very concrete way it puts us in touch with the process of life and the natural world around us. Watching it grow takes us outside of ourselves and helps reestablish our own capacity for appreciation and wonder. But even more than this, we believe that paying attention to how a puppy grows is important for the health and vitality of the puppy himself. Studies have shown conclusively that the first sixteen weeks of a dog's life are of vital importance in determining his later behavior as an adult. Negligence by a breeder or new owner during this time can scar a puppy for life. Thus, if you hope to raise a puppy that will be a trusted companion and friend for the next ten to fifteen years, we believe that you can lay no better foundation for yourself and your dog than to understand thoroughly how he grows during this time of early change and development. That way you will be able to provide him with every available aid to help him grow to his potential.

A Miniature Adult?

Recently we were speaking with a gentleman who had come to us for help with his rambunctious three-and-a-half-month-old golden retriever puppy. As we sat talking about the difficulties he was having adjusting to his new pup, the conversation kept returning to his former golden, a calm, well-trained dog who had died several months earlier at the age of twelve. The man's eyes filled with tears as he recalled this dog, explaining how he had obtained her at seven months of age and how quickly the dog had been house-trained, learned her obedience exercises, and adapted to the rhythm of his daily routine. Then he pointed to his new pup, Argus, now wildly jumping up for attention at his side and nipping at his hands. Without trying to hide his frustration, he launched into a detailed account of the trials of the first month and a half, the disappointments and irritations he had experienced, and his growing fear that Argus was simply a deficient representative of the breed. He was at the point of giving up.

Listening to the man, it became clear that he was overlooking a very important point. All of the problems that he was having with Argus were being measured against the stability and maturity of his first dog, one he had obtained after a good deal of her development had already taken place. In fact, the pup that was now giving him so much trouble appeared to us to be a normal, energetic dog that was simply being mismanaged and misunderstood. When we asked about the circumstances in which he obtained the first dog, he replied that she was sold to him by a man whose sudden job transfer had required that he and his family move to Europe. Regrettably, they were unable to take the puppy with them. But from his description it was clear that the family had been very conscientious in raising their puppy, providing a sound basis for the relationship that had then developed with her. When we pointed this out, he was surprised. He had assumed that it was simply a "good dog." Not having shared with his first dog the initial months of growth so critical to adult behavior, he did not appreciate how dynamic an organism a young puppy is. As a result, he was now transferring a mistaken set of expectations onto Argus, based on what would be normal for an older, properly socialized dog. He was treating Argus as a miniature adult instead of as a fourteen-week-old puppy.

The Development of Individuality

It is not uncommon for puppy owners to have such misconceptions about early growth. Because they have not had a breeder's experience in observing young puppies' development, they usually have only a vague understanding of how it occurs, which can lead to the type of misunderstanding displayed by Argus's owner. To help prepare yourself for the proper reception and intelligent raising of a new puppy, you must take the time to examine the growth process in detail in order to gain some necessary insight into this otherwise obscure period.

The birth of a litter signals a new opportunity to observe ever more deeply a remarkable series of events: the passage of a totally dependent puppy into a fully mature dog, capable of true companionship. If you have the good fortune of such companionship you will no doubt understand how life enhancing it is. What you may not realize, however, is that the seeds of this capacity are planted very early in your dog's life, well before the dog has been placed in your home. The development of a puppy is not an automatic process that takes place precisely the same way in each dog. Rather, it is a dynamic unfolding of life, which, while following general patterns, reflects the subtle and ultimately mysterious interaction of three factors: type of breed, genetic makeup, and environmental influence. The results of this blending produce the wide variety of canine personalities. This is why raising puppies defies routine: each puppy is unique; each is an individual.

This insight is at the heart of what has become one of the most authoritative studies on dog behavior, *Genetics and the Social Behavior of the Dog,* by Drs. John L. Fuller and John Paul Scott. When these men began their research in Bar Harbor, Maine, on the effects of heredity on human behavior, they chose the dog as the subject of their work precisely because, like human beings, it shows a high level of individuality. Although their principal interest was in understanding why human beings behave the way they do, they believed that by studying the parallel development of dogs, they could make observations that would be of value in raising children to become psychologically better adjusted, healthier members of society. Their research helped distinguish the important relationships that exists between genetics, early experience, and adult behavior. Further, it illuminated as well the process of how a dog becomes an individual, unique creature. This work provided a more comprehensive and accurate view of canine behavior than had existed previously.

The complete results of the research, exhaustive and quite technical, go well beyond the scope of this book. Yet one finding in particular is important to single out because of its profound effect on our understanding of development and on the way conscientious breeders raise their puppies. It also provides a helpful framework in understanding how a pup grows. Over the course of the seventeen-year study, Scott and Fuller followed in detail the development of litter after litter of pups. From their data, they discovered that puppies pass through four clearly identifiable stages on the way to their full adult personalities. Each of these periods begins with natural changes in the puppies' social relationships, identified by the way the puppies relate to their environment. Taking into account the slight variations present from individual to individual, they noted these periods as follows: *the neonatal period*, from birth until the opening of the eyes at about thirteen days; *the transitional period*, from the time the eyes open until the opening of the ears at twenty days of age; *the socialization period*, which extends from approximately three to twelve weeks of age; and *the juvenile period*, lasting from this point until sexual maturity, which may occur from six months to a year or more.

Furthermore, in trying to determine why some dogs matured into happy, sociable pets while others did not, they found that the timing of early experiences played a vital role in the development and shaping of behavior. Events that occurred at a certain stage of a puppy's life affected its development more than if they had happened at other times. This suggested to them the presence of critical periods, special times when "a small amount of experience will produce a great effect on later behavior." Though somewhat ambiguous as to precisely how many of these periods there are, they singled out as the most important the period between three and twelve weeks of age, the "critical period of socialization," when a puppy has certain social experiences that exert the maximum influence on its future personality and temperament. Through correct socializing at the critical period, puppies could be conditioned naturally to behave as friendly, people-oriented pets.

While acknowledging the overall value of Scott and Fuller's study, not everyone is comfortable with the term "critical period." Critics argue that it is too absolute and seems to rule out the possibility of rehabilitating the animal that is the unfortunate victim of abuse and neglect during infancy. Instead, they prefer the term "sensitive period" as a clearer expression of the reality. Understood in this way, timing and quality of experience, though undoubtedly important factors in influencing behavior, are not straitjackets that frustrate any future attempts to modify behavior. Development is much more complex than that. These periods simply approximate the time when a pup is most naturally susceptible to socializing influences.

This does not change the main point; everyone is in agreement over the important role early experience plays in the development of personality. It follows that if you are serious about purchasing a puppy, you should try to get as clear an idea as possible of the sort of background it comes from. The more you can learn about a puppy's early experiences, the genetic heritage that it carries, and the general characteristics proper to its breed, the better prepared you will be to understand your pup and help it develop to its potential. Nevertheless, keep in mind that this knowledge will still not completely solve the riddle of your dog's individuality. There are limits to what science can teach us about our dogs. Ultimately, we must leave room for mystery.

Fathoming the way a dog develops means recognizing that our knowledge reflects general patterns and not absolute rules. We can never understand fully why a dog is the way it is. In fact, "the dog" does not exist, only individual dogs and the unique way each develops. Thus, in every stage, though the process of growth is basically the same, the particular way it manifests itself varies from pup to pup. This is why littermates, raised under the same conditions, will develop differently. The very nature and chaos of life disposes them to behave and develop in individual ways.

This diversity is not without purpose. The dog, like its chief ancestor the wolf, is a pack animal. While each dog has its own individual personality, it also has a pack identity that is manifest at a very young age, while still within the litter. These personality differences are important, for they highlight the fact that a pack is dependent upon mutual cooperation for its survival. Each member has its own role and importance; each is worthy of respect.

This is seen most clearly with wolves. Were a wolf pack made up entirely of *alpha,* or leader, personalities, its ability to stick together would be pressed beyond its limits. Continual infighting and challenging of one another would make pack unity impossible. Conversely, were all members submissive types, the pack would lack the leadership necessary for effective hunting. In both cases, survival would be jeopardized. What gives the pack its strength are the different personalities that exist within it. Yet these are linked directly with the experience of puppyhood. It is the diversity of developing personalities within the litter that forms the basis of an efficient, coordinated pack wherein each member's strengths and abilities are used to serve the whole, while benefiting each.

This insight is vital to understanding the domestic dog. As we return to Anka and her puppies, it will provide us with a general framework for discussing puppy growth and various related issues. Yet it is important to remember that we are dealing here with a litter of German shepherd pups. Having already spoken about individuality, it follows that the size and breed of a puppy can affect the rate of physical and behavioral growth. For example, toy breeds like the Chihuahua tend to mature sexually at around six months of age and reach adulthood at about a year. Larger, more slowly developing breeds, such as the Irish wolfhound and mastiff, do not reach sexual maturity until about a year and a half and reach adulthood from between two and three years of age. Every breed has a natural growth rate you should be aware of when you obtain your puppy. The purpose of following Anka's litter is not to make a standard of their growth rates, nor to chronicle every detail of their growth. Rather, it is to provide a real-life background for our discussion and to help you better understand the early development of your own pup.

Ordinarily, it is not our practice to give nursing puppies proper names. Here, however, for the sake of clarity, we have decided to give each pup a name so that it will be easier to follow his or her individual growth. The first two males born we named Sunny and Kairos, the next two females Oka and Yola, and the last male, who at birth was the smallest puppy in the litter, Kipper.

CHAPTER THREE

More than Meets the Eye

Neonatal Period: 1–13 Days

We are now standing next to Anka's nest, pausing a moment from kennel chores to observe her nursing her pups. They are two days old. Over her, a heat lamp glares down, ensuring that the room temperature is kept warm and constant. Anka is lying with her underside fully exposed, and the puppies are lined up next to each other in an orderly fashion, each on a teat, each kneading gently with its paws to stimulate the milk flow. They look like little sausages attached to her side, their smooth black coats giving off a sheen under the light. Anka pants heavily as they suckle; she is unconcerned by our presence, her gaze fixed on a solid white wall that borders the nest.

Minutes pass.

Finally the calm is broken as Anka shifts herself and stands up in the nest. As the pups lose their hold on her teats, they roll off to the side, helplessly landing on their backs, squealing at the sudden disruption. This lasts only for a moment. Quickly they right themselves, and after a few moments of crawling, they fall fast asleep next to each other. Anka, meanwhile, lies down on the opposite end of the nest and looks up at us.

After the excitement of Anka's whelping only two days before, the quietness of the following days might easily lull us into overlooking the critical importance of this time, when the principal activity of the litter is the alternating rhythm of sleep and nursing. In this quiet, however, a great deal occurs

A three-day-old
Oka nursing.

that provides the essential foundation for the future development of the litter.

Vulnerability

Entering a world they can neither see nor hear, newborn pups exist in a sensory desert, necessarily well insulated from harsh disturbances. They are entirely dependent on their mother; without her (or the equivalent care by humans) the pups will die. Anka knows this. During the first days she is continuously in the nest, leaving it only to eliminate. As mother, she is a portrait of concentrated, faithful attention to every detail of the puppies' lives, reflecting her profound awareness of just how vulnerable they are at this stage. It is a vulnerability that she is prepared to defend with her life.

An example: while the puppies are asleep, Anka remains awake in the nest, occupying herself with a rawhide bone. Suddenly her ears stand erect and she begins to growl tentatively. Strange voices drift into the kennel from outside. At once, she is out of the nest and flying through the kennel hatch into her outdoor pen, ferociously barking out her alarm. As she paces back and forth, her hackles are fully raised the length of her back and her tail stands straight up. Through this natural illusion, she appears substantially larger than life to the strangers, tourists who have inadvertently wandered too close to the kennel building. Quickly, they hurry off in the other direction, convinced of her seriousness. Anka, however, continues the warning, her bark echoing throughout the monastery grounds for several minutes. It is only when she is satisfied that the danger has passed that she returns to the nest and the pups huddled in the corner sleeping, oblivious to all the commotion.

The fact that the pups lie huddled together should not be interpreted as evidence of neonatal sociability. It is simply a way to conserve heat. Newborn pups have poor control over their body temperature, so they tend to gravitate to the warmest area of the nest. As soon as the first pup, Sunny, awakes, he begins a restless search for a nipple by inconsiderately piling over the others, ignoring their presence. His stirring causes a chain reaction of mad maneuvering, each pup struggling to reach one of Anka's teats. The scene confirms that the pups have no direct awareness of each other; their behavior is confined largely to reflex actions that they have been equipped with at birth, such as sucking, crawling, attraction to warmth, and distress vocalizations arising from pain, hunger, or cold.

Development

Conventional wisdom, reflected most authoritatively by Scott and Fuller, sees the newborn as an essentially tactile creature, incapable of any real learning, and relying exclusively on the sense of touch for getting nourishment. Other astute observers, such as Dr. Michael Fox, however, have demonstrated that this view needs to be broadened in several respects. First, it has been shown that a newborn puppy also possesses a well-developed sense of smell. In a cleverly conceived experiment, Fox coated a nursing mother's teats with aniseed oil, a rather unpleasant-smelling substance, and then let the newborn pups nurse. Twenty-four hours later these pups would crawl toward a Q-tip dipped in aniseed oil, held close to their noses. Other pups, who had not received this

The pressure of a four-day-old pup nursing on your finger is surprisingly strong.

previous exposure while nursing, recoiled sharply from the odor.

In addition, neonatal behavior reveals a capacity for the simple learning necessary for survival. A newborn puppy will instinctively begin a burrowing motion with her muzzle when she first contacts something warm. This helps her find her mother's teat, which can sometimes be hidden beneath her hair. Watching Yola behave this way shortly after she was born, and then again several days later, shows quite a difference. While at first she was awkward and clumsy, after three days she is quite adept at it. Proficiency clearly improves with time.

Over several days she also develops strength and assurance in nursing. It is interesting to feel the difference in sucking ability of a pup shortly after birth and then again after several days. We did this with Yola by letting her nurse briefly on our finger. Initially, after birth, the pressure was a little weak, unsure. When we repeated the exercise a few days later, the pressure was surprisingly strong and forceful. This shows us that what is taking place is an elementary learning that forms a basis for later, more complex, learning.

Regardless of how one interprets infant behavior and what constitutes *true* learning, the fact remains that the pups' brain, motor, and sensory capacities are all immature during this period. The pups exist in a naturally protected environment where they possess only the basic abilities necessary for their survival. None of the behavior we most commonly associate with dogs is present: no barking, tail wagging, walking, or play behavior. In fact, the most dominant impression we receive of newborn pups is their need for sleep. During the neonatal period puppies spend about ninety percent of their time sleeping, waking only to nurse or be cleansed by their mother.

This abundance of sleep is an absolute requirement. It is vital to the development of the central nervous system and the brain. A pup's brain waves measured with an electroencephalograph (EEG) during the first three weeks of life will show no difference whether the pup is awake or asleep. This indicates how immature the brain is at this time. In particular, the reticular formation, the section of the brain that controls sleep and wakefulness, has not yet developed sufficiently to keep the puppy awake for any significant amount of time. It is only after the third week that a marked change begins to register on the EEG, showing a clear differentiation between wakefulness and sleep, and only after four weeks that pups are able to stay awake for any sustained amount of time. Early in this initial phase, it is the quietness of sleep, combined with regular nourishment, warmth, and elementary movement, that establishes the proper climate wherein the brain and central nervous system may mature.

Gross immaturity characterizes the way newborn puppies look; they have an appearance entirely unique to this period in their life. The shepherd pups born to Anka bear no resemblance at all to the familiar image we possess of a noble German shepherd. At six to eight inches from their pug noses to the tips of their tails, they have rounded, oversized heads, barrel-shaped chests, and short, stumpy legs. Their ears are quite small and seem stuck to the sides of their heads. Their eyes are closed tight. If you did not know better, you could easily mistake them for members of a different species!

Even the ability to eliminate is a reflex completely

A four-day-old puppy.

controlled by the mother, since newborn pups are unable to urinate or defecate on their own. During the first three weeks of life they require the regular stimulation of their anal and genital areas by the mother's tongue to eliminate bodily waste, which the mother licks up immediately. This keeps the nest completely clean and avoids the serious health risk of waste buildup. It is also thought that this behavior may have another important function. Wildlife biologist L. David Mech, in his study on the wolf, points out that this activity may also establish the postural and psychological beginnings of submission in a pup once it matures. Although he was speaking specifically of the wolf, we have observed the importance of this in our own shepherds. Living as they do in a semipack environment, younger, more submissive dogs often assume the identical posture of a pup when submitting to an older, more dominant pack member. They roll over on their backs and expose their undersides while the other dog proceeds to investigate and sniff the anal-genital region. This posture defuses the threat perceived by the submissive dog and establishes pack hierarchy.

Two puppies in the later part of the neonatal stage, starting to investigate each other.

Individuality

All of these details form the background for the later growth of each pup. Overall, we now can see that what is occurring lays the foundation for the future, despite the obvious immaturity of a pup at this stage. It is a simple fact: life is growth. And even now, so early in life, the individuality we spoke of begins to be apparent. In keeping daily records of weight gain, we notice that Sunny and Oka are gaining the most weight and appear to nurse the most vigorously. In the nest they are the two who consistently manage to nose out the others when competing for a teat. These are preliminary signs of dominance that we pay attention to throughout their puppyhood.

Daily weighing also gives us a chance to note which puppies are more reactive, more vocal over being handled. Anka's second female, Yola, for example, seems quite sensitive to touch and squirms vigorously when held. When we place her on the cold scale, she cries more loudly than the other pups, who are not so alarmed by this experience.

The presence of this type of behavior in Yola raises an important issue about puppy development. Though some breeders and scientists claim that physical handling has no effect on a puppy during the first three weeks of life, our experience suggests otherwise. Over the years we have found it beneficial to introduce the pups to moderate amounts of human handling throughout the course of puppyhood, not simply during the period of socialization. This handling is actually a mildly stressful experience, though one that in no way reaches traumatic levels. Contrary to what might be expected, mild amounts of stress are beneficial to the development of puppies, provided the levels are not excessive.

Puppies exposed to mildly stressful experiences from a very early age (1–6 weeks) usually develop into dogs possessing superior problem-solving ability, with less emotional imbalance than their counterparts raised without such stimulation. In the young pup, in addition to raising the heart rate, stress causes an involuntary hormonal reaction in the adrenal-pituitary system, a help in resisting disease and handling stress. The overall effect of this is to prime the entire system, building it up and making it more resilient to emotionally challenging experiences later on in life. We find that at each particular stage of growth, specific types of handling enhance the development of pups and orient them in a positive manner to later life. When puppies receive consistent, nontraumatic handling, they become more outgoing and friendly and show less inclination to be fearful once they are older. When the time comes, you may want to ask your breeder what type of early handling your pup has received.

Here at the monastery, we schedule regular periods of handling with each litter, making sure that the pups receive daily handling from different brothers. This is possible because all of us work in varying degrees with the puppy program. Each brother is known by all of the mothers, who allow the pups to be touched and handled without becoming agitated. When we observe a pup who is extremely reactive to touch at this early stage, as Yola is, we make sure that she receives a little more stroking and handling than normal, though without overdoing it. Usually we do this once or twice a day, stroking the pup's body and gently massaging the stomach. We also like to lift a pup up and hold her next to our face, allowing her to rub against the texture of a beard as well as the softness and scent of skin. In general, we find that with such regular exposure, even pups that are initially very sensitive to touch show noticeable improvements in reactivity, becoming quieter and more accepting of these mildly stressful experiences over the course of the following weeks.

The final type of mild stress we introduce during the neonatal period involves the reduction of the puppies' body temperature. During the second week of life, we routinely administer a brief *thermal stress* by placing the pups in a separate, cool room away from the nest. The pups are placed in separate cardboard boxes for three minutes. This allows their bodies to sense a temperature fall, causing the adrenal system to respond with a brief output of corticosteroid hormones, which helps the pups resist disease later on. When we do this exercise, the pups begin to squeal and make a ruckus. When the period is over, each pup is returned to the warm nest and stroked gently. Immediately, all signs of agitation stop, and the pups are clearly relaxed and comfortable once again.

One additional point needs to be made in connection with early handling and development. Occasionally a whelping occurs that produces only one or two puppies. In such cases, we find that the pups can be prone to greater touch sensitivity because they do not have the ordinary amount of physical contact and stimulation with other pups that is present in larger litters. As we have mentioned, when there are a number of pups, they quickly become accustomed to tumbling and squirming over one another, and they adjust naturally to a variety of sensations. When such contact is absent, it is important for the breeder to take the time to handle the pups more often, introducing mildly stressful experiences into an overly sedate environment.

CHAPTER FOUR

Light Shines in Darkness

Transitional Period: 13–20 Days

On the twelfth day after birth, the first major change becomes visible in one of the puppies. Kairos, Anka's second male, starts to open his eyes. This signals the start of the transitional period of development, a week when many of the pup's sensory capacities begin to function. Contrary to what you might expect, this is no small accomplishment. A puppy's eyes do not open all at once. Instead, it is a gradual process that may take well over twenty-four hours to complete. At first, his eyes seem like dark little slits, begging to be pried open. Then, slowly, as if waking from a deep sleep, they become more visible, their grayish-blue, semiopaque color giving them an unworldly appearance. It is only after about five weeks that they will become clear and distinctive, reaching their adult coloration.

By the fifteenth day, all of the puppies in the litter have their eyes wide open, and a parallel increase in activity occurs. They crawl around the nest and continually bump into each other. Despite the fact that their eyes are open, the pups still do not see very well. Shining a penlight into Kairos's left eye causes the pupil to contract; quick hand movements in front of his eyes, however, evoke no reaction, and a sudden movement directly toward him does not make him blink. It is not until about twenty-eight days of age that a puppy is able to begin clearly distinguishing forms, though occasionally we have seen puppies become startled by quick, threatening movements as early as the seventeenth day, apparently the result of the quick movement of shadows.

Thus, during this time we take care not to make sudden movements that could frighten the pups.

Kairos at thirteen days old, just starting to open his eyes.

The process of eye opening is symbolic of everything that happens during this stage — a steady, gradual transformation. It is the first clear sign of the passage from the insulated newborn stage to the fully social existence of an adult. This is why this period is termed transitional. It is a week of dramatic change. By the end of this stage, albeit at an immature level, the pups will have received all the basic tools of life: sight, hearing, walking, the ability to eliminate by themselves, chewing, and a more refined sense of smell. This means that the pups will become much more sensitive to their environment than they were before.

For example, in the neonatal period, puppies have no sense of place. If you remove one and place him in a different room, alone, at the same temperature and on a comfortable surface, the pup will show no sign of distress, provided he is not hungry. Now, however, since they are becoming aware of each other and of their nest, when we repeat this same experiment with Kipper we see a marked change. After poking his head around for several moments, he suddenly begins to whimper and show signs of distress. The whimper then turns into a wail. Clearly he has no taste for being alone!

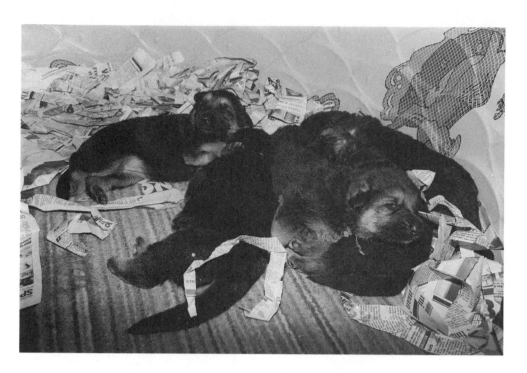

The litter huddled together at the beginning of the transitional period.

Once their eyes are fully open, the puppies begin investigating the small world of the nest. Looking at them now, you see that they are trying out life for the first time. They start to crawl backward as well as forward, and quickly move on to the first clumsy attempts at walking. This reflects the basic pattern of a puppy's becoming aware of himself and his surroundings.

At the daily weighing session on the sixteenth day, Oka and Sunny are the first to try walking. As they attempt to stand on the scale, they shake the platform precariously and are unable to maintain their balance. This, however, is just the beginning. The efforts continue when they are returned to the nest. Standing up ever so tentatively, wobbling from side to side, Sunny finally takes two brave steps forward only to flop over onto a sleeping Kipper, creating a very cranky outburst. Quickly crawling backward, Sunny barks indignantly in a comically high pitch and tries to stand up once again. Meanwhile, Oka is a little less adventurous. She simply tries to remain standing without falling over. Lacking the confidence to actually try walking, she finally crouches back down, crawls over to the other pups and falls asleep. Throughout all this, Anka looks on from outside the nest, with what seems to be mild amusement.

The seed of example has been planted. The following day,

all of the pups except Yola are beginning to give walking a try, basically following the same pattern. Together they are like a group of youngsters learning how to ride bicycles for the first time. They have little coordination and make numerous false starts, but their proficiency improves daily. By the end of a week they will be able to walk around the nest without much trouble at all.

About this time we also notice something else: the puppies are beginning to sniff around the nest. The refinement of the sense of smell that has been occurring since birth stimulates their curiosity, and they are soon snuffling each other, the newspapers, and Anka. If we pick them up and hold them close to the face, they sniff and try to suckle the skin, awkwardly probing the side of our cheeks. To reinforce this contact, we put an old cotton sock or unwashed cotton T-shirt into the nest so that the pups will be continuously exposed to human scent as they grow.

Given the fact that the olfactory area of adult dogs is fourteen times as large as a human's and that their overall ability to smell has been estimated conservatively as being one hundred times more sensitive, we can begin to realize the role scent plays in a dog's understanding of the world. While we depend more on our eyes for information about our world, dogs rely on their noses, learning much about their environment from the currents of air that pass their way.

Connected with this rise in inquisitiveness is the emergence of the upper canine teeth, which can be felt around the eighteenth and nineteenth days. Not only does this development set the stage for a transition to more solid foods, it is likely that the pressure of the incoming teeth prompts puppies to begin exploring each other. As Sunny's upper teeth begin to emerge on the nineteenth day, he starts to chew and suck on the other puppies' ears, paws, and muzzles. This happens in slow motion and is accompanied by the first signs of tail wagging. Like a chain reaction, the other pups begin to reciprocate. Thus the first real sessions of play begin.

Hearing is the last sensory faculty to develop, with the ears opening at about twenty days. Beginning with the seventeenth day we check for this by periodically clapping our hands over each pup's head. The noise elicits no response until the twentieth day. Then Oka and Kipper both react to it, especially Oka, who yips a little and starts moving backward — an understandable expression of alarm. She recovers quickly, however, taking several steps forward with an inquisitive look on her face as she mutters under her breath.

An elevation exercise. This is a mild stress during the transition period.

When testing to see if they can hear yet, we are careful not to clap too loudly, because what the pups hear for the first time can leave a strong fear imprint. Emerging from a silent world into one of sound should happen as naturally as possible to allow the pups to adjust without excessive trauma.

The type of mild-stress handling that we expose the puppies to during this week follows the same principle. Our purpose is to stimulate the puppy, not traumatize him. We find two exercises especially beneficial. In the first, an elevation exercise, we hold the pup up in midair until he begins to squirm and protest. We then draw him close and stroke him gently to allow him to settle down. In the second, a dominance exercise, we place the pup on a soft surface, roll him onto his back, and hold him there for ten to fifteen seconds. After the pup begins to struggle and squeal (and most do!), we turn him upright again and stroke him gently. After a week of this the pups associate the gentle petting with the end of stress. It also helps dispose the pups to human presence and handling, which we increase in the upcoming weeks.

One final observation: during the transitional period we begin a weekly grooming session that teaches the puppies how to be handled and touched; ears are cleaned, nails clipped, and the fur lightly brushed. At first, the novelty of the handling causes some minor protestations from the pups, but after a few sessions they come to enjoy it. We continue this practice at least once a week until the puppies are placed in their new homes. As you can imagine, this type of handling can make all the difference in your early attempts to groom and handle your puppy.

In this week of transition the newborns become more recognizably puppies both in the way they look and in how they act. They now stand poised for the move into clearly social existence. Yet this phase is transitional not only for the pups. Anka's behavior now shows a change of role. Before, she was in the nest continuously, jealously guarding and caring for her whelps; now she modifies her vigilance by spending time outside the nest, resting while her pups are asleep. She also wants to play. In the first two weeks even the sight of her much-loved tennis ball could not coax her away from the pups; now, a little bored, she eagerly jumps up at the gate to greet her master, trying to get him to play and take her for a walk. She has no worry about leaving her pups briefly. This is the beginning of her natural disengagement from the pups over the next several weeks until they are on their own.

CHAPTER FIVE

Opening Up to the World

Socialization Period: 4–12 Weeks

Twenty-two days have passed. Thus far, the only world the puppies have known has been a small, circular nest that replaces the ordinary den found in the wild. For the infant pup, the nest provides the stable, confined environment needed for all of its primary needs to be met.

Until now, that is.

For the past several days the pups have been much more animated in the nest, almost restless, indicating their growing sense of confinement. With Anka spending longer periods away from them, they start pawing at the sides of the nest in an effort to follow her. This morning, Sunny finally resolves to overcome the barrier. Slowly inching his way up the side of the nest, enough to place his front paws on top of the edge, he peers over and spots Anka snoozing on her dog bed nearby. He yips impatiently, but in vain; Anka ignores his calls. This is just the incentive he needs. With fearless determination and daring, he stubbornly attempts to scale the side. Hoisting himself up, his rear legs pumping wildly against the side of the nest, he manages to clear the top, only to tumble down onto the hard floor of the whelping room. This unexpected drop elicits a series of high-pitched shrieks that rouse Anka to his aid. Licking him reassuringly, she settles down next to him and lets him nurse. Meanwhile, the commotion rouses the other pups, who now peek over the edge of the nest. They quickly become a chorus of screaming, impatient siblings. It is only a matter of time before each of them will join his or her brother.

Sunny's venture out of the nest occurs near the beginning of the all-important *socialization period* — nine weeks of intensive exposure to life during which the puppies' personalities blossom. Practically overnight their behavior changes. Their growing abilities to perceive and move about, which we began to see in the transitional period, suddenly become coordinated. Clearly, they have reached a milestone in their growth. Though still requiring plenty of sleep, the pups are more energetic and awake for longer periods. They now become animated and curious. Their play with each other includes the barking and tail wagging we identify with adult behavior. Though still immature, the brain and central nervous system have developed enough for the pups to interact seriously with their surroundings. Now they begin to learn quickly!

What Is Socialization?

By socialization we mean two things: first, the positive adjustment a puppy makes to the many aspects of her life, whether other dogs, people, places, or objects; second, what we do to foster this. A puppy is extremely sensitive to socializing experiences between three and twelve weeks of age, when their effects are permanent for better or worse. Previously the puppy was psychologically isolated from her environment, protected by the lack of sensory development. Now that has changed. She is vulnerable in a new way.

Naturally the pups are not aware of this. At the beginning of this stage, their basic orientation is one of openness. Their senses are receiving an abundance of stimuli whereby they gain an immediate perception of their surroundings. Everything is new and interesting, and the pups start to show real curiosity. They are ready to form their first genuinely social relationships with their mother and littermates.

Because of this positive thrust toward life and growth, we keep the pups' environment stable and capitalize on this natural inquisitiveness with a proper blend of new experiences. The mother should still spend the majority of her time with the pups. Since they are in the process of adjusting to their newly found senses, we do not overwhelm them with excessive stimulation and noise during the first week and a half of this period. At this time, though they are naturally disposed to investigate their small world, too much stimulation can cause fearfulness. Normal fear and avoidance of new experiences arises naturally later in the period, once the brain and central nervous system have matured to their adult levels. This is commonly referred to as the "fear period" and is discussed later in the book.

In the wild, this natural rhythm of attachment and avoidance initially bonds a pup to its pack, then later makes it wary of strange animals and new, potentially dangerous circumstances. It is a survival mechanism that instinctively keeps puppies away from predators. During the first twelve weeks of life, the only social contacts a wolf pup has are with its mother, littermates, and immediate pack members. This keeps the pup safe, reinforces attachments to the pack, and thus creates a greater pack solidarity and security. In domestic dogs, the pattern is the same: attachment, then displays of avoidance.

Ideally a pup is raised with a variety of the right kinds of social experiences, first with his mother and littermates and subsequently with the wider world. Since domestic dogs are expected to behave in ways that are socially acceptable to humans, a puppy needs plenty of human contact and exposure to all sorts of common, everyday things. This lays the foundation for a positive attitude toward new people and new experiences and teaches the puppy that human beings and their world are part of his pack. If deprived of these contacts, a pup will develop fearful reactions to people and grow up socially maladjusted and emotionally disturbed. At that point reconditioning, even if possible, is extremely difficult (and very expensive).

This explains why adult wolves are almost impossible to domesticate. While there have been numerous accounts of wolf pups that were raised and socialized by humans into trusted companions, it has long been known that adult wolves are extremely resistant to being tamed. Lacking any exposure to humans during the critical period of socialization, they have no basis for making the connection. Quite understandably, when faced with the prospect of an encounter with a human being, their tendency will be either flight or, when cornered, displays of aggression.

In *Understanding Your Dog*, Eberhard Trumler, a noted ethologist in Germany, recounts the story of how he deliberately raised a litter of dingoes (Australian wild dogs) in such a way that they had no contact with human beings between their third and seventh weeks of life. Except for the presence of other pack members, they were raised by their parents just as they would be in the wild. The results were predictable. They developed into shy, wild dogs who avoided any contact with humans and would hide whenever Trumler entered their yard. Since one of Trumler's purposes was to observe the behavior of dingoes in an essentially natural setting, the deprivation did not matter. The animals acted in an ordinary fashion. Similar deprivation for domestic dogs, however, has more serious consequences.

When Scott and Fuller raised a number of litters in large, open fields, they found that pups raised without human contact would show fearful reactions to humans at five weeks of age but could readjust over two weeks' time if handled often. Puppies first exposed to human contact at twelve weeks of age, however, immediately reacted very fearfully and fled from the experimenters. They acted essentially like wild animals and were socially irretrievable. They had missed the vital contact during the critical period.

A practical application of this discovery was made by Clarence Pfaffenburger at Guide Dogs for the Blind (San Rafael, California) during the 1950s and 1960s. Operating a breeding program specifically designed to produce qualified guide dogs, and working closely with John Paul Scott, he confirmed the necessity of regular socialization if pups were to have any hope of becoming successful guide dogs. Pups needed regular human contact to acquire the emotional stability necessary for such work. Without it, not only were they unsuited for guide work, but they made poor companion dogs as well. The implications for all dog breeders were self-evident.

Pfaffenburger also found that the initial benefits of socialization could be lost if puppies were left in the kennel too long after the conclusion of personality testing at twelve weeks of age. If a properly socialized pup spent three additional weeks in the kennel without deliberate socialization and then was placed in its new home, chances were high (70 percent) that it would be unable to take responsibility for its blind master as an adult guide dog. Pups placed in homes immediately after the testing, however, had a 90 percent success rate.

These examples underscore the importance of what happens in the life of your puppy before you obtain him or her, as well as the absolute importance of socialization. We believe that we can use this information to distinguish two phases within the period as a whole. The first centers on a pup's interaction with other dogs and takes place roughly between four and six weeks of age. During this time, though human contact should not be absent, it is not the main focus. Major changes in behavior come about as a result of the puppies' interactions with each other and with their mother. This period flows into the second phase, when the pups begin to focus on socializing with people. This interval extends from five to twelve weeks of age, thus allowing for a week's overlap when the pups require both forms of social exposure. These two phases highlight the basic social adjustments most pups need to make if they are to live happy, balanced lives.

Phase One: Socialization with Dogs
(4–6 Weeks)

To make these ideas clear, let us return to Anka and her pups. Once the pups start getting out of the nest, we remove the nest and leave them on the floor, with Anka's comfortable dog bed in the corner to sleep on. As they move around now much more freely, they begin to eliminate on their own, away from the bed, on newspapers that cover the floor. Their instinctive aversion to messing where they sleep is connected with their mother's meticulous care of the nest earlier.

Wildlife biologists observe the same behavior in the wild with wolves. There, three-week-old pups emerge from their den and start playing with each other in front of the entrance. As they do so, they urinate and defecate on their own, gradually learning to pick spots away from the den. By six to seven weeks of age, the pups select particular "scent posts," areas where they will consistently relieve themselves. The movement away from the nest, coinciding with the ability to eliminate by themselves, reveals the natural tendency of both wolves and dogs to keep their sleeping areas clean. Knowing this will help later on when you begin housetraining your puppy in his or her new home.

This is why a filthy, disorganized breeding kennel not only reflects badly on the breeder, but could also spell future health and behavioral problems for you as well. When soiled papers are not picked up regularly, the pups wrestle and stomp in their own feces and lose their natural aversion to soiling where they play or sleep. They also quite likely will begin eating their own excrement. This may lead to health

Anka nursing her five-week-old litter. At this stage, she begins to wean them naturally, allowing them to nurse only for several seconds.

problems as well as habitual stool eating (coprophagy) as adults. Thus, kennel cleanliness is essential for proper socialization and should be an important consideration in determining where you purchase your new puppy.

A Gentle Weaning

During the fourth week, the puppies grow so rapidly that their requirements for food increase beyond Anka's ability to produce. Anka becomes more and more impatient with their constant demands. She is reluctant to let the pups nurse and avoids them by escaping into the outside holding pen where they have not yet learned to follow. If confined to the pen with them, she no longer lies down but moves constantly and snaps when they try to nurse from her. When she finally relents, she remains standing, forcing the pups to nurse standing up. But not for long. After several minutes she ends the session and moves away, leaving the pups yipping and barking as they stubbornly follow after her for more.

Because their sharp little teeth have begun to emerge, Anka's ability to let them nurse for long periods of time diminishes. It is simply too uncomfortable for her. This is a

Anka's litter gobbling up its meal.

sign that it is time to wean the pups. During the next several days we will introduce the pups to semisolid blends of cottage cheese and high-quality canned meat, gradually working up to moistened puppy kibble (dry puppy food). The weaning process should occur gently, giving the pups time to get accustomed to a new diet as well as to prolonged absences by their mother. To grant Anka some relief, we place an elevated platform in the whelping room that allows her to retreat from her pups while still remaining with them. Three- to four-week-old pups still require the stabilizing and secure presence of their mother. Since they are being bombarded with an abundance of new experiences and stimuli, abrupt separations would be harmful.

Finally, we bring the pups their first solid meal, a gruel of cottage cheese and warm water that is easy to digest. As we approach the pen, however, we notice that they are already huddled around what we discover to be regurgitated food. As they eat this, Anka sits content in the far corner. This strange sight is actually the most natural of procedures, and the puppies are perfectly satisfied with the fare. Sunny and Oka adapt to the new diet almost immediately. The others, however, pause and cough frequently as they chew and swallow.

Anka pinning Oka to the ground when she tries to nurse.

Soon Kipper tires of the feast. He looks up, pauses, then walks straight through the middle of the pile toward Anka, disturbing the others and tracking food all over. Seeing his intentions, Anka curls her lip and snaps purposefully at him. This show of force has its desired effect as Kipper yips and retreats. The others continue eating.

This is precisely how weaning begins with wolves. In the wild, however, the regurgitated meal is provided by other pack members as well as the mother. Once the pups are about three weeks old, the mother resumes hunting with the pack while the pups stay in their den. When the pack returns, all the adult members regurgitate a semiliquid gruel, which the pups gobble up eagerly. This is a normal transitory stage until the pups can begin eating solid food. The pups solicit regurgitation from the adults by submissively licking at their mouths. This is the principal method of feeding for wolf pups, even though the mother continues to provide milk until seven to ten weeks.

Weaning also initiates a new emphasis in social relation-ships. By the middle of the fifth week, the periodic absence of the wolf dam* associated with weaning gradually causes the pups to focus their attention more on each other than on their mother, and they learn to be less dependent on her care.

*"Dam" is the usual way of referring to a canine mother.

The litter in the exercise yard. Here, Kairos is trying to take the small box away from Sunny and Yola is starting to lick submissively at Oka.

It is the same with Anka's pups. For several days we progressively lengthen the time Anka spends away from the litter, and the pups make the adjustment easily. Now, as we pass the litter while doing chores, we see that if they are not sleeping together they are playing together, inventing innumerable healthy games, visibly behaving like a pack. As we watch, Oka parades around the pen with a squeak toy. The other pups follow her, eagerly trying to pull it from her mouth. Sunny manages to pry the toy away from her, and the game continues until a noise from outside causes them all to stop and listen. Kairos is the first to go outside and investigate, and the others follow.

Puppy play is anything but frivolous. Not only does it develop muscle coordination, it also exposes the pups to spontaneous social situations they must learn to handle. When Sunny has Kairos rolled over on his back and is playfully biting him, they are beginning to learn social roles — in this case, dominance and submission. If Sunny bites too hard, Kairos retaliates in defense, letting Sunny know that he has gone too far. This happens often with all the pups and teaches them how to use their mouths gently. Playfighting is usually kept friendly, and, particularly early in this period, pups easily exchange roles as play-fights become highly ritualized periods of learning. For example, during the

Play-fights are highly ritualized periods of learning. Through play, pups learn the basics of appropriate social roles.

fifth week, Yola, the most submissive pup in the litter, stands over Sunny with her jaws buried in his neck, growling and shaking her head. Sunny accommodates this, acting out submission by remaining on his back and gently pawing her face.

This constant interaction with each other gradually establishes a loose hierarchy within the litter. The pups learn whom they can dominate and whom they cannot. Were this development allowed to continue uninterruptedly, roles would be completely defined by about four months.

This initial interaction is the basis for the healthy adjustment of pups with other dogs, as well as their own self-identity as dogs. Puppies need this time of familiarization with each other and with their mother. If a puppy is separated from her mother and littermates before six weeks of age, she will not have learned the basic social behavior proper to her species. Serious behavior problems can suddenly develop as the dog matures. One client brought us his seven-month-old American Staffordshire terrier for training after he had attacked another dog in a local park. The horrified owner, totally unprepared for such a spontaneous outburst of aggression, could not understand how this wonderful pet, so gentle and friendly with people, could ever have done such a thing to another dog.

We discovered that the man had obtained the pup from a

Dominant behavior in a six-week-old puppy as Sunny begins to mount Kairos.

friend at only four and a half weeks of age. From that time on, the puppy had been raised exclusively with people and had been given no real exposure to other dogs. Since he had formed no social bonds with other dogs, he did not recognize his kinship with them nor learn the basic social interaction proper to dogs. The result nearly cost the man his dog.

Between four and six weeks of age, if the primary social focus is on people, the pup will be oversocialized and tend to identify only with people. This inclination can even be expressed sexually. One woman contacted us after her young keeshond mounted a guest's leg at a dinner party she was giving. The embarrassing incident had not been the first of its kind, although former occurrences had been confined to immediate family members, who were amused. Now, however, the problem had come out of the closet. Again, questioning revealed that the dog had been obtained at a very early age. Since the people lived in an apartment in New York City, the dog was always walked on leash and was prevented from interacting with other dogs. The owner was afraid of his "catching something," even after four months of age, when all his vaccinations had been completed. Lacking this ordinary experience with other dogs, the dog had begun to identify exclusively with human beings, even to the point of displaying overt sexual behavior.

Never adopt a puppy under six weeks of age. The interaction occurring within the litter at that time is too critical to a pup's development. Puppies depend on these natural relationships in order to grow up normally. Then they can enter fully into the next stage of socialization, that of adjusting to the presence of people in their lives and learning to interact with them.

Phase Two: Socialization with People
(5–12 Weeks)

The sixth week of life (35–42 days) is pivotal in puppy development. The main emphasis of socialization begins to shift from mother and littermates toward human beings and the world beyond the nest. Building on social behavior already developed, the pups refine their abilities by playing together and manifest new behavior that helps them experience the world. Sexual play now becomes apparent, with mounting common in both male and female puppies. This is an ordinary part of puppy development that helps teach them normal sexual responses in maturity. In addition, mounting is used to communicate dominance. Even among females it is not unusual to see a dominant female mounting a subordinate. This happens from time to time with Oka and Yola, another sign of Yola's more submissive nature.

By now the pups have developed sharper eyes and ears. They have much clearer depth perception. Their muzzles are beginning to elongate, permitting greater facial expressiveness, and their vocal patterns cover a wider range. Their legs are stronger and more coordinated, allowing them to move where they will. They show an eagerness to explore and investigate everything, approaching new objects and people without hesitation. The brothers working at the kennel take short breaks between chores to play with the pups, and regular times are set aside each day for specific types of handling, with individual pups as well as the entire litter. During this time, puppies require all the attention they can get, and their reactions help us gauge how they are developing.

Whenever we approach the outside holding pen, whistling, talking, hand clapping, or jingling of keys brings the puppies charging out to greet us. As we crouch down, they paw at the fence to get our attention and yelp with excitement while we pet them. We intentionally make eye contact with each of them, since puppies instinctively focus on the faces of those they greet, human and canine alike. As we do so, their gazes are fixed and unconcerned, showing no signs of fear. Our animated, friendly facial expressions and voices, combined with patting and stroking, reinforce the contact in much the same way that a human mother playfully coos at her infant. Anyone who has experienced the silent, absorbing gaze of a faithful companion dog during a relaxed moment or its focused attentiveness during obedience work understands its value. Fostering nonthreatening eye contact in puppyhood lays a solid foundation for training and for long-term relationships.

A Special Pup

The greeting ritual with Anka's pups reveals some differences between them. After the initial eye, voice, and hand contact ceases, most of the pups are distracted by other things. Kipper, however, is different. He continues to yip long after we have stopped the greeting. He is very people oriented and repeatedly tries to weasel in on our attention. He nudges in and crowds the other pups out of the way, mouthing and pawing playfully at our hands.

What is remarkable is that Kipper, at six and a half pounds, is the smallest in the litter. With Sunny the largest at nine pounds, there is enough of a size difference to warrant destroying the widely held belief that the smallest in the litter, the "runt," is an inferior puppy. While the expression "runt of the litter" is commonly used to designate the smallest pup, as a technical term it refers to an animal that is stunted, that fails to grow to a size within the normal characteristics of the breed. Though a true runt *may* have a congenital defect affecting the heart or digestive system that explains its small size, this is not necessarily the case. It may be perfectly healthy and normal in every respect other than its unusually small size.

When the term is incorrectly applied to the smallest in the litter, it presumes deficiency. Variations in the size of newborn pups can be the result of large litters, positioning in the womb, breedings that occur over several days, or the particular genetic makeup and growth pattern of the pup. We know many runts who have matured into marvelous companion dogs, and we have seen numerous instances in which the smallest pup in the litter turns out to be the biggest at maturity. One of the more memorable dogs in our program, Caralon's Elko von der Lockenheim, was the smallest pup in his litter, yet he matured into a large shepherd, bigger than all his littermates.

In addition to a marked orientation toward people, Kipper displays a strong survival instinct brought out because of his size. At feeding time he refuses to be bullied by his bigger brothers and sisters. As they ravenously attack the food, Sunny suddenly snaps at Kipper in an effort to scare him away from his fair share. Kipper, however, yields nothing, snapping back quickly and convincingly, and Sunny retreats back to his side of the dish. Occasionally when a dominant puppy becomes overly aggressive toward its littermates during feeding, we intervene, giving the offending puppy a brief shake by the scruff of its neck, just as its mother would when disciplining it. If necessary, we feed it separately. Kipper, though, knows how to take care of himself.

Puppies need to be looked at individually and not prejudged according to simplistic criteria. If you are considering adopting a pup of normal temperament who happens to be the smallest in the litter, there should be no problem with this provided you have the option of returning it should a veterinary examination reveal a defect.

A Growth Environment

Full socialization extends well beyond ordinary encounters with people. We conceive of socialization as contributing actively to the emotional development of each puppy by providing him or her with as wide a range of safe experiences as possible. There should be plenty of variety, with care taken to offer different sights, sounds, and textures. The pup's world needs to be enlarged by exposure to surroundings different from the familiar whelping room. It is of no benefit to the pup to be left cooped up all day in a monotonous kennel room with only a few toys and limited opportunity for play and investigation. Life in the puppy kennel needs to be balanced by other experiences and environments that challenge curiosity and intelligence. Since this is so, when you are

We get the pups accustomed to a variety of surfaces early on. Here, the pups learn to come on concrete steps as Olga Barnet, a puppy tester, claps her hands enthusiastically.

looking for a puppy, be sure to discuss with prospective breeders how they accommodate this requirement with their pups.

We begin by getting the pups accustomed to a variety of surfaces — gravel, grass, woodchips, tile, cement, linoleum, and dirt. Anka helps with this because the pups are inclined to follow her. She leads them over the gravel, dirt, and grass surrounding the puppy building, romping and playing with them, occasionally pinning one playfully to the ground with her mouth or herding an errant pup who has wandered a little too far from the main pack. After several days of these sessions, the pups fearlessly and confidently march around as they play together on any of these surfaces.

We can easily lead the pups on short walks to the edge of the woods to let them explore a new world of sight and scents. The pups do this with obvious enthusiasm, investigating the plants, branches, insects, and animal odors at their level, things they have no contact with in the puppy kennel. Sunny picks up a leaf and mischievously taunts Yola,

For a young puppy, a walk in the woods exposes him to a new world of sights and sounds.

who cannot quite get her mouth on the other end. Several yards away, a robin lands on a bare branch close to Kairos. He stares at it quizzically, then backs up and mutters threateningly under his breath. The robin flies off, leaving Kairos bewildered over its sudden disappearance. The other puppies, involved in their own explorations, take no notice.

Since the pups are still young and tire easily, after ten minutes we start jingling keys (a practice we have already begun at meal times) and the pups begin yipping excitedly as they eagerly follow us back to the kennel. Before placing them back in the pen, we conclude the session with lots of praise and pats on their heads.

This technique of conditioning the pups to sound teaches them to associate a specific noise with a particularly pleasant experience. We like to use keys, since dogs respond well to their high pitch. As soon as the pups begin eating regular meals, at weaning, we jingle keys right before placing the food in front of them. The pups quickly learn to recognize the keys and connect them with food. Soon it is possible to link the keys with any pleasant experience. We simply jingle them and follow up with the pleasant experience, usually petting and praise. This conditioning also forms a helpful foundation for teaching the recall, which will be described later in detail.

Sound conditioning. Puppies can be conditioned to come by jingling a set of keys and following up the recall with lots of praise.

It is important to vary environments. During the day, we let the pups stay outside to play. In special outdoor fenced-in areas behind the kennel, we create play spaces that are interesting and mentally stimulating. Old tires and large clay conduit pipes make excellent, safe obstacles and tunnels for the pups to explore and play in. The pups will play there for hours with large cardboard boxes, clean used plastic bleach bottles, old tennis balls, and squeak toys.

Even the puppy room itself can be made stimulating. Aside from providing plenty of toys, we also suspend a tennis ball or nylon ring from a fine chain at their eye level. When the pups tug at it, a cowbell attached to the top of the chain rings loudly. Not only does this develop eye coordination, it gets the pups used to unusual noises that might otherwise frighten them.

We tune radios to classical-music stations in the puppy rooms and periodically blow whistles, clap together wooden blocks, jingle bells, or turn on the vacuum cleaner throughout the day. In private sessions with each puppy, we encourage him or her to sniff, lick, and examine the noisemaker before and after the noise, making sure never to praise or comfort a puppy who shows fear. A puppy is praised only for reacting positively to a stimulation with alertness and

Puppies love to investigate and play in tunnels in their play yards.

Puppy rooms should be mentally stimulating, utilizing toys and safe objects to help the pups develop.

It is vital to expose puppies to a variety of different situations. Here, two seven-week-old pups learn to walk up and down stairs.

curiosity. It is vital that exposure to a variety of sounds be an important aspect of socializing. In our increasingly noisy world, dogs must deal with the constant stress of loud noises. Exposing puppies to a variety of unusual sounds at this point in the socialization process helps them get used to this and prevents fearful, nervous reactions later on.

Each litter requires plenty of individual attention and handling. Breeders must make sure pups get accustomed to men, women, and children. Here, a young pup is socialized with a visiting family.

Individual Attention

From the fifth to the seventh week it is imperative that each pup be handled individually by different people, both men and women, every day. Dealing with the litter as a group often masks significant traits that are visible when a pup is forced to relate to a human being alone. Puppies derive confidence and security from each other. A pup that appears lively with her littermates and comfortable in her puppy area may act hesitant and fearful when placed by herself in a strange room with an unfamiliar person. By spotting poor reactions early in the socialization period, breeders can make sure certain puppies receive the personalized attention that helps them better adjust to people.

Our practice is to make sure each pup receives sufficient individual handling every day at this age. During these sessions we combine simple play with a concluding restraint/ petting exercise that helps familiarize the pups with having their front and back paws touched, mouths opened, and muzzles held. Combined with weekly grooming sessions, this helps modify any touch sensitivity.

We also utilize community members who are ordinarily not directly involved with raising the puppies, namely the nuns, the married Companions, members of our parish —

Young pups cannot get enough handling and love.

even retreatants. We bring the pups over to the monastery for a community gathering once a week, allowing them to interact with a wider circle of people in an unfamiliar environment.

This requires time and effort. There is no magical shortcut, no room for compromise when it comes to the emotional growth of puppies. Breeders who are genuinely concerned about their pups set aside quality time for daily encounters because they understand how much of a pup's future personality is shaped by these seemingly insignificant moments. This play is creative in the deepest sense of the term, allowing the finest elements of a puppy's personality to develop.

CHAPTER SIX

Testing the Puppies

By the time the puppies are six weeks of age, much of our attention is devoted to the critical issue of placement: where are the pups going and why? Puppy placement should never be arbitrary. Rather, it should be the result of careful consideration and planning, something that evolves out of a respect for puppy and person alike. Different puppies are suited to different circumstances, and it is important for a breeder to come to an accurate appraisal of each pup's possibilities.

You will want to consult your breeder regarding placement procedures. At New Skete we appraise puppies in several ways. First, since we take notes on each litter from birth and are fully aware of its genetic background, we have a sizable amount of information on each pup by the time it is six and a half weeks old. Its development is looked at in detail, and a general impression is formed about its adaptability to various circumstances.

We also interview many of our puppy clients well in advance of the time they receive their puppy. This allows us to reach a mutual agreement on the type of puppy that will be best for them, as well as to measure how serious they are about certain responsibilities. Unfortunately clients are not always realistic about their true needs. For example, people often say they want a *Schutzhund* puppy — with no real understanding of what that means. Schutzhund is a highly challenging form of training that involves competence in three separate areas: tracking, obedience, and protection. It requires a high level of dedication and knowledge on the part of an owner and should never be undertaken without the support of a reputable club and qualified trainer. Because of its demanding nature, puppies suited for this type of work must be more confident, more competitive, more alert, and much more aggressive than the normal companion puppy. A novice handler could get far more than he bargained for by purchasing a Schutzhund puppy without a serious commitment to the sport. In the wrong hands, a strong, dominating puppy could easily develop into an overly aggressive dog with serious behavioral problems.

We strongly encourage personal interviews before the purchase of a puppy. By understanding what you are really looking for in a dog, the breeder can work more effectively to provide you with a puppy you will be truly satisfied with.

Puppy Aptitude Testing

We also administer puppy aptitude tests to each puppy at seven weeks of age. Over the past fifteen years, there has been a growing appreciation among breeders of the value these tests have in indicating the situations to which the puppy is best suited. The test is intended to guide the placement process by identifying general personality traits. As an aptitude test it allows us to evaluate puppies on the basis of sociability, dominance, and obedience potential.

Actually, evaluating puppies is nothing new. It goes back hundreds of years to cultures in which dogs were used for specific tasks: herding and guarding sheep, hunting, transportation, protection, rescue, even pulling carts and boats. In our mechanized and technological society it is difficult for us to appreciate the vital importance dogs once had for people's survival. Working dogs were critical to the economic well-being of their owners, and farmers and breeders had to learn by experience how to spot puppies best suited for various tasks, as well as how to cull those who lacked promise. They had to acquire a breeder's intuition in order to perpetuate and develop the breeding lines they were using. Puppy evaluation has long been at the heart of selective breeding and the establishment of purebred dogs.

We have used the Volhard Puppy Aptitude Test (see appendix) successfully for ten years, finding it an invaluable aid for placing puppies in homes where they will thrive. Though no one test can ever be considered faultless, when combined with all of the previous information accumulated on each litter, a clear picture of puppy personality and potential emerges that makes the likelihood of successful placement high.

Testing Anka's Litter

On the fiftieth day after the puppies were born, Olga Barnet, a friend who is unacquainted with Anka's litter, comes to the monastery to test the pups. We always have someone who is a complete stranger to the litter do the testing, in a location the pups are unaccustomed to. This prevents the results from being biased by a pup's familiarity with the tester or the location of the test, since the purpose of the test is to obtain an accurate picture of each puppy's raw temperament. Puppies will behave differently in various circumstances, but we can accurately chart a pup's true temperament by observing his or her reactions during a broad spectrum of new experiences and minor stresses.

The best time to test puppies is as close to the forty-ninth day as possible. By the time they are seven weeks of age, EEG readings indicate that neurological development has reached adult levels, thus allowing us to obtain a true reading of their behavioral tendencies. If testing is done earlier, results will be inconclusive because neurological development is still too immature; if testing is done later, between eight and ten weeks of age, pups will be in the fear period, making assessments of temperament subject to serious misinterpretation.

We conduct the test late in the morning, well after the pups have eaten, during a period when they are lively. The test takes approximately ten minutes, and each pup is tested individually, going through the entire test in one session. To assist the tester, one of the brothers watches from a hidden location and records the puppies' responses.*

Yola is the first pup to take the test. The first phase evaluates social attraction, testing the degree to which a puppy is willing to approach a stranger. Once Yola has been placed in the room, Olga crouches down several feet away from her and begins clapping her hands gently. Though Yola's tail

---

*For clarity's sake, we will discuss individual responses to each phase of the test together.

The restraint exercise of the puppy test. In this picture, Dorothy Updike, a community puppy tester, tests the pup for the degree of submissiveness.

initially goes down, she approaches readily, and when she reaches Olga, she circles back and forth between her legs, squirming affectionately as she is petted. This is a submissive reaction, indicating a certain lack of self-confidence that is blended with a gentle disposition toward humans. The other pups are bouncier, coming readily to Olga with their tails wagging high and licking at her hands. Sunny even jumps and paws at Olga's leg, displaying a more dominant, self-confident nature. None of the pups bite at her hands.

After several seconds, Olga stands up and begins the following exercise, which measures the pup's sociability as well as its willingness to accept leadership. As Olga walks away, Yola pauses a moment, then walks after her with her tail

The elevation dominance. The pup is held in midair for thirty seconds.

wagging gently, though she does not get underfoot. She stays about a foot behind Olga and follows her around the room, suggesting her willingness to accept her leadership. Kairos and Oka score about the same, while both Kipper and Sunny end up getting underfoot, a sign that foretells dominance with their future owners.

The next two phases, the restraint and social dominance tests, are given right after each other and measure puppies' tendencies toward dominance or submission, as well as their willingness to forgive. Olga crouches down and rolls Yola over on her back, looking at her calmly. As she does so, Yola remains passive, offering no resistance and licking her hand several times. After thirty seconds, she is placed back on all fours and is stroked gently from the top of her head on down the back. While she does this, Yola licks at Olga's face once and seems to melt under the petting. This series of reactions shows a high degree of submissiveness and sensitivity, and suggests that Yola will be a dog that is quick to forgive after being disciplined. Her response differs from that of the other pups, who offer more initial resistance on the restraint test, struggling to escape for at least fifteen seconds before they settle. Except for Sunny. Sunny struggles and squirms to get free, tossing his head back and forth in protest as he is held to the ground. When time is called, Olga lets out a sigh of relief, and Sunny immediately rights himself and briefly walks away. He comes back quickly, however, and as Olga pets him, he jumps up toward her and starts pawing at her arm. Sunny's response to the restraint test shows a high orientation to dominance, and, though he was forgiving after it, he was also somewhat pushy. The other pups did not show this characteristic; they simply allowed themselves to be stroked, cuddling up to Olga to lick her face.

In the final phase of the temperament section of the test, an elevation dominance, the puppy is evaluated in a situation in which he or she has no control. Cradling Yola with both of her hands under her rib cage, Olga lifts her up and holds her in midair for thirty seconds. Yola shows no signs of struggle; she is passive, fully accepting of the handling. The other pups score exactly the same, even Sunny. Not one manifests any inclination to struggle, a sign that they will be easy to handle when placed in a situation such as a veterinarian's office or a professional groomer's parlor.

At this point, the tone of the test shifts to obedience aptitude. The first test is a retrieval exercise and demonstrates a puppy's willingness to work with a human being. Olga takes a crumpled-up piece of paper and jiggles it playfully in front of Yola. She then tosses the paper about four feet away. Yola goes to investigate it, sniffs it for several seconds, and then returns to Olga without having picked up the paper. This shows a modest aptitude for obedience, since she did investigate and show some interest but did not bring the paper back. The other pups do, though not in identical ways. Kipper and Kairos trot over to the paper immediately, pick it up, and return with it to Olga, who praises them enthusiastically. When Oka picks it up, she meanders around the room, showing a little independence, but after about thirty seconds she brings it to Olga, who is still clapping her hands and calling her. Sunny's response is the most precocious. Running after the paper, he picks it up in his mouth and shakes it vigorously back and forth. Pacing sideways with it for several moments, he then shakes it some more and brings it back to Olga, who praises him. These reactions all show various degrees of obedience potential, with Oka's response being the weakest. Her delay in bringing the paper back suggests a bit of independence we do not see in the other pups.

After the retrieving exercise, we test the puppy's touch sensitivity. The purpose of this is to determine a pup's level of pain, giving us an idea of how difficult it will be to control and train. Puppies who are very touch sensitive will respond to the slightest pressure from the collar. Those who are insensitive will probably require more strength and perhaps

A puppy bringing back an object to the tester during the retrieval exercise of the puppy test.

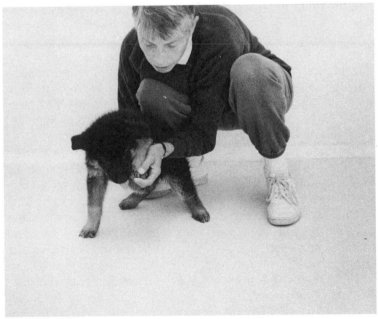

Testing touch sensitivity. Squeeze the webbing between the pup's toes and count to ten. Release when the pup responds to pressure.

Testing sound sensitivity. Drop the sleigh bells close to the pup and observe his reaction.

different types of training equipment. Olga crouches down next to Yola and lifts her front leg up. Taking her paw, she squeezes the webbing between her toes and counts, increasing the pressure as she does so. After a brief two-count, Yola gives a quick yip and tries to pull her paw away. Her pain threshold is low, indicating that it will not be necessary to use a great deal of force with her in training. The puppy with the highest count is Sunny, who yips at six. Nevertheless, this is still a medium sensitivity reading and does not indicate potential problems with obedience training.

The next test measures sound sensitivity and is intended to show how a pup responds to sharp noises. This is especially relevant for puppies who will be living in busy cities. Olga takes Yola and faces her away from the source of the noise. Then she takes a group of sleigh bells that have been strung together and throws them to the floor. Yola acts a bit startled and very cautiously takes several steps in the direction of the bells. She then stops, looks over at Olga, and walks away, deciding not to investigate any further. The other puppies are more confident, going over to the bells and sniffing them. The most interesting reaction comes from Kairos. After hearing the sound, he walks over to the bells and picks them up in his mouth, carries them over to the corner of the room, and lies down. This manifestation of courage and intelligent reaction to sudden noises demonstrates his ability to adapt to any type of living situation.

The final exercise is the sight sensitivity test, which gives

The sight sensitivity test. Pass the strange object near the pup and observe his reaction.

us an indication of a puppy's reaction to a strange object. We use an old cloth that is attached to a string and have Olga tauntingly jerk it across the floor so that Yola can see it. She hesitates for a moment, ducking her head down in a cautious movement and tucking her tail. After Olga makes several passes with the cloth, Yola starts to trail slowly after it, though she does not pounce on it. Her response is very tentative in contrast with Sunny's. He immediately pounces on the cloth and puts it in his mouth, shaking it vigorously. Olga gives a few tugs on the string and Sunny pulls back with delight, revealing a feisty, spirited pup who could become aggressive if put in the wrong circumstances. The other pups simply walk over to the cloth and try to sniff it, showing self-confidence but less inclination toward aggression.

After finishing with each test, Olga briefly praises the puppy on the way back to the puppy pen. Then she confirms the recorded score with the brother. When all of the tests are completed, several brothers involved in puppy placement discuss the results and begin planning each pup's departure.

As you might guess, the purpose of puppy testing is not to judge which pups have good or bad temperaments, but to help indicate where they should be placed to reach their full potential. A pup with a good temperament for an outdoorsman might have a poor temperament for working as a therapy dog in a nursing home. So much depends on an owner's needs and desires.

Analyzing the results of Anka's litter (see appendix for score sheet), we see no real surprises; each pup's scores confirm our own general impressions from the previous weeks. Because the litter comes from two parents of solid working lineage, the results suggest that the pups will require people who are familiar with handling active, intelligent dogs. We can now carefully review the applications of people who are waiting to obtain a puppy from us and try to match them with what is available from the litter.

Sunny, who scored mostly twos on the test, is the dominant pup in the litter. He possesses all the qualities found in a successful working dog: spirit, self-confidence, intelligence, and poise. We placed him with an experienced handler who is seriously involved in Schutzhund work.

Kairos, the second male, scored mostly threes, indicating a lively, outgoing dog. Since he showed no difficulties with either people or noise, we chose to place him in a suburban setting, with a family that has three teenagers. They had owned shepherds in the past and were committed to having him well trained.

Oka, scoring mostly threes and fours, is also lively, though with a mild tendency toward independence. We felt she would adjust well in a situation in which the owner would be gone part of the day, so we placed her with a single woman who spent part of her day counseling clients in her home.

Kipper, who also scored primarily threes, is a pup we felt confident could fit into a family situation because of his strong orientation to people. He was placed with a family that had two children and one other dog, an active Labrador retriever.

Yola, who scored mostly fours, is a perfect puppy for an elderly couple. She is gentle and submissive but not fearful, so we placed her with a recently retired couple who had plenty of time and love to spend on her.

By the end of the eighth week, all of the pups are gone. Ordinarily, we send puppies to their new homes between seven and ten weeks of age, depending on particular circumstances. Though some books make a point of identifying the seventh week as the ideal time for placement, we have found that departure dates can be much more flexible, provided regular socialization continues at the breeder's. When puppies stay beyond the seventh week, we continue to follow a regular schedule of socialization, making sure they receive plenty of exposure to people, dogs, and different environments, and we have seen no ill effects from this. By the time they leave, they are ready to make the transition to life with their new owners.

Earlier, we alluded to a natural part of the socialization process that occurs between eight and ten weeks of age called the fear/avoidance period. During this time, puppies that a week earlier were confident and precocious can suddenly appear tentative and cautious, making one question whether something is wrong. This is especially so for new owners, who can fearfully wonder whether such behavior indicates that their breeder pulled a fast one on them, or that they are somehow mistreating their new charge. Be reassured. What is most likely occurring is merely the pup's natural adjustment to full adult sensory capacities; this lasts for several weeks. Because most breeders place their pups between seven and ten weeks of age (the optimal time for pups to bond with their new owners), you must be conscious of this phase and use it to your advantage. Your patience and understanding strongly encourage the eight-and-a-half-week-old pup to come out of this period with a strong bond with you.

Despite the fact that this phase is normal, however, it is important not to expose a pup to highly stressful experiences during this time. Significantly, specialists have discovered that in this period pups are especially sensitive to traumatic experiences and poor handling. These may result in long-lasting emotional scars. Whereas five- to six-week-old pups bounce back quickly from a sudden fear experience, the impact is much more profound during the fear/avoidance period.

This does not imply keeping the pup insulated from new people or new experiences. Socialization is essential throughout the entire period. However, it must be done intelligently, with care. New experiences must be nontraumatic and easy for the pup to deal with. By taking a positive, encouraging attitude toward your pup and safeguarding him from frightening, stressful experiences, you will see him make a natural recovery back to his normal self toward the end of the tenth week.

One final remark: The fear/avoidance period is just one more reason the early environment of a pup, of necessity, must be balanced and healthy to begin with for a positive adjustment and transition through puppyhood. If a puppy was never in a normal, healthy situation early on, if he did not receive the necessary socialization at each stage of his young life, then there will be no solid ground for him to return to now — the effects of this period will be much more pronounced and long-lasting. Furthermore, if the circumstances and attitudes in the pup's new home are not conducive to guiding him through this period, the pup usually suffers emotional scars that affect his behavior for life. Prospective puppy owners must be careful where they obtain their pup and about the manner in which they introduce him to his new home. We will examine these issues in detail in the following chapters.

CHAPTER SEVEN

Deciding to Adopt a Puppy

To form a healthy bond with someone requires that we take into consideration the genuine needs and possibilities of the other. This is true not only of people but of dogs, too. Certainly dogs should not be thought of as human, but they still have a unique value of their own. Many people fail to recognize that having a dog involves what any true relationship involves. We most successfully adopt and raise a puppy when we build on a clear-sighted respect for the kind of creature a dog is; then we can understand and accept the responsibilities of caring for one properly. Such an attitude flies in the face of the "ME" mentality, a one-dimensional mindset that fails to respect a dog in its integrity as a dog and instead sees it only in terms of "my" own wants and desires.

So before rushing out to buy a pup, we recommend that you step back for a moment to challenge yourself and your family on the seriousness of this step. Play devil's advocate! Examine your motives. Why do you want a dog? What type of owner will you be? What return are you prepared to make your dog for the pleasure of her company? Far better to raise the issue of responsibility and care before you get a pup than to learn of your mistake later, when you have a twelve-week-old puppy who is suddenly making demands on you . . . at three o'clock in the morning!

The One-dimensional Owner

Recently we received a telephone call from a married couple inquiring whether we could find a new home for their five-month-old German shepherd puppy, Wolf, whom they were no longer able to keep. Though we explained that we did not offer that type of service, we asked them why they were giving up on their puppy. Embarrassed, the husband said he and his wife lived in a suburb of a large city and had purchased their pup after several local burglaries convinced them that a watchdog would be desirable. They had gone to a reputable breeder and had obtained a bright, affectionate puppy they assumed would easily meet their needs. "Yet," the man confessed, "we had no idea what we bargained for." This was their first dog.

Being professional people, they had to be away from the apartment at least nine hours a day. In itself, this wasn't a problem since Wolf had been successfully house-trained in a matter of days, and they had arranged for a dog-walker to take him out for a half hour at midday.

"Then what is the problem?" we asked.

"He won't leave us alone," the man replied.

Having Wolf around, he complained, was like adding four more hours onto an already hectic day. When he and his wife got home from work, they wanted to relax and be with each other, yet Wolf's need for attention made that quite impossible.

"I mean, he has to be fed, walked, played with . . . it's worse than having a kid . . ."

". . . and all that licking," the wife chimed in on the other line. "It's disgusting! He simply won't settle down and be a good boy. The two of us are even starting to get into arguments because of the dog, and the neighbors are complaining about his barking and whining during the day. It's just a pain having him around. I mean, who needs it?"

What the couple discovered too late was that they did not need a dog but a high-tech burglar-alarm system. They never really wanted a dog in the first place; they only thought they did. They were unwilling to accept (because they never dreamed of it!) the real demands a dog would make on their lives, specifically its need for love and companionship. During our conversation it became obvious that it had never occurred to them to try to see things from Wolf's perspective, to try to see *his* needs in the relationship. Wolf was bought for protection, period. When it did become clear that Wolf's needs exceeded what they were willing to give, that Wolf was becoming a pain, an inconvenience, their solution was to get rid of him.

This is a frequent scenario that appears in many different

disguises. Though nobody intentionally purchases a dog only to keep it for several months, it can easily turn out this way. Sometimes this is connected with the onset of specific problem behavior in the dog; at other times it is merely the result of the owner's fading interest. The common thread in so many failed owner/dog relationships is the belated discovery that having a dog is not what the owner thought it would be. Cold reality clashes with their one-dimensional expectations, and so they bypass the responsibility by opting for the easier solution: giving up the dog.

Who Should Have a Dog?

When it comes to dogs, romanticism abounds! Certainly one of the effects television has had on our culture is to create highly idealized images of what a dog should be like. Rin-Tin-Tin, Lassie, Bullet, Benji, and Big Red are all presented as ideal companions who require no training and are faithfully devoted to attending to their owner's every need. They never have soiling accidents; they do not need to be taken out for walks; and they are always obedient. They mind their own business when they are not wanted and are always ready to give love and affection when it is asked of them. What could be easier or more wonderful?

The truth is that the Hollywood dog exists only in the movies. What we never hear about is the long and difficult training process these dogs go through to perform the amazing tricks and stunts they do, and the patience, love, and perseverance required on the part of their trainers! If you expect your puppy to rise effortlessly to the standards set by Lassie, you will be sorely disappointed.

Many people are simply unprepared for the changes that will take place in their life once they adopt a puppy. In fact, our experience teaches us that anyone who thinks he or she wants a dog should postpone the decision until after thinking the matter through completely.

Not everyone should have a dog. Because of a variety of circumstances, many people simply do not have the time or ability to care for a puppy or even an adult dog. A pup will take us outside of ourselves and our own little world. Ordinary personal decisions that previously concerned only you or your family will now always have to take into account the presence of the puppy. Free time that was once for yourself alone must now be shared with your pup. How do you feel about that?

Caring for a dog is a lot of hard work. *Canis familiaris*, the pet dog, cannot take care of itself. From the moment of its adoption until the day of its death (which, barring accident or illness, can be after fifteen years or more), it is a highly dependent creature that will count on you for all the essentials of canine living: food, water, shelter, exercise, training, and periodic veterinary care. But beyond these, the principal need a puppy has throughout its life is social. It requires an owner who is a companion in the fullest sense of the word. Can you see yourself or your family in such a role?

From this perspective, the old injunction is as relevant as ever: Know thyself! People who are willing to look at themselves honestly and who try to find a dog that blends in with their lifestyle and living environment stand the best chance for developing a healthy, long-term relationship with their puppy. Any normal puppy has a unique personality; it will naturally and actively seek out a relationship. Though there are a number of legitimate, practical reasons for getting a pup (working, sport, show, breeding, protection, etc.), none of them should ever exclude or override the chief one, the desire for companionship and therefore the willingness to accept the obligations this entails. Taking the time to consider the choice realistically and listing the demands and responsibilities beforehand will bring results that are more rewarding for both puppy and you.

So You Really Want a Dog?

Frequently visitors to our monastery are interested in obtaining one of our shepherds. On one such occasion, after meeting many of our dogs and talking at length with one of the brothers, a woman asked what she should do next in order to get a puppy. We explained to her that there would be a waiting period involved and that she would first have to fill out a puppy application form. This is a detailed application that we use to help match prospective customers with individual puppies. As she looked over the form, the woman expressed real amazement, saying, "My heavens, you'd think I was adopting a child!"

*   *   *

This is precisely the point. Though a puppy is not a child, the decision to adopt one involves a similar sort of seriousness. It is entirely appropriate for breeders to question potential clients thoroughly, since their answers will help indicate what sort of puppy is best suited for them. Any conscientious breeder feels a personal sense of responsibility for the pups she has bred; her interest is less in selling them than in placing them in the right homes (that is, right for the owner and right for the puppy). Thus, if we prefer to use the term "adopting a puppy" instead of buying one, it is only because it puts the emphasis squarely where it belongs: bringing another member into your family.

All canids live naturally in packs, which correspond to the immediate members of their social circle. With domestic dogs, this means that they will treat those human beings with whom they live as fellow pack members, even if the "pack" involves only one other individual. There is nothing sentimental in regarding a new puppy as an additional member of your family: this is how *it* will view *you*.

This makes it important that your choice be more than just a hit-or-miss proposition. It should involve serious thought and planning. Personal circumstances and those of the dog also must be considered. Dealing as we do with a large variety of dogs and people, we have files of case histories that repeatedly demonstrate the effects of poor selection on the human/dog relationship. Making a smart decision regarding a puppy is more complicated than most people imagine.

Dogs are the most varied of all the species we know of in the animal kingdom. There are currently 130 breeds officially registered by the American Kennel Club (AKC), and natural historians of dogs can identify more than four hundred breeds internationally. Of the purebred dogs recognized by the AKC, six general breed categories are distinguished that reflect the general orientation of each breed: Sporting Dogs; Hounds; Working Dogs; Terriers; Toy Dogs; Nonsporting Dogs. In addition, there are any number of mixed breed* combinations that draw physical and behavioral characteristics from diverse genetic backgrounds. With all this to consider, what is the best way to determine which is the best puppy for you?

---

*We prefer the terms "mixed breed" or "random bred" for dogs whose immediate ancestry involves two or more breeds to the more demeaning designation of "mongrel" or "mutt."

DATE _____

AKC Reg.
GSDCA
OFA Cert.

NEW SKETE SHEPHERDS
POTENTIAL PUPPY/DOG CLIENT INFORMATION

Thank you for your interest in our dogs. We would appreciate your answering the following questions so that we can more easily test and select the right puppy/dog for you. All information is confidential and used only by the monks. Thank you for your cooperation and help in answering our questions.

Your name _____

Address _____

City _____ State _____ Zip _____

Phone Number (Home) _____ (Work) _____

Good time to call if we need to reach you _____

How were you referred to us? _____

Are you interested in a puppy ( ) _____ Older trained dog ( ) _____

Male _____ Female _____ No preference _____

Pigmentation desires (Circle)   Blond Face   /   Blond Face with mask   /   Dark Face
    Additional Information _____

Structure/Size preference (Circle)   Large   Standard   Small   Long-haired   None
    Additional Information _____

Why are you interested in obtaining one of our shepherds? (Circle One)
    Companion   /   Show and Breeding ( )   /   Obedience Ring   /   Protection
    Additional Information _____

What qualities do you like in the GS breed? _____

What don't you want to find in a GS? _____

Is this your first German shepherd? _____ Previously owned dogs _____

Animals present at home now _____

Have you examined our Sales Policy? _____ Are you committed to caring for this dog for its lifetime? _____

Have you ever had to euthanize (put to sleep) a dog? _____ If so, why? _____

Are you willing to spay/neuter this dog? _____ If not, why not? _____

If you are considering breeding, do you promise to have this dog X-rayed for dysplasia and to consult the monks prior to breeding? _____

FAMILY DATA: Are you   M   S   D   (Circle)   Your age _____ Children _____ Ages _____

Occupation of adult(s) in family _____

Others in household who will have contact with dog _____ Where will dog stay during the day? _____

Where will the dog stay during the night? _____

Do you live in: (Circle)   Urban   Suburban   Rural   Environment / Own Home   or   Apt.

Further information _____

Have you read our book on dog care and training? _____ Other books you've read on dogs _____

Please use the reverse side of this sheet to add any further information you wish us to consider in placing one of our German shepherds with you. We would appreciate if you would give us a little insight into the expectations you may have for this new addition to your family. Thank you again — your interest is deeply appreciated.

Mixed or Purebred Puppy?

There are many opinions within the professional community regarding the desirability of a mixed-breed puppy over one that is purebred. Some veterinarians, for example, maintain that mixed-breed pups make better family pets because they have calmer temperaments and by nature are more adaptable to a wider variety of living circumstances. They also point out that they are substantially less expensive (usually around $10–$20) and are less apt to have congenital defects. If you add to these factors the consideration that buying a puppy from an animal shelter will most likely save it from being euthanized, adopting a pup of mixed breeding has considerable merit.

Other specialists, however, disagree, pointing out that random-bred pups are far less predictable with respect to future size and temperament than their purebred cousins. Since they come from breedings that were more than likely unplanned and unwanted, there is often no way of foreseeing what the puppy will be like when it grows up. Thus, an owner may be adopting a puppy he is especially unsuited for. The advantage of adopting a purebred pup is that you can reasonably predict what the pup will be like as an adult, in size, color, and behavior. This is not necessarily the case with a pup that is random bred. What may initially appear to be a scrawny terrier mix at eight and a half weeks could well end up being a 95-pound mammoth by the time it is full-grown. Choosing a purebred helps prevent "surprises" that end up badly for owner and dog alike. Also, because random-bred litters are often unwanted, it is likely that the puppies have not been raised with the consistent care administered by dedicated breeders.

So who is right?

The truth is that either a random-bred or purebred pup can become an ideal companion, provided that the right elements are present. We have known too many good mixed-breed dogs to doubt the possibility of finding one that can become a wonderful companion. Nevertheless, it is deceptive to state that random-bred dogs are calmer or more intelligent than their purebred counterparts. It is simply not the case. While one random-bred dog may be superior in intelligence and trainability when compared to an individual purebred, there is a basic standard of quality among purebreds (from *reputable* breeders) that does not exist in the gamut of random-bred dogs. Puppies can only inherit the genes of their parents. The results of unplanned breedings between dogs of differing breeds are difficult to predict. Conscientious breeders of purebred dogs, on the other hand, study pedigrees, analyze previous litters, and purposefully breed into lines that demonstrate intelligence, good health, and overall soundness. This is one reason service and working organizations involved in Seeing Eye, support for the handicapped, search-and-rescue, protection, and so on, all use purebred dogs. There is greater reliability and certainty of an individual dog's capacities.

Taking these factors into account, we believe that for the individual who wants to be responsible in choosing a pup that will be right for him or her, the best course to follow is to adopt a purebred puppy. It is always wiser to adopt a puppy in full knowledge of what it will be as a full-grown adult than on the basis of what it appears to be as a pup. This is most easily done with a purebred pup.

If you do decide on a mixed breed, however, you should keep several things in mind. First, plan on neutering or spaying your pup between six and eight months of age: no random-bred dog should be allowed to reproduce, since it only perpetuates the sorry cycle of unwanted pups that are annually destroyed. Second, a random-bred dog has the same needs as a purebred dog. It is never, under any circumstances, a second-class citizen. It requires the same commitment, the same amount of love and care from you as would any purebred. Never think that because it is a less expensive investment the burden of responsibility is lessened. Regardless of what kind of puppy you adopt, your love and informed attention should be constant.

Pet Shop Puppy?

If you have decided to get a purebred puppy, where is the best place to obtain it? A pet shop? Pet stores are a curious phenomenon in American life. Frequently tucked away in shopping malls, they do a decent job filling the needs pet owners have for supplies. Take a walk through a typical shop, and a wide variety of colorful specimens vie for your attention: cats and kittens, reptiles, mice, gerbils, birds, tropical fish, and . . . puppies. The puppies, all kinds, are in separate cages lined up against the wall for shoppers to view easily; elsewhere, older pups in larger pens lie forlornly on dog beds. While Muzak drifts through the store, the birds in the center of the shop whistle at the browsers, jealous of the attention the puppies are receiving.

The puppies all seem cute enough, like the young of all species. They look up toward their admirers for several moments, seemingly begging for liberation, and then go back to playing with squeak toys provided for their amusement. Maybe a well-dressed couple chats before the springer spaniel puppy, putting their fingers through the cage for it to lick as they try to decide if this is the one they really want. Nearby, two children tug at their mother's skirt, pointing to a Labrador retriever pup while they pester, "That one, Mommy, that one!" Shop attendants in practical white smocks move throughout the store, politely answering questions, while another employee routinely makes sure that all the cages are clean. Everything seems so civil. It has all the order of a supermarket, and, we might think, all the quality as well!

So what is wrong here?

We could first focus on the source of many of these pet-shop puppies, "puppy mills" where dogs are bred in cramped, fetid, factorylike conditions and where basic health standards are nonexistent. These establishments, located primarily in the American Midwest, are often run to supplement ordinary farm income by mass-producing puppies for pet shops throughout the country. The preponderant motivation for any puppy mill is pure profit and not the breeding of sound, healthy animals. Large numbers of male and female purebred dogs, jammed into filthy kennels, are bred as often as possible and with no consideration whatsoever for quality. Dogs that are nervous, hyperactive, shy, vicious, or who have one of any number of inherited defects are not prevented from breeding. That would simply be bad business.

The puppies themselves are forced to spend their first critical weeks in abominable conditions: they must walk around and sleep in their own filth; vaccinations are rarely given, human contact is negligible, and when they are shipped out at five to six weeks of age they must spend up to a week in transit, stuffed into cages or crates with insufficient food, water, or veterinary care. Often they arrive at the pet shop weak and dehydrated, stressed, and suffering from infections picked up in transit. After a superficial cleaning up, they still lack the vigor and spark of really healthy pups. By the time they are offered for sale, customers pay approximately the same price they would to a private breeder, though for a much less reliable dog. Though it is true that some pet shop puppies are purchased from local breeders who raise their puppies in responsible ways, it is more likely that they come from outside the immediate area of the store. This makes checking up on where the puppy came from next to impossible.

Thus, for the prospective customer looking at a pet shop puppy, there is seldom any reliable information available on its background, genetic predispositions, or how it was raised. Even if a pedigree comes with a puppy, the names rarely involve top dogs; it is more a smoke screen designed to impress clients. More serious is the impossibility of seeing the parents, or at least the mother, firsthand. Without realizing it, the customer may be buying into a host of unseen medical and behavioral problems that will surface months later.

Finally, it is reasonable to question how humane it is to have a puppy "on display" in the store itself, isolated from its mother and littermates, in a separate cage, lacking adequate exercise and handling, and exposed to any number of germs and infectious diseases. Think about it. Who would want to buy a friend at the local supermarket? A pet shop is fine for buying goldfish, gerbils, or pet supplies, but it is the last place a person should look for a new puppy.

Adopting a Puppy from an Animal Shelter

We are often asked whether it is a good idea to look for a puppy at an animal shelter. Though animal shelters offer a humane and economical way of getting a pup, the absence of a breeder's background information plus the presence of a number of potential dangers in the shelter itself always make adopting such a puppy risky business. The fact that a puppy has been left in a shelter in the first place represents a certain measure of "unwantedness," suggesting the possibility of inadequate care before it arrived there. Shelters operate on a policy of withholding background information on all dogs offered for adoption, so there is simply no way of determining what the early experience of a puppy was like.

In addition to this, animal shelters are places where diseases can easily spread. All sorts of dogs pass through the facilities: problem dogs, strays, abandoned or sick dogs, and many puppies. Particularly with puppies, there is no way of knowing what their previous exposure to disease has been. While some shelters do give puppies shots and check for worms, this is done only after the puppy has been sold, since they cannot afford to give shots to puppies who will be euthanized within a couple of weeks. Thus, the adopted puppy might well have been exposed to a disease without any protection. By the time the shots are given, the incubation period may have progressed to the point where the shots will have no effect. This could mean that you will have a very sick puppy on your hands shortly after your arrival home. The amount of money you saved buying the pup from the shelter would then go into a sizable veterinary bill to nurse the puppy back to health.

In saying this, we also point out that these are only possibilities. It is just as possible that in a shelter you will find a healthy, affectionate puppy who will grow into a wonderful companion. Just be aware of the risks.

Where to Get a Puppy

It should be apparent from the foregoing discussion why we believe it is preferable to get a puppy from a reputable breeder rather than to risk adopting one from another, perhaps more convenient, source, such as an animal shelter or pet shop. Though it will doubtlessly cost you more, the advantages make the additional expenditures worth it. Aside from providing you with a guarantee of health and temperament, a pedigree going back at least three generations, and an AKC registration slip, a good breeder will take the time to explain to you how the puppy was raised and socialized during the important early weeks of growth. She will introduce you to one or both of the parents and accurately describe the results of similar breedings, so that you will be able to judge the immediate temperamental background of your pup. This information will give you a realistic picture of what to expect as your puppy grows. Good breeders are intensely interested in the pups they produce and will want to stay in touch with you to find out how the puppy matures. Because of this, they can be a valuable source of information, advice, and assistance should you run into difficulties down the road.

In his well-known book *Man Meets Dog*, the famous etholo-gist Konrad Lorenz goes out on a limb when he makes this remarkable statement:

> A bitch is more faithful than a male dog, the intricacies of her mind are finer, richer and more complex than his, her intelli-gence is generally greater. I have known very many dogs and can say with firm conviction that of all creatures the one near-est to man in the fineness of its perceptions and in its capacity to render true friendship is a bitch.

We respectfully beg to differ categorically! It is futile to discuss gender differences in terms that suggest that a com-panion dog of one sex is superior to the other. Not only is this untrue, it fails to account for the many exceptions to gender stereotypes: the highly affectionate and trainable male, the overly protective female, the male that does not fight with other dogs, and the female that does. While some loose generalizations can be made about gender differences, these are only generalizations, not absolutes. Especially when considering puppies, the general behavior depends more on you and the way you raise your pup than on its particular sex.

Deciding on a male or female is primarily a matter of indi-vidual preference, and there are advantages and disadvan-tages to each. Female dogs are smaller than males and tend to mature more quickly. This is why they are easier to train at an earlier age, not because they are more intelligent. They come into season (proestrus and estrus) twice a year for a period of three weeks, during which time they secrete drops of blood-tinged vaginal discharge (spotting) that sexually attracts male dogs. During this period, if puppies are not desired, you will have to keep the female locked indoors to prevent "accidental" breedings. This can be a nuisance. Also, when a bitch is in season, she will need to be confined to linoleum or hard surfaces because of her spotting. Blood spots are difficult to remove from carpets and fabrics. It is recommended that she be spayed between six and eight months of age if she is not to be bred or exhibited at shows. This prevents unwanted pregnancies and incidences of uter-ine and ovarian disease, and it has beneficial behavioral side effects as well. Many owners observe a mellowing in their spayed female dog that reflects a calmer, more focused attitude.

The high spirits and self-assurance of many male dogs leads them to dominate weaker owners, especially in larger breeds, where the males are bigger and stronger. They generally exhibit more independence than females, and, particularly in the earlier phases of obedience training, will require firm yet patient handling. Though males who are not neutered are inclined to roam and fight more than females, owner negligence significantly contributes to this behavior. Neutering a male you do not plan to breed is a wise course to follow and will diminish roaming, aggression, and generally boisterous activity.

Which Breed Is Best for You?

Among dog fanciers it is quite common to hear good-natured ribbing over what breed of dog is the best. Understandably, personal prejudices often color these judgments and allow mistaken notions to spread. There is no "best breed." The principal reason there are so many breeds today is that they have been bred selectively over the centuries for specific tasks and characteristics, always bred only from those dogs possessing the desired qualities. As a result, different breeds emphasize different qualities, and some are better suited than others for specific situations and living environments. For example, a dog that fits in beautifully with a suburban family with several young children may not be the best dog for a single woman living in a high-crime neighborhood of a big city. Or a very active dog may be perfect for a young, athletic couple but would be particularly ill-suited for an elderly couple who are quiet and sedentary. So much depends on the circumstances of your life.

However, you should also remember that no dog conforms rigidly to the behavioral standard of his breed. Within the individual breed there can be a wide range of personalities and aptitudes. However, certain bloodlines can be expected to produce dogs with specific behavioral orientations. This is especially important to keep in mind when dealing with individual breeders. Any conscientious breeder wants the puppies she raises to be placed intelligently and will be more than happy to discuss a particular puppy's family background. She will want to make sure that the puppy she is selling you will fit into your life.

Despite these complexities, there is hope. While no one can provide you with a surefire method for picking a perfect puppy, you can increase the likelihood that the pup you do choose will be a good companion by following several guidelines. The decision to adopt a puppy should be made from a sober look at the whole of your life, and not simply on the basis of your own personal preference. Face the reality around you and within you. Do not assume that because a particular breed appeals to your aesthetic tastes, it is therefore the right one for you. That decision needs to be weighed in a careful, critical manner.

The following recommendations are intended to help guide you through the complex process of choosing a puppy. They represent an integrated approach to adopting a puppy, an approach that we believe will help prevent poor selections and start you in the direction of responsible ownership.

Personality What is your own personality like? What about the people you live with? Just as each dog is an individual with particular characteristics and personality traits, so are we, and recognizing what our basic personality is like should always be connected with the decision to adopt a pup. Companionship involves mutual compatibility and, on a human level, our most lasting relationships are with people we connect with, whose personalities harmonize or complement our own. It is the same with a dog. Part of our natural preference for a particular type or breed of dog will often be based on the type of person we are. Matching your own personality with representatives of any particular breed is the intelligent way to decide on a puppy. A quiet, low-key individual, for example, may find a high-strung, always-on-the-go terrier a little too much to handle. Or someone who is lighthearted and affectionate may be more oriented to a breed that has more need for affection than one that is independent and aloof.

Look at yourself. Ask some basic questions: Are you extroverted or introverted, high-energy or laid-back, strong-willed or easygoing? How affectionate are you, how demonstrative with your emotions? Are you reserved, or do you spontaneously express yourself through touching and physical contact?

As you answer these questions and others they will provoke, remember that there are no ideal answers, just as there are no superior personality types. What makes us individual human beings is our variety, our different abilities and talents. However, since breeds vary widely in such areas as trainability, playfulness, protectiveness, as well as in the need for exercise and affection, it is important to take those characteristics that make you the kind of individual you are and match them with what you would most like to find in a companion dog. Taking the time to reflect seriously on yourself first will provide a good foundation for beginning to consider individual breeds.

Lifestyle How much time will you have available to spend with a puppy? Whatever your lifestyle, it is subject to a certain routine. The puppy you adopt will not only have to fit into that but will alter it dramatically, forcing you to take into account new priorities and needs. Are you flexible enough so that this will not be a problem?

It is possible the way you live may make owning a dog unwise. For example, imagine that you and your spouse are dedicated environmental lawyers who work away from home ten hours a day. You are also socially active, involved in the local chapters of the Sierra Club and Greenpeace, which take up most of your remaining free time. While this type of lifestyle may be rewarding and desirable, it is entirely *inappropriate* for a young puppy. What will the pup do? Who will take care of it while you are away?

Dogs are social animals who require plenty of human contact and respond poorly to isolation and confinement, unlike cats and tropical fish. Being left alone in the basement, confined to a utility room for ten hours a day, or stuck outside on a chain is no life for any dog. While it is good to have a large fenced-in area for a dog to play in, with a well-insulated kennel, this should only be in addition to plenty of ordinary socialization. It is never a dispensation, absolving you from spending quality time with your dog.

As owner, you should anticipate walking your dog at least three times a day (10–30 minutes each), feeding and playing with it (one hour a day), basic training (15–30 minutes a day), and grooming needs that will vary according to the breed you select. An Old English sheepdog, for example, may require as much as thirty minutes of grooming daily to keep it free of mats and tangles. How would these needs fit into the way you live? For the daily jogger, the thought of having a dog along might be fine; if, however, you are less active and are occupied with other concerns, you may discover these needs present problems.

Most dogs will have to adjust to a certain amount of time

alone each day. This should not be a problem if the periods are reasonably short. If, however, your dog will be home alone for ten hours a day, at least consider hiring someone to take him out for a good walk at midday. In most cities, professional dog-walkers can be hired for forty to sixty dollars a week. In suburbs, responsible teenagers can sometimes be hired for the same purpose. If this sounds unreasonable (or impossible) to you, you should reconsider adopting a pup. "Latch-key" puppies that spend most of the day alone learn to take out their boredom on your furniture, linoleum, carpeting, and anything else within reach! Owners should remember that weekends will require extra quality time with your pup for exercise and companionship.

If you have a family, it is usually easier to share the responsibility to ensure that the puppy receives proper attention, but you should not be blind to potential problems. Our experience has been that most children under the age of fourteen are unable to take *full* responsibility for a dog, even when it is officially theirs. Mom usually ends up with the biggest share of the duties of daily care. When parents merely go along with their children's wish for a family dog and are uninterested themselves, they may discover that the burden falls on them once the kids lose interest. Thus, it is important to educate children beforehand to the responsibility they will share once a new pup comes into the family.*

A close look at how you live will also suggest characteristics to look for in individual breeds. For example, if you enjoy hosting dinner parties or casual evening get-togethers, you should consider a breed that is confident, good-natured, and not overly protective. Otherwise, you will be forced to isolate your dog every time you have guests. Similarly, if you have children, you should anticipate the presence of playmates romping in and out of the house. Right from the start, you will be looking for a breed that is good with children. One couple we know wanted a companion dog for the wife, since the husband traveled frequently in his work. They also lived in a high-crime suburb, so they were more inclined toward breeds that demonstrated high levels of protectiveness,

---

*An excellent children's book on this topic is a short picture book entitled *Some Swell Pup, or, Are You Sure You Want a Dog?* by Maurice Sendak and Matthew Margolis. Mr. Sendak's drawings delightfully highlight the basic issues involved in caring for a puppy, and the text is simple and direct enough to be appreciated by parents and children alike. This should be read well ahead of the actual adoption.

trainability, and loyalty. An Akita fit this profile, and the well-bred pup they obtained worked out well.

There are endless possible situations. The point to remember, however, is basic. An examination of your individual lifestyle can provide you with important information to help discern which breeds are most compatible with you.

Environment   Where do you live? Whether in the city, suburbs, country, or in different places at different times, be clear about what your living environment offers for walking, exercising, and caring daily for your dog. While there is no such thing as an ideal setting for raising a dog (every environment presents its own problems and challenges), be realistic about how your living environment will affect the development of your puppy's behavior. All dogs require a certain amount of exercise every day, in every season, regardless of the weather. Depending on the breed, that need may be substantial. Be careful to select a breed whose size and general activity levels do not exceed the opportunities your environment offers. Many canine behavior problems can be traced to high energy that is not allowed to be expended in proper exercise. Instead, it is released through destructive chewing, excessive barking, aggression, and hyperactivity, behavior that can abruptly end a dog's welcome.

Many small breeds adapt well to city life because it is easier to satisfy their exercise needs than those of bigger dogs. While it is true that many of these same breeds are highly active and demand their share of exercise, a mile walk for them can be equivalent to a four-mile walk for a big dog, due to the difference in leg spans. High energy can thus be held in check, preventing many problems from developing.

Still, there are no absolutes here, either. Your surrounding environment need not automatically determine what size dog you get. We know many people who live happily in urban environments with large dogs such as German shepherds, Dobermans, Rottweilers, and Akitas, because they go out of their way to ensure that their dogs are well cared for and properly exercised. We once worked with a young man from New York City who owned a Hungarian vizsla, a highly energetic sporting breed that ordinarily would be poorly suited for city life. This relationship, however, was exemplary. Since the man was a jogger, he went out with his dog twice a day, five miles in the morning and three in the late afternoon. He also owned his own business and was able to keep his dog with him during the day. Since puppyhood the dog had been worked with faithfully in basic obedience training, and the owner spent weekends at his upstate home, giving the dog even more room for exercise. The success of this relationship demonstrates how dogs *can* adapt to unlikely circumstances, provided their basic needs are attended to.

Another aspect of your environment to consider is your personal living space. Is it an apartment, house, studio, town house, or farm? How big is it? Is there yard space available that could be fenced in to give your dog freedom for play and exercise? Also think about your neighbors. How do they feel about dogs? Are they so close that barking would be a problem? If so, look at breeds that rate low in chronic barking.

Small environments, such as city apartments, are nevertheless generally incompatible with breeds that are big and bulky, and when forced to adapt to them, some dogs develop neurotic behavior. We knew a young woman who lived in a small studio apartment in Boston. When she was a young girl, her family always had Great Danes, and when she moved away from home, she decided to adopt a pup she named Hulk. When she first got the pup, it was 35 pounds and full of fun. In four months, however, it had grown to 80 pounds with no sign of letting up. Left alone in the studio while his owner was at work, Hulk became extremely destructive, forcing her to crate him for unreasonably long periods during the day. This confinement resulted in general unruliness that made walks unpleasant, contact with people exceedingly rare, and dramatically increased aggressive, over-protective behavior. The only place Hulk could run was a small playground several blocks from where his owner lived — and then only late at night, when there weren't any people around.

The young woman finally realized that she could no longer keep Hulk. Fortunately, she was able to place him with a middle-aged couple who had a country home and who were experienced in keeping Great Danes. With plenty of exercise, consistent handling, and faithful obedience training, Hulk overcame his problems and blossomed into a happy companion dog. Many dogs, however, are not so fortunate.

As we pointed out in *How to Be Your Dog's Best Friend*, dogs can be happy almost anywhere, provided you structure their lives in accord with the demands of your particular environment and with sensitivity to the general characteristics of each breed. Weighing the practical issues of your environment before getting your puppy will give you a balanced idea of what to look for in a breed.

Do Your Homework

After all this, let us not seem to imply that finding a breed that matches you well is an impossibly burdensome chore. It is a matter of attitude. It can be a fascinating and enjoyable process that involves you and those you live with. You may already have a good idea of exactly what breed you are looking for. If you do not, there are several things you can do to help narrow your possibilities.

First, pay a visit to your local library. Most public libraries have well-stocked sections on dogs that will help give you a general idea of the possibilities available to you. Start by looking through a dog encyclopedia. Each section will have a short profile and description of the breed with a photograph reflecting the standard. Another valuable reference book to check is *The Complete Dog Book,* the official publication of the AKC. This gives the official standards of those breeds recognized by the AKC and provides profiles of what their temperament and personalities should be like. Also, be on the lookout for books on individual breeds. Howell Book House (845 Third Avenue, New York, NY, 10022) is well known for the many fine books they publish on individual breeds. These provide detailed accounts of breed history and use, suggestions about proper care, and other valuable tips on each particular breed.

Several books offer a comparative look at different breeds as they relate to different behavior categories and living environments. These are invaluable for helping you determine how realistic a particular breed may be for you. Though these profiles are not absolute (different books sometimes conflict in their evaluations of some breeds), they do provide a good idea of how obedience judges, veterinarians, and breed fanciers look at various breeds. We recommend three books that should be easy to locate at either your library or local bookstore:

The Roger Caras Dog Book, by Roger Caras. Holt, Rinehart and Winston, New York, NY, 1980.
This comprehensive book is readable, easy to use, and offers valuable insights into more than 120 different breeds. It also evaluates each breed according to exercise and grooming requirements and its adaptability to urban/apartment living. The photographs by Alton Anderson are a beautiful supplement.

The Perfect Puppy: How to Choose Your Dog by Its Behavior, by Benjamin L. Hart, D.V.M., and Lynette Hart. W. H. Freeman and Co., New York, NY, 1988.

This book focuses on fifty-six breeds, ranking them according to thirteen key behavioral traits that are of concern to most dog owners. The text is clear, easy to use, and informative. Its fault, in our judgment, is that it covers fewer than half of those breeds recognized by the AKC.

The Right Dog for You: Choosing a Breed That Matches Your Personality, Family and Lifestyle, by Daniel Tortora. Simon and Schuster, New York, NY, 1980.

The scope of this book is broad and complex. It surveys 123 breeds and ranks them according to numerous behavioral criteria. It is packed with valuable information, though it occasionally lapses into technical jargon that makes it less readable than the other two books. The persevering reader, however, will be rewarded with a multi-dimensional look at any of the breeds reviewed.

The information you uncover in your research should take you a long way in narrowing down your preferences. However, don't make any final decisions on book information alone. What you have learned now needs to be balanced by seeing the dogs themselves.

Attend some all-breed dog shows. These are usually scheduled on weekends and make ideal outings for families and friends. Call your local newspaper or breed club for schedules and upcoming events. Going to a show will give you the chance to directly observe adult representatives of the breeds you are interested in and to talk with people who are involved with them. Do not be bashful; dog breeders love to talk about the virtues of their particular breeds and can be quite candid about potential difficulties. Besides learning a lot, it will also give you the chance to make personal contacts with breeders from whom you may later wish to purchase your puppy.

Finally, a good veterinarian or an experienced dog trainer can be an invaluable resource for information about the breed you are most interested in. Aside from offering you personal insights from their own experiences, they may be able to direct you to a breeder they know to be conscientious and reputable. If you call ahead to schedule an appointment, they will be able to make time available to help you with your decision.

CHAPTER EIGHT

Finding a Dog Breeder

Once you decide on a particular breed, take the time to locate a breeder who is committed to breeding excellence. Purchasing a puppy involves a large amount of trust, so it makes sense to deal with breeders who have established reputations for high-quality dogs. In addition to checking with local veterinarians and trainers, write the AKC or the national club of the breed you are interested in for a list of registered breeders in your area.

Be a little cautious. Before settling on a particular breeder, get as broad a perspective as possible. Visit several breeders and meet as many of their dogs as possible. Compare the dogs you meet as well as the conditions in which they are kept. Do not expect to handle the puppies, for any conscientious breeder is aware of the risks of transmitting diseases before puppies are fully vaccinated. Instead, observe the pups in their pens and ask the breeder how they are raised and what sort of socializing they receive. Healthy pups appear curious and lively, with glossy coats and clear eyes. Be wary of breeders whose kennels are a mess. Central to the overall quality of any breeding program is the cleanliness of the kennel. Filthy conditions often mean unhealthy dogs and puppies that are especially vulnerable to infectious diseases such as parvovirus and coccidiosis. There might be behavioral side effects with these pups as well, such as coprophagia and house-training problems. A dirty, disorganized kennel not only reflects badly on the breeder, it could spell future health and behavioral problems for you as well.

Good breeders will be able to show a clean environment, healthy puppies, and breeding dogs with sound temperaments. They will be both knowledgeable and sensitive to health issues within their breed and will always use only OFA-certified* breeding animals. Because of their desire for excellence they will belong to their national breed club (for example, the German Shepherd Dog Club of America) and probably be involved in showing their dogs in obedience, conformation, or field trials. They will allow you to return a puppy if a veterinary examination reveals a problem (usually within forty-eight hours of purchase), and their sales policy will cover your right to return a puppy with crippling hip dysplasia or genetically unsound temperament within the first year.

Most important, however, they will be interested in you. Good breeders do not peddle their puppies to just anyone. They are concerned that the pups they raise go to good homes, and they will spend time planning good match-ups based on personal interviews and detailed application forms. Most often, reputable breeders prefer to select puppies for their clients instead of relying on the client's choice, which is often overly emotional and mistaken. The breeder's experience in placement is usually more objective and will serve the client's needs better.

Buying a puppy from a breeder is much more than a standard business transaction. The pup you take home with you is a living creature and will have a profound effect on your life, so it pays to be careful. If you find a breeder who fits the profile described above, you have an excellent chance of getting a puppy you can live and work with successfully.

---

*The Orthopedic Foundation for Animals evaluates hip and elbow X rays to determine the presence and degree of a genetically transmitted condition known as dysplasia. Dogs that are certified by the OFA are acceptable for breeding.

CHAPTER NINE

First Things First

Having decided on a breed and chosen a breeder you can trust, you may still have to wait a while before getting your puppy. Often the puppies you see during preliminary visits are already spoken for, so you must wait for a pup from a future breeding. This is just as well, for you can use this time for preparation and learning. Your breeder can recommend a book on her breed as well as general introductions to dog care and training, such as this one. Look for several other training books on your own, making sure the ones you choose cover puppy behavior and training. Different approaches provide different insights, and no one book can ever give the last word on training.

During the waiting period, you may find it helpful to attend some local K.P.T. (Kindergarten Puppy Training) and obedience classes as an observer to get a feel for what is involved in these types of training. Without the distraction of a puppy of your own, you can discover a lot just by watching different owners and their dogs and listening to the trainers. At local obedience trials you can see the actual results of conscientious obedience training. A well-trained dog at work is certainly a beautiful sight, and it is worth it to see for yourself the successful and harmonious interaction of dog and master. Check with local obedience clubs for the dates of trials taking place in your area, and make it a point to attend one for some firsthand experience.

When you hear from your breeder that your puppy will soon be ready to be taken home, you should make some specific preparations. Before you actually pick up your new puppy, gather the family or household members together to discuss future responsibilities for the pup. Make sure that everyone is clear about how the puppy is to be managed, since owner consistency is one of the biggest factors in a smooth adjustment to the home. The separation of your puppy from its littermates will be stressful; everything familiar will be gone. Conflicting signals from different members of the household would only compound this distress. Consistent handling by everyone will prevent confusion and give the puppy a clear set of expectations right from the start.

To accomplish this, set up some basic ground rules: How many times a day will the pup be fed, walked, and played with? Who will do this? Where will the pup eliminate? Which rooms of the house will the pup be allowed into and where will she be kept when she cannot be supervised? Where will she sleep? Best to resolve all of these issues before the arrival of the puppy.

If there are young children in the house, discuss with them their role in welcoming the new pup to her home. Both before and after adopting a pup, owners must educate their children in proper behavior. Kids have a tendency to maul puppies and to contribute to stress by their squealing, roughhousing, hugs, kisses, and teasing during the first few days. Explain to them that it will take several days for the puppy to get used to her new home, and that during that time they will have to be calm and quiet around their new friend.

It is best to plan on having the puppy arrive during a vacation, when someone can be with her most of the time for the first week or two. Most puppies are adopted either just prior to or during the fear period (8–10 weeks of age), when a close bond with a new master or mistress develops most naturally. Take advantage of this. It is never wise to make a new puppy spend large blocks of time alone when you first adopt her, since the stress of such abandonment can lead to serious problems.

Naming

It is best to decide on a name for your puppy prior to her arrival in your house. Why not spend some time considering the different possibilities and including everyone in the decision making? Though picking a name is enjoyable, do not take it lightly, since the name is the doorway to communication with your pup. Her name not only reflects a dog's individuality, it also reveals the way you look at her.

This is worth considering seriously. Many people do not realize when choosing a name that dogs are not *people*. A dog does not understand a name the way we do. She does not identify herself with her name nor take her self-identity from it. She recognizes the particular sound we have imposed on her only as a call to attention, having learned to associate it with our desire for expectant attentiveness. A dog, then, makes no judgment on her name. Thus, the poetic qualities of the name, its psychological associations, are important only for us and serve as a sign of our mental and emotional bond with our dog.

Instead of choosing human names for our dogs, we should select names that speak to a dog as a dog yet respect her own dignity and uniqueness. Otherwise we can easily forget that a dog really is a dog and fall into the trap of giving her human status. The dog becomes one of us, a "Fred," an "Oscar," or a "Betty," and we end up anthropomorphizing our pets, forgetting how differently they see things.

The chief rule is to pick a name easy for the pup to understand and for you to pronounce. In general, we suggest short, two-syllable names that end in a long vowel or a soft *a* (for example, Nero, Anka, Ola, Ivy), because they are clear and easy for the pup to distinguish. This helps the puppy tune in to you quickly and is essential later on when you are teaching obedience, especially the recall.

Naturally, you should avoid names that rhyme with or sound like obedience commands, and do not select one over three syllables long; complex and exotic names can be clumsy or confusing and often must be repeated to be understood. Similarly, we find excessively sweet or joke names totally inappropriate for a dog. Dogs are remarkably intuitive; they sense when they are being made fun of or when they are the objects of suffocating sentimentality. When you choose a name that wears well and reflects common sense, you and your pup will be the better for it.

Though you should avoid the temptation to go out and spend a fortune on equipment for your new pup, it is still a good idea to have a number of essential items on hand before you bring your puppy home. These include food and water bowls, collar and leash, grooming tools, shipping crate or metal cage, chemical deodorizer/cleaner, and toys. Do not wait until you already have the puppy to do this, since you will be using them right from the start. Try a pet-supply store or mail-order catalogue, as opposed to a department or hardware store — the products are usually sturdier and of better quality.

Food and Water Bowls   We recommend tip-proof bowls, either heavy ceramic or stainless steel. Make sure the bowls are big enough to be used when the puppy grows up. Beware of cheap plastic or metal bowls — they can splinter or develop jagged edges if the puppy starts chewing on them. Remember that certain breeds with long, floppy ears (like hounds and spaniels) do best with a specially tapered bowl that prevents the ears from resting in the bowl as the pup eats or drinks.

Collars and Leash   Most puppies grow quickly. By the time they are adults, medium- to large-size dogs have outgrown at least two collars and two leashes, so keep your initial purchases simple. We suggest two collars to start with: either a flat nylon or rounded leather collar to hold an identification tag and dog license (in case your dog gets lost), and a braided nylon training (slip) collar for preliminary obedience work. We prefer nylon collars to metal ones, since they are easier on a dog's coat and stay up higher on the neck.

For puppies, lightweight nylon show leads (six-foot) are excellent. They introduce the pup to a leash gently, without trauma, and are relatively inexpensive (about $3). As pups grow, they require a more durable training leash. We suggest a six-foot braided leather leash without sewn parts that could separate. The width you choose (⅜", ½", ¾") depends on what size your pup will be at maturity.

Grooming Tools   Proper grooming tools depend on the breed of dog you select. Ask your breeder about any tools specific to your breed. Some basics are a wire slicker brush,

Some important equipment for you and your pup. Pictured are two nylon training collars, a flat nylon collar, a six-foot braided leather leash, and two flexi-leads, one sixteen feet, the other twenty-six feet in length.

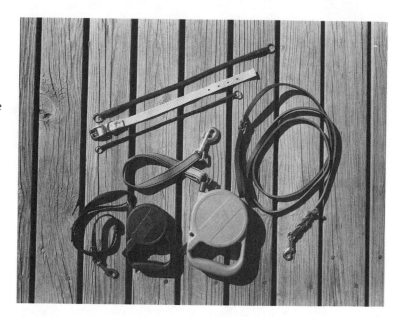

undercoat rake (no German shepherd owner should be without one!), a dematting tool, comb, nail trimmers, and ear cleaner (such as Ear-Rite or Otic liquid).

Shipping Crate or Metal Cage　We feel strongly that shipping crates and metal cages are effective, humane aids in house-training a puppy. They provide the young pup with a secure den and capitalize on its tendency to keep its sleeping area clean. They also are the safest way to transport a dog by car, preventing injury due to sudden stops. We recommend either an airline-approved kennel made of high-density plastic, or a slant-front metal cage designed especially for transporting dogs in hatchbacks or station wagons. These are lightweight and can be disassembled easily for cleaning. Since they are expensive, get a crate that will be big enough for your pup to use when she is fully grown.

Chemical Deodorizer/Cleaners　During the house-training of your puppy there are bound to be some "accidents." Because puppies tend to return to the scene, where they detect the smell of urine and feces ("scent posts"), it is important that these spots be cleaned properly, using a product that effectively neutralizes the odor. For cleaning puppy accidents on nonporous hard surfaces, as well as on carpeting, it is best to use a pet deodorizer/cleaner designed for this purpose, which you can obtain at a pet shop.

Toys Every pup needs several toys to play with. We like to expose our pups to a meat-scented nylon bone, tennis ball, and play ring to avoid boredom and control chewing. We like to start puppies out on nylon bones as opposed to rawhide ones, since they are much more durable and less expensive in the long run.

Optional Items These optional items, while not absolutely necessary, can be helpful.

- Pooper scooper: to make cleanup of the soiling area easier. More handy if you separate the two parts.
- Bitter Apple: a product designed to keep dogs from chewing objects in your house or from licking boredom sores on themselves.
- Flexi-leash: a retractable leash that extends up to 30' in length. Invaluable for leash-training a puppy in a firm yet gentle manner.
- Dog bed: these are excellent for giving pups a secure sense of place when they sleep. The best dog beds use a combination of cedar chips and fiberfill; cedar chips are a natural repellent to fleas and ticks, and fiberfill helps preserve the bed's shape and softness. Make sure that the cover is removable, washable, and durable.
- Folding gate: to confine a pup to a particular area. The gate should be sturdy, made of a material other than wood (which is chewable) and have slats that are small enough to prevent a puppy from sticking her head through and getting caught.

Finally, before buying a large quantity of dog food, it is best to speak to your breeder and veterinarian. Choosing a high-quality dog food is an important factor in your dog's health, and it pays to check with professionals before you make your decision. We will have more to say about nutrition in chapter seventeen.

CHAPTER TEN

A New Beginning

In my beginning is my end.

— T. S. Eliot, *Four Quartets*

The day you go to get your new puppy always has a bit of magic about it. It is a day of anticipation and excitement, dreams and possibilities, hopes and aspirations. Puppies have a way of reducing even the most serious adult to spontaneous displays of childlike delight. It is part of their charm. A puppy touches something very deep in us, and when we first hold one in our arms it is easy to be swept away with blind enthusiasm. Who would suspect the challenge that awaits us?

Nevertheless, magic is deceiving. Whether this day is *truly* blessed remains to be seen, and so we offer a word of caution: enthusiasm that is not grounded in reality, supported by knowledge and understanding, has a way of fizzling when ordinary problems develop. Once the puppy passes the novelty stage, once he becomes a familiar part of your household, the true nature of the relationship becomes apparent, and second thoughts may arise. New owners can quickly lose interest. A more substantial foundation than mere enthusiasm is required to sustain this relationship.

Beyond the joy and emotion of getting a puppy, beyond the good feelings this new bundle of life inspires in us, lies a deeper, more profound reality that should be the anchor of any relationship with a puppy: adoption. Adopting a puppy means bringing him into the heart of your life, and developing a healthy relationship demands plenty of hard work and dedication from you — especially now, at the beginning. The day you adopt a puppy begins a new phase in his life, one rooted in his earliest experiences, yet now poised to take fresh expression in *your* life. How he develops now depends largely on you. The puppy is no longer the breeder's, no longer his mother's. Today he becomes your puppy, a new member of your family, and this means you become parent, companion, pack leader, peer — the puppy's closest friend.

If this sounds sentimental or idealistic to you, think again. Canines are among the most sociable species in the animal kingdom. Whereas a wolf pup is naturally integrated into the wider pack with his brothers and sisters, your pup does not have that possibility. Instead, he adapts himself by establishing his closest social bonds with you and those you live with, treating you as his fellow pack members. It is now up to you to teach your pup his proper role in *your* pack family, a process that begins the moment you adopt him.

As we have seen over and over again, a puppy builds on previous experiences, and this is no less true of his first few days in your home. Good habits start from the beginning. Planning ahead, taking the time and energy necessary to help your pup make a smooth transition to his new home, increases the probability that his good behavior will continue to develop into maturity. The opposite is also true. High amounts of stress, careless house-training procedures, pampering, and improper discipline, to name just a few potential problems, can get the relationship off to a rocky start and lead to serious problems later on. Since it is reasonable to assume that this puppy will be an intimate part of your life for the next ten to fifteen years, it makes sense to put serious thought and effort into these first few days in order to establish a sound framework for the future.

With this in mind, let us take a detailed look at your pup's first few days with you. During this time, the guiding principle underlying your approach to the pup should be to minimize unnecessarily stressful experiences and to establish a natural rhythm that your puppy can easily adjust to. Since there are many things to remember, having a clear set of guidelines to follow will help bring order and understanding to a potentially chaotic period and reduce the stress you and your puppy experience. The following suggestions will get you and your pup off to a good start, one that you will appreciate in the months and years to come. "In my beginning is my end."

A puppy should be adopted only when someone can stay with him most of the time during the first week to promote house-training and socialization. This may mean sacrificing a week of vacation time; however, the long-term benefits make it worthwhile. Speak with the breeder ahead of time and arrange to pick up your puppy in the morning of the first day of a long weekend or planned vacation. This will allow the puppy to spend most of the first day with you and will hasten his adjustment to you and your home.

Ask your breeder not to give the puppy food or water the morning of pick-up. Most do this routinely, but it is best to check ahead. Fasting will not harm the pup and reduces the likelihood that he will get carsick and vomit on the way home. Also, we advise that you drive to the breeder's with at least one other adult, since it is difficult to drive and watch the puppy at the same time. If you have a long car trip ahead of you, you might consider carrying a crate in the car; however, if you do this, the pup should be exposed to a crate several days beforehand by the breeder.

If your puppy has already been selected for you, you will naturally want to spend some time with him when you arrive at the breeder's. When you first meet your pup, sit or crouch down to his level and start playing with him. We like clients to spend ten or fifteen minutes making friends with the pup before we start answering particular questions they may have and going over the necessary paperwork. This gives the initial excitement and anticipation a chance to settle down and helps everyone pay closer attention to instructions during the interview.

New owners ordinarily have lots of questions to ask the breeder, so it is wise to make a list of them beforehand. Aside from specific questions about the way the puppy was raised and the type of personality he possesses (in the litter as well as by himself), you should also ask how he scored on his Puppy Aptitude Test. These results will suggest specific guidelines for handling this particular pup and will help you to avoid management errors during the first weeks.

Make sure that you get a written record of the immunizations and wormings that your puppy has received. If your puppy is purebred, you should receive a copy of his pedigree and the AKC registration slip. Though you may have a particular type of dog food in mind for your pup, it is always best to continue feeding the brand that the puppy is currently eating for at least several more days, gradually changing to the new brand. Sudden changes in diet add to stress and can lead to diarrhea or loss of appetite. If you do not plan to use the brand chosen by the breeder, ask if he could give you several days' supply to help wean the puppy onto the new food.

The Ride Home

Keep the ride home as relaxed and low-key as possible, allowing whoever accompanied you to do the driving. Unless you are using a dog crate, cover your lap and the seating area next to you with a towel or old bedsheet in case the puppy gets carsick. Let the pup ride in your lap or lie on the seat next to you, and keep one hand in gentle contact with him. It is best to avoid any kind of coddling or doting behavior, especially if the pup starts to whine, since this only reinforces whining as an attention-getting behavior. A certain amount of whining is to be expected; if things get too noisy, try putting the pup on the floor between your feet: the vibrations of the car often have a calming effect. Do not punish the pup for whining or vomiting. On the way home, stop periodically and let the pup stretch its legs, but stay away from any area that is frequented by other dogs, since your pup is not yet fully vaccinated and is vulnerable to contagious diseases.

Introduction to the House

When you arrive home, first take the puppy outdoors to the spot you have chosen for his soiling area and wait for him to eliminate. Normally after a car ride the puppy will have to relieve himself, and when he does so, be sure to praise him enthusiastically. Then take the puppy into the house and allow him to walk around and explore, keeping a close eye on him from a distance. Do not be surprised if the pup seems a little disoriented at first. Even the most outgoing puppy will experience strain or confusion in a strange environment, separated from his littermates. Be calm and reassuring, and allow the pup to adjust at his own pace.

If, while exploring, the pup shows interest in chewing something inappropriate, gently distract him by focusing his attention on a squeak toy or meat-scented nylon bone. *Do not discipline the pup at this time.* Should the pup not seem interested in the bone, entice him to play by some play-inducing gestures such as quick hand clapping or rubbing your hands along the floor. If he starts to follow you around the house, encourage him. Tap the side of your leg (or use keys if the pup is used to them) and call his name as you walk, praising him as he comes along and investigates the different rooms. During these first days, whenever your pup begins to focus his attention on you, either to follow or to simply look up at you, say his name in a cheerful, pleasant tone of voice that encourages him to hold the eye contact. These simple dominance exercises quickly teach your pup his name while presenting you as his leader in a way that builds confidence and trust. Conclude the session by crouching down and playing with him on his level for a while.

Keep the introduction to your household quiet and unforced, allowing the process of bonding to develop in a relaxed and gradual manner. For the first few days, it is important not to overwhelm the puppy with visitors who are curious about the new arrival. Save introducing your pup to friends and relatives until you are certain he has made a smooth transition, usually after two or three days. Then you may initiate a variety of important socializing experiences, described later.

Usually puppies are not interested in eating as soon as they get home, since everything is unfamiliar. Hold off feeding your puppy for at least a couple of hours until he has begun to settle down. Then, offer him some food, and when he has finished eating, take him out to his soiling area and wait for him to eliminate. Puppies typically have to urinate and/or defecate following eating and drinking, waking (short naps included), vigorous play activity, and chewing a bone. If you should wait ten to fifteen minutes and the pup still has not eliminated, take him back into the house for several minutes and then try again. Repeat this procedure as necessary. When he has finished, praise the puppy and bring him back into the house. He should now be ready for a nap.

Young puppies still require plenty of sleep and should have several naps during the day. Choose an area where the pup can be kept safely when he cannot be supervised and which is not isolated from family activity. Usually, the best

The correct way
to hold a puppy.

location for this is the kitchen, since it is large enough for the
puppy to move around in and can be easily blocked off with
one or two dog gates. Make sure the area is puppy-proofed
from anything that could be dangerous for the puppy when
left alone, such as electric cords, small and chewable objects
(rubber golashes, shoes, etc.), and anything made of wood.
We also recommend keeping a shipping crate there to serve
as the pup's den during the day. As described in the next
chapter, throughout the early stages of house-training, you
will be alternately keeping your pup in either of these two
confined areas. For this first nap, leave the cage door of the
crate open (you can tie it so that it does not shut if the pup
knocks into it) and have comfortable bedding or fake fur in

the crate itself. Puppies will naturally seek the security of the den atmosphere on their own. Do not be concerned if the puppy initially starts to whine in his confined area; wait for him to relax and fall asleep and then periodically check on him to see when he wakes up. When he does, take the puppy out to his soiling area and let him eliminate.

During these first few days, it will be necessary to pick the puppy up from time to time; young puppies are rarely conditioned to a leash at the breeder's, and this will take you at least several days. While you should encourage a pup to walk on his own whenever possible, unfamiliar experiences such as walking up stairs may require some initial help. There is a right and wrong way to do this. Whenever you pick your puppy up, always use both hands. Place one hand between the forelegs to support the chest and the other behind the thighs to support the rear. This ensures that he is perfectly balanced and unable to wiggle free. *Never* pick a puppy up by his front legs alone (since this could dislocate his shoulder) or pick him up by the scruff of the neck (which could be traumatizing). Also, puppies occasionally solicit attention by approaching their owners and whining. A good response to this is occasionally to pick the pup up and pet him briefly, making eye contact at the same time. This reinforces the positive dominance of the owner and is an effective way of having your puppy key into you.

The First Night

The first night a puppy spends away from his littermates is often traumatic for both owner and puppy alike. The pup's incessant whining and squealing, restlessness, inability to sleep, and the need to eliminate can all contribute to making your first night together miserable. In the face of such disturbances, the temptation will be simply to isolate the pup in a basement or far corner of the house and face the consequences the next morning. We hope that you will not do this. This only compounds his sense of isolation and may make it difficult to teach him to be alone in the future.

It is helpful to understand that when a puppy becomes anxious during this first night, he is reacting naturally, according to a separation reflex. In the wild, when a wolf pup is separated from his pack, he becomes highly emotional and begins to whine, bark, or howl. This is instinctive behavior that helps reunite the pup with his pack, which is essential if he is to survive. This same instinct is at work in your pup.

The best method we have found to prevent night trauma is to let your puppy sleep in your bedroom on an old sheet or blanket, tethered next to your bed. This works because the pup will want the security of being with you. We prefer this to using the crate, since most pups will not be used to the crate this first evening and will tend to make a lot of noise in it. Before retiring, take your puppy out to eliminate and walk with him around the backyard for a while. Give him the chance to get a little tired. When you are ready to go to sleep, tether the pup with a leash and place him on the bedding so that he is right next to you. This does two things: first, it helps the pup to adjust to you as part of his new pack. In a seven-hour block of time, the pup continuously smells you, listens to your breathing, and accepts the security of your leadership. Second, it prevents the puppy from getting up in the middle of the night to eliminate away from his bed. Remember, puppies ordinarily will not soil in their sleeping area.

It is normal to expect some whining this first night. Should the pup start to do so, reach down and quiet him without a fuss. Do this calmly, soothing him at first. If whining persists, a gentle scruff shake along with a low "No, go to sleep" may be necessary (see chapter sixteen for more details). *Do not put the puppy in bed with you.* The pup will come to expect this and the practice can lead to a number of behavior problems later on in life. If the pup has been quiet for several hours and then begins to whine, he probably has to go out. Dealing with all this is part of being a new parent and may be necessary for the first few nights.

As soon as you rise in the morning, get dressed quickly and take your pup immediately to his soiling area. Let him empty completely; puppies will sometimes eliminate several times first thing in the morning. When he has finished, praise him cheerfully and return to the house.

Trip to the Veterinarian

For as long as your puppy lives with you, he will require periodic veterinary care for routine shots and check-ups, treatment for minor illnesses, and possibly emergency health care. All will mean trips to your veterinarian. Your puppy's first experience at a veterinary clinic is important, since it often leaves a lasting impression that conditions future visits. An initial visit marked by a traumatic, negative experience will most likely establish a pattern, making future ones repeatedly unpleasant. One of the most common behavioral complaints we receive from clients concerns their pet's behavior at the veterinarian's. Usually this is deeply ingrained, going back to puppyhood.

You can avoid this by making your pup's first visit to your veterinarian as pleasant and untraumatic as possible. Schedule an appointment with your veterinarian for the day after you purchase your puppy, so that he can receive a thorough health examination and any vaccinations that are due. Ask if it is possible to bring your puppy right at the beginning of clinic hours, since it is not a good idea to be sitting in a waiting room with other people and their possibly sick pets. Having not yet received the full cycle of vaccinations, your puppy is still vulnerable to infections. Be sure to take a fresh stool sample with you (in a paper cup) to have examined for parasites. It is common for pups to have worms, and often they require several treatments to show a parasite-free stool sample.

Keep the visit itself calm and cheerful. Praise your puppy gently as he is examined, and, especially afterward, make sure your behavior toward your pup is happy, keeping the tone of your voice pleasant. Do not be overly sympathetic or indulgent if your pup gets upset, as this only reinforces whining, spoiled behavior. Simply try to distract him with playful gestures. You want your pup to form a happy, enjoyable association with the experience.

CHAPTER ELEVEN

House-training and Preliminary Obedience Exercises

During the first days, there is no more pressing task for you than to see to it that your puppy acquires proper elimination habits. Nothing is so tiresome as a dog who has not learned to use her designated area for elimination, and statistics show that more puppies are abandoned every year because of house-training problems than for any other reason. Have no illusions about this: starting off house-training correctly is one of the pillars of a healthy relationship with your pup, and it is your responsibility to follow sensible guidelines to establish good habits.

Fortunately, there are natural instincts in dogs which, when combined with understanding and consistency on your part, make house-training a relatively straightforward process. Dogs that are raised properly as young puppies have an innate tendency to keep their den areas clean. As we have seen, young puppies instinctively move away from the nest to eliminate. In doing this, they naturally create "scent posts," places where they will consistently eliminate. Whenever dogs urinate or defecate, scent chemicals called pheromones are also passed with the waste. When dogs smell these on subsequent occasions, an eliminative reflex is triggered that disposes them to repeat the process. Besides being a necessary bodily activity, this process also develops into a form of social communication with other dogs. A dog defines her territory by leaving these scent marks for herself and other dogs to sniff out. When your pup smells her own mark, she repeats the "marking" and forms the habit of using the same area for elimination.

Understanding this allows us to devise a preventive, humane, and effective approach to house-training that avoids the common mistakes new owners make and is in harmony with a pup's natural instincts. Successful house-training depends on several things: sound behavioral principles, a balanced, nutritious diet that produces firm stools, and faithful attention by you. The following guidelines provide you with an integrated program that will house-train an eight- to ten-week-old puppy in one to three weeks and help prepare for the time when your dog will be able to be trusted alone in your house.

Using a Crate

We are decidedly in favor of crate-training puppies. Though many of our clients are initially horrified at the prospect of using such "barbaric, medieval devices to stuff their puppies into," once they come to understand a crate from a dog's perspective, their attitude changes.

All canines are den animals; they naturally seek out spots for rest that are sheltered and secure. This is why family dogs often lie under dining room tables, underneath beds, or in dark closets: they are simply following a deep-seated den instinct.

By using a crate, you provide your pup with her own den and capitalize on her innate tendency to keep this area clean. This is why house-training with a crate is so sensible. A puppy kept in her den for a *reasonable* length of time (no more than three hours at a time during the day) will refrain from soiling and will learn to hold herself until you let her out. Consistently doing this helps your pup quickly acquire a regular schedule for elimination.

There are other benefits as well. Crates prevent young puppies from getting into mischief when you cannot watch them and confines their chewing to objects you have provided. Also, crates are ideal for transporting your puppy by car, keeping her safe from sudden stops and swerves, as well as providing safekeeping whenever you stay at motels. There

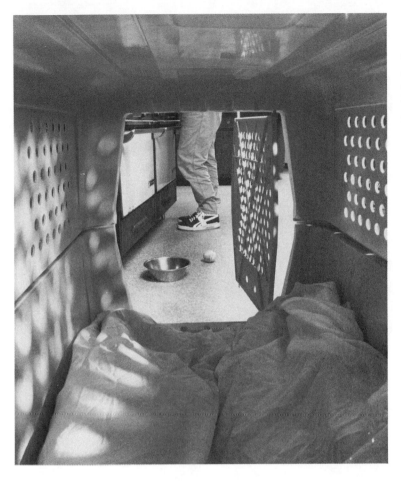

Think of the crate from your pup's perspective. Dogs naturally seek out denlike spots that are sheltered and secure.

will always be times when you will not be able to supervise your pup. Having a crate simplifies these situations and provides your pup with a spot that she will always be comfortable in because it is familiar.

Introducing Your Pup to a Crate

As with all things in puppyhood, it is important to introduce your pup to the crate gradually. Go out of your way to make her first experience with this a pleasant one. Begin by placing an old blanket over the floor of the crate. *Never force a puppy*

A pup who is gradually introduced to a crate will feel relaxed and comfortable in it.

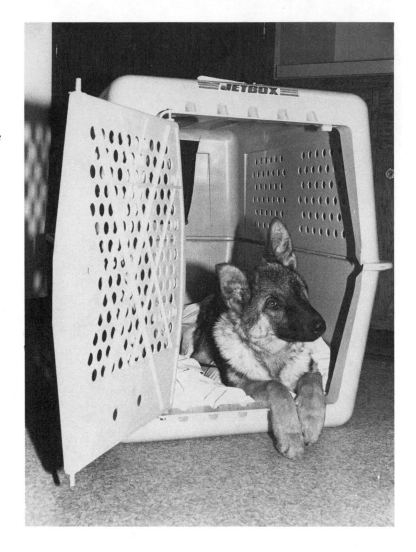

in, shut the door, and leave during the first session. Instead, allow your pup to explore around the crate. Then place several pieces of kibble in the crate as your pup watches. If she goes into the crate after the food, praise her enthusiastically. If not, gently lift the pup up and place her inside the crate, without shutting the door. You can pet the pup if she needs reassurance. Next, call the pup out and praise her when she comes to you. Repeat this for several minutes. Assuming that your pup shows no signs of disturbance, try closing the door for a minute. Conclude the session by opening the door and praising her.

The next time you feed your pup, feed her inside the crate,

luring her inside with her food bowl, and then close the door. When she finishes, your pup may start whining and barking to get out. This should be discouraged by firmly striking the front of the cage door with your hand, and saying "No!" in a deep voice. Wait for your pup to be quiet for five minutes before opening the door and escorting her out to her soiling area to eliminate.

As your puppy becomes comfortable with the crate, you can increase the time that she spends there, realizing that it is important not to overuse it. *Your pup should not live in her crate — she should live with you.* However, let her spend periods of time there when she cannot be watched, when she is resting, eating or traveling, and while she is being house-trained, since during this time staying in the crate will teach her to hold herself. Remember, dogs normally will not soil in their nests. Used this way, a crate is an important aid in your pup's adjustment to its new life.

A Consistent Schedule

Dogs are creatures of habit and quickly adapt to scheduled routines. Be a fanatic about your pup's schedule. Starting your puppy off immediately with set times for feeding, watering, and elimination creates a rhythm that allows you reliably to anticipate when she will have to eliminate, thus reducing accidents.

First thing every morning, take your pup immediately to her soiling area to eliminate. Do not let the pup out by herself, even if your yard is fenced. Taking your pup out ensures that she will always use the same spot and that the praise is properly timed. Always use the same door and route, and for the first several months leave one or two stools in the soiling area each day for her to smell. Watch her carefully as you let her sniff and circle around. As soon as she appears ready to eliminate, softly repeat a simple word or phrase (such as "Do it!" or "Hurry up!") to coincide with the act. Repeat it softly several times; once you begin the command, do not stop until she actually begins to eliminate. When she does, *quietly* change from the command word to soft praise until she finishes.

Puppies often have to go several times when they first wake up, so make sure your puppy is completely finished before you take her back into the house. When you are certain she is done, conclude with a "Good girl!" and walk her back. Follow this same procedure every time you take your pup out to eliminate, using the key word and praise as the conditioning factors. After fifty to seventy-five occasions of well-timed commands and praise, your pup will have a conditioned reflex to eliminate anything in her bladder or bowel whenever she hears her trigger word. This is a great aid to house-training and avoids long waits late at night or in inclement weather.

Feeding Schedule

Plan on feeding your young puppy three times daily, at the same times each day. An ideal schedule is 7 A.M., 12 noon, and 5 P.M., because it ensures that your pup will be empty by the time she goes to sleep and can pass the night without having to go out. Keep to this schedule until the pup shifts to two meals daily, between fourteen and eighteen weeks of age.

When you feed, be certain that your pup receives the correct amount of a nutritionally balanced, high-quality *puppy* food. Avoid generic or bargain-brand foods you see in supermarkets, as well as prepackaged, semimoist foods that contain high amounts of glucose (sugar). These foods generally lack the proper nutrients necessary for puppies, disrupt their normal growth, and often cause diarrhea. Training manuals frequently underestimate the importance of good diet in house-training. It is of little value to a pup to go through a detailed house-training program if she is suffering from either loose stools or constipation connected with poor diet or overfeeding. Take the time to find a top-quality kibble designed for puppies; ask your veterinarian and breeder about particular brands and amounts to feed, and consult the General Care section later in this book for more detailed information.

We suggest feeding your pup in her crate; this forms another positive association with the crate and allows her to eat without distraction. It also helps prevent the pup from eliminating immediately on finishing her meal. Give a pup fifteen minutes to finish her meal, offer her some water, and then take her to the soiling area.

Sample House-training Schedule for a Young Puppy

6:30 A.M.	Rise. Walk pup briefly.
7:00 A.M.	Feed pup and offer a drink of water. Walk pup. Return home and play briefly with pup. Pup stays in crate.
Midmorning	Walk pup. After walk, pup stays with owner 15 minutes. Pup returns to crate.
12 noon– 1:00 P.M.	Feed pup second meal and offer water. Walk pup. Return home and play with pup. Pup returns to crate.
Midafternoon	Offer pup water. Walk pup. Pup returns to crate.
5:00 P.M.	Feed pup third meal and offer water. Walk pup. Allow pup to play in kitchen while dinner is being prepared.
7:00 P.M.	Walk pup briefly. Return home and play with pup. Pup returns to crate.
Before bed	Walk pup. Pup sleeps in crate or on a tether in your bedroom.

After elimination sessions, it is a good idea to spend some time playing with your pup in the house. Do this either in the gated kitchen area or in some other area of the house, as you prefer. Since your pup has just finished eliminating, you can be relaxed, without having to worry about "accidents." When the playtime is over, lead your pup to her crate and let her rest for an hour or two, leaving one or two toys with her.

During the house-training period, plan on taking your pup to her soiling area once every hour and a half. Before you go out, always offer her some water. Keeping to this schedule, you will discover that your pup will gradually be able to hold herself for longer periods of time, establishing a sense of confidence. This is another reason why adopting your pup during a vacation period makes sense.

House-training and Preliminary Obedience Exercises | 117

Inevitably, some puppy "accidents" are bound to occur. No matter how watchful you are, how careful about looking for warning signals, your pup will probably have several episodes of house-soiling during her first weeks with you. When these happen, it is of the utmost importance to deal with them correctly, in a manner appropriate to your pup's age.

One of the most frequent mistakes new owners make with their pups is the tendency to overcorrect for house-soiling errors that have already occurred. Puppies live entirely in the present. They do not "remember" acts of house-soiling, and punishments given after the fact only confuse the pup and harm your relationship. That is why it is important to have your pup either with you or safely confined and not to allow her to wander around the house unmonitored. Punishments based on poorly thought out "folk remedies" such as rubbing a pup's nose in her mess, beating her belatedly at the site of the mess and then isolating her, or letting her lie in her own mess when she has soiled her crate, are absolutely inappropriate ways of dealing with the problem. They give the pup the wrong message and end up producing a pup that is terrified of you.

For a correction to be meaningful, you must catch your pup *in the act*. If you see your pup starting to eliminate in the house, quickly raise your voice enough to startle her (use "No!" or "Ahh!"); shake her firmly by the scruff of the neck and sweep her up in your arms, taking her immediately outside to the soiling area. Wait for her to eliminate, following the method we have already described. Most pups will stop what they are doing as soon as they are startled. If your pup requires more, throw a set of keys in her general direction or use a shaker can (an old soda can with some pennies in it).

Young pups have to be watched constantly when they are not confined. Learn to look for telltale signs that your puppy needs to go out. These include restless pacing, intense sniffing of the floor, whining, or scratching at the door that leads to the soiling area. If you should come upon an accident that has already occurred, count it *your* mistake. Take your pup to her den so that she does not see you cleaning up the mess. You do not want her to think of you as her maid.

From our discussion of scent posts, it should be apparent why cleaning up accidents thoroughly is so vital to the success of house-training. With scent capacities estimated conservatively as being a hundred times greater than those of human beings, dogs can easily detect lingering odors of feces and urine in areas that have been already cleaned with conventional products such as detergent or ammonia. The result can be a distressing pattern of repeated accidents in the same spot.

To prevent your pup from making scent posts of locations in your house, neutralize urine and feces odors with a chemical deodorizer/cleanser that breaks them down chemically. Whether on carpet, vinyl tile, linoleum, or wood, after you thoroughly clean up the mess, spray the spot with a chemical deodorizer and cover the area with an overturned chair until it is completely dry.

The City Puppy

For a new puppy owner living in a city, house-training presents specific difficulties that must be handled differently from those used in suburban or rural environments. While it is always preferable to house-train a pup to a safe outdoor location (usually a spot in your yard), often in urban environments this is neither possible nor advisable. Aside from the difficulties living on the fourteenth floor of an apartment building creates for getting your pup outside quickly, city puppies are particularly vulnerable to diseases such as parvovirus and canine distemper, which are communicated through urine, feces, and vomit. City veterinarians are rightly insistent that clients not walk their pups on the street until they have received their full series of immunization vaccinations, at sixteen weeks of age.

In these circumstances, paper-training is the only real alternative. To do this properly, begin by placing several layers of newspaper over the entire confined area (if possible, over a large plastic sheet), to prevent urine from seeping through onto the floor. Naturally, make sure the confined area has easy-to-clean surfaces such as linoleum or ceramic tile, never an absorbent surface such as carpeting. We still advise keeping a crate available for the pup's use in this area, since it gives her a secure spot of her own.

Instead of taking the pup outside to her soiling area after feeding and watering, simply wait for the pup to soil, praise her, and then change the papers. When you first change the papers, leave a soiled paper underneath the fresh papers in the area where you wish the pup to relieve herself. The scent will draw the pup to the spot, helping her to eliminate exclusively in that location. Leave a little bit more of the floor unprotected by the papers after each paper change, until you finally have an area the size of four sheets of newspaper. In a few days the pup should be conditioned to seek out that spot to relieve herself. Keep in mind, however, that once your pup is fully immunized, at sixteen weeks, you will want to shift her soiling habits from papers to an outside location. This is usually done by strictly confining a pup to her crate as described in the original schedule. When the scheduled time for elimination arrives, whisk her out and wait for her to eliminate outdoors. Praise her effusively if she does this. If she does not relieve herself in a reasonable period of time, take her back to her crate, wait five minutes, then take her back out. Patience is important here. For a pup who has difficulty making the transition, try putting one of her soiled papers outside until she gets the point.

Leash-Training and Preliminary Obedience Work

Puppies are rarely accustomed to a collar and leash when they first arrive home, and though it is important to begin using them right away, if you do this too abruptly and without adequate preparation, their first reactions will probably be fearful and belligerent; they will balk and fight all your efforts to get them to walk with you. A more sensible approach is to make the introduction gradually, over the course of several days, building up the pup's self-confidence as she learns to accept the leash. Done in this way, the leash becomes a means of bonding, of communicating with your pup, and not an instrument of compulsion.

Begin by having your pup wear her flat buckle collar around the house for a day or two. Do not be concerned if she initially scratches at the collar or shakes her head. Though a collar might be uncomfortable at first, puppies quickly forget they are on.

Introducing the leash follows naturally. First, let your pup begin dragging the lead around the house, getting her used to the feel of minor pressure on her neck. As the pup walks

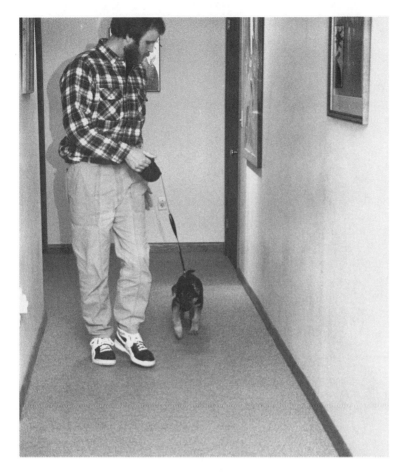

Retractable leashes are excellent for preliminary leash-training.

around, follow her, then gently pick up the lead and walk with your pup, keeping the lead held high and speaking in a friendly, encouraging manner as you walk.

You can follow a similar routine in your backyard. Start by following your pup around the yard without a leash, praising her as she investigates. After a short while, reverse the roles, getting your pup's attention by clapping your hands and enticing her in cheerful, encouraging tones. Praise her enthusiastically when she follows. Next, try the same sequence with the lead attached. If the pup should balk and start to play tug-of-war, crouch down with your arms wide open and call your pup in a pleasant voice (that is, say her name and the word "Come"). Do not force the puppy to come as if you were reeling in a fish, since this will only cause more fight and resistance. Simply clap your hands and encourage your

House-training and Preliminary Obedience Exercises | 121

Retractable leashes are also excellent for conditioning a young pup to come when called. When the pup is some distance away from you, call him cheerfully, saying "Frodo, come." If he does not come immediately, give him a little tug to get him going, and pat your leg enthusiastically. As he comes, the leash will recoil automatically.

pup to come. Most pups will come immediately. This is excellent foundation work for the "Come" command discussed later.

This exercise can be easily adapted for several family members by doing circle work. First, have the participants sit in a large circle or triangle, about five feet apart from each other. Attach a light nylon line to your puppy and then toss the end of the line to one of the handlers. Have the handler call the puppy in, praising her enthusiastically as she comes and gently easing the pup into a sit. The end of the line is then tossed to the next handler and the exercise continues around the circle for five to ten minutes.

Retractable leashes (flexi-leads) are now widely available for walking dogs in a safe, relaxed way. These are also excellent for preliminary leash-training and teaching the come; they allow a pup to get used to the leash and an occasional tug without feeling the constant pressure of the lead on the

An effective bonding technique. Tie your leash to your belt and have your pup accompany you throughout the day.

neck. This eliminates virtually all rebellion, since you can immediately release the tension on the leash after a mild tug. The result is a puppy who quickly learns to walk with the leash in a relaxed, unthreatened manner, and to come willingly from a distance of up to twenty-five feet.

Once your puppy is walking nicely with you on lead (this will probably take a week), try this effective exercise for bonding. Tie your leash to your belt and have your pup accompany you for various periods throughout the day (preferably after she has eliminated). You will be able to go about your business for an hour or so without having to worry about the pup needing to go out. With the puppy accompanying you all around the house, she learns to stay right with

House-training and Preliminary Obedience Exercises |

you and focus her attention primarily on you. This exercise will naturally develop a pup who chooses to be with you in a calm, collected manner, and is the groundwork for the "Heel" command described later.

An observation: At this early stage, do not look for the disciplined precision of a formal heel. Your goal is simply to get your pup comfortable with the leash and to walk with you without protestation. For this informal walking, instead of the command "Heel," use the phrase "Let's go," which will mean that your pup is to walk with you without pulling, though not necessarily at heel. Be sure to be animated and encouraging. If she starts to pull out in front, gently reverse your direction and say "Let's go, Fleeta," clapping the side of your leg in a happy tone. Everything should be geared toward conditioning your pup to remain close to you.

Right from the start, in addition to introducing your puppy to coming when called and to preliminary leash work, you can also begin teaching the "Sit" and "Down" commands by using simple, noncoercive techniques that familiarize her with moving into these positions without the use of force. At this early stage, it is always wiser to refrain from using compulsive techniques; we are concerned only with a gentle, positive introduction to the exercises.

To teach the concept of sit, get your pup's attention by snapping your fingers above her head or by using a ball as an object of attraction. When she looks up toward your hand, move it slightly over her head. By following the movement of your hand, your pup will move naturally into a sit. As she does, say "Sit," following immediately with lots of praise. If after several attempts your pup is still standing and simply looking up at your hand, repeat the exercise, and with your other hand tap her rear end lightly. Follow up with praise. Avoid using treats to induce the sit; instead, provide your pup with plenty of praise and encouragement, incentives that are more effective for long-term training. Most pups will very quickly become conditioned to sitting when you use this technique.

For teaching the concept of down, use another noncoercive method. With your pup in a sitting position, get her attention by showing her a ball or toy. As she focuses on it, bring it down to the ground dramatically about six inches in front of her feet, saying "Down" at the same time. As your pup follows the object down to the ground praise her gently. You may have to pat the ground several times to get her all the way down, and do not be concerned with making her

Teaching the sit to a young pup. Get the pup's attention with the tennis ball and move it slightly over her head. As she follows the movement of the ball, say "Sit" at the same time that she moves into the sit position. Be sure to reinforce this with praise.

stay down at this time. This is simply a preliminary exercise. If your pup does not follow the object to the ground, simply put a small amount of pressure on her shoulder as you give the command. Once she is down, immediately release her with plenty of praise. This will gradually teach her to be comfortable with the position.*

Remember, a house is only as good as its foundations. Taking the time to start off right with your pup is in the best interest of both of you. It sets the stage for teaching your puppy the basic elements of obedience and companionship in the weeks and months ahead.

*For a clear photographic demonstration, see our earlier book, *How to Be Your Dog's Best Friend*, page 117.

CHAPTER TWELVE

The Foundations of Training

The first months of puppy rearing pass quickly — so quickly that before you know it, your puppy is practically full-grown. From adoption to six months of age, your pup will grow to three quarters of his adult size and pass through a series of developmental stages that have a strong effect on his future behavior. Do not let this growth find you unprepared. Understanding how this period of development unfolds will allow you to anticipate your pup's behavior and plan training that will be effective. You must learn to harmonize your handling of your pup with the particular stage of growth he has reached, thus giving him the best chance of maturing into a happy, well-adjusted companion.

The Socialization Period Concludes

As we have seen, most people buy their pups between seven and ten weeks of age, in the middle of the socialization period. Because of this timing, new owners often notice their pups manifesting fear and avoidance shortly after they bring them home, usually in connection with new experiences. This fear/avoidance period (8–10 weeks) is a normal part of socialization and is indirectly responsible for puppies' bonding quickly with new owners. A puppy that experiences this touch of insecurity tends to seek the presence and security of his master; he gladly follows you around and stays close by your side.

Through this close contact his self-confidence grows steadily, so that when he enters the final two weeks of the socialization period (10–12 weeks) he acts like a little adult. This is a particularly enjoyable time to spend with your pup. He learns quickly, yet still looks upon you as the central figure in his life. Occasions of fearfulness are infrequent. Even though the pup appears to be well adjusted, it is important not to relax into a careless, laissez-faire attitude with your pup. Within the parameters of safety, continue intensive socializing; invite friends and neighbors to your house to meet your puppy, and make sure to plan these encounters ahead of time so that your friends know what to do. A good practice is to set up a greeting routine that your pup will become quickly accustomed to. When the doorbell rings, bring your puppy to the door on leash, so that he is under control. After you open the door and greet your friend, have your friend *crouch down* to greet your puppy, praising him in a pleasant voice. It is much easier for pups to approach a crouching figure than one who is towering over them. Make sure your guest makes no sudden movements toward the pup that could be frightening.

Also, take the pup on short car trips around the neighborhood to get him accustomed to the car. Use a portable crate (or have a friend stay in the back seat with him), and keep the trips short enough so that he does not get sick. Follow up each excursion with praise and a session of play so that he learns to associate the car with a pleasant experience. Pups who are conditioned to riding in the car early in puppyhood become quite comfortable doing so and rarely have difficulties later on with motion sickness.

If you can walk him safely (remember, until your pup is fully immunized you must be careful about exposing him to other dogs and areas where they defecate), let him explore your surrounding area while on leash, and take him to meet people in the neighborhood, especially children. We cannot overemphasize this: providing your pup with as many new experiences as possible should be a major priority for you at this time in his life. This should also include conditioning to a wide variety of common household appliances: electric blender, dishwasher, garage-door opener, waste-disposal system, and vacuum cleaner. Make initial exposures gentle, switching on the appliance when your pup is well away from it, so that he can make a gradual approach. Do not force or drag him. Instead, let your pup get accustomed to the noise and movement in his own time.

All young pups need to be socialized in a variety of situations and with a variety of people. Make sure your pup meets plenty of children.

These daily episodes of socializing build up his self-confidence and foster a healthy attitude toward life. Also, if you have not already started, now is the time to begin teaching your pup the basic obedience exercises (see chapter fifteen). Although a puppy at this age has a short attention span and requires plenty of patience, he is quite capable of learning and will benefit from short training sessions that are kept positive and nonpunitive.

The above holds true for city pups, as well, though it is easy to imagine how socializing a puppy under these circumstances can be a real challenge. Since urban apartment dwellers most likely will not be walking their puppies in public till at least sixteen weeks of age, they must provide safe alternate social experiences. For clients living in apartments without private yards, we recommend several procedures that ensure proper socializing without jeopardizing a puppy's health. First, as part of your daily routine, take your pup on walks around the neighborhood, using a large tote bag that the pup can be comfortably carried in. Small and medium-size breeds have no difficulty fitting in these kinds of carryalls throughout puppyhood, and large breeds can easily be carried till between ten and twelve weeks of age. Doing this prevents your pup from coming into contact with urine and feces but exposes him to the sights and sounds of city life. City puppies have to become used to honking horns, jackhammers, sirens, busy traffic, as well as to large crowds of people walking along sidewalks. Often if an owner is sitting with a puppy on a park bench, people will ask to meet or pet the pup. These experiences will provide a pup with controlled exposure to the world and nurture its normal development.

Another safe socializing exercise for pups in cities is to use the lobby area of your apartment building for random encounters with all sorts of people. With your pup on leash, walk it around the lobby, letting it investigate and mingle naturally with the whole environment. Simply offering your pup the opportunity to see people coming in and out of the building has a very beneficial effect. If people come over to greet or admire your pup, introduce your puppy to them, taking care not to allow it to jump up. Finally, after the adjustment of the first several days, invite friends and relatives over to meet your puppy. This is extremely important if a large number of the social experiences it will be having before sixteen weeks of age will occur in your apartment.

The Juvenile Period
(12 Weeks to Sexual Maturity)

The juvenile period of development corresponds to that time in the wild when wolf puppies make their first excursions away from the nest area, showing a new curiosity about their surrounding environment. They become increasingly independent, and existing behavior patterns are refined as the pups grow in strength and skill. Prior to this, the pups have stayed within twenty yards of the nest and their primary focus of attention has been their mother. Now that changes: the nest is abandoned and the pups are taken to "rendezvous" sites, where they stay while the pack is hunting elsewhere. There, within an area that can be as large as one half acre, they become adventuresome and begin learning how to hunt, practicing on field mice and other small animals. Their running skills improve steadily, and their gait progresses from awkward bunny-hopping to a smoother, more coordinated trot that results in greater stamina and higher activity levels. Social behavior also matures; by fourteen weeks of age the dominance order of the litter is fixed and the pups have developed a keen sense of their rank and status within the pack. Over the following months their permanent teeth come in, and they are introduced gradually to adult life, beginning to hunt with the pack around ten months of age, after their bodies have grown strong enough.

These same behavioral changes occur in the life of your puppy, though they can make for trying times in a domestic context. Many owners are quite unprepared for the challenge of these months, when puppy behavior fluctuates over a broad range of possibilities. Beginning at thirteen weeks, you will notice more pronounced expressions of independence; the pup that only last week was your shadow, who seemed well on his way to being trained, now begins to ignore you when you call, and during training and play sessions you have to work extra hard to keep his attention. His rapid growth produces a corresponding increase in activity that makes him highly excitable and difficult to manage; while he does need plenty of exercise, for most owners this translates into walks with lots of pulling and lunging. Bad habits develop quickly. When guests come to the house, the juvenile pup turns into a juvenile delinquent, jumping up and making himself a pest, continually demanding attention. It is also common for pups at this age to become very mouthy, so that by the teething period (4–6 months), they are chewing on everything, people included. To top things off, your puppy will probably go through a *second* fear period, when his behavior swings from being independent and bratty (12–14 weeks), to being periodically cautious and fearful (16–24 weeks), even of things he had formerly been comfortable with.

Patience alone is not sufficient to get through these months. Now, more than ever, your pup needs the guiding, stabilizing presence of a competent and understanding pack leader (see chapter fourteen). Take an active role in this process. Preliminary training, appropriate discipline, and a reassuring attitude from you are all key elements in helping your pup through this challenging period of his life. Perhaps the biggest mistake you can make with your pup is to put off this early training under the mistaken assumption that training is what happens to a dog *after* six months. That common misunderstanding is responsible for all sorts of unnecessary behavior problems. When owners fail to begin puppy training as soon as they adopt their pup, the pup begins to train himself. After several months of the pup doing as he pleases, "untraining" will most likely involve sterner training techniques that, while effective, could have been avoided had puppy training begun immediately. An illustration of this is the case of Rory.

Rory

A six-month-old German shepherd puppy lunged through our giftshop door with its owner, a young graduate student, following in tow and desperately begging the rambunctious pup to "heel." As she pulled the leash back and forth in an attempt to restrain him, the pup forged around the room, excitedly sniffing the carpet and furniture. When she finally managed to get the puppy under control and collect herself, the student looked up at the attending monk nervously and said, "Hello . . . uh, . . . I have an appointment to bring my pup, Rory, for training . . ."

When she had first contacted us by phone, the woman had described the bind she was in: she had unexpectedly received an important grant to study in Europe for two months, which left her no choice but to board Rory during that time. Since Rory had not yet received any training, the woman was looking for a kenneling program that could do two things: board Rory, and train him in a "kindly, gentle way," as well. She confessed that the idea of training made her very wary, but she also admitted that she was having real problems controlling Rory and that, among other things, he was becoming highly destructive.

In response, we outlined the services we could offer, and we were frank with her about what would be involved in training him. From her description, it appeared to us that despite his basically friendly nature, Rory was spoiled and used to getting his own way; he was the boss in their relationship, and if a real change was to take place in Rory's behavior, he would have to learn to become a follower. In all likelihood, this would mean firm, yet fair, discipline, particularly early on.

This response made her nervous — she did not like the idea of training Rory by force. We explained that it was she who had inadvertently made that choice by delaying training till now. By allowing Rory to grow up without proper direction and leadership, she had made the task of training a more difficult proposition. She said that this had never occurred to her and that she was under the impression that training should not begin before six months of age, anyway. We then explained to her the reasons why this was not true. Finally, almost reluctantly, she agreed to bring Rory.

As the brother greeted the two of them, Rory playfully tried to jump up several times, and the student had to use all of her strength to restrain him. Soft-spoken and polite, she kept pleading, "Stop it, stop it!" but Rory seemed completely oblivious to her corrections, merrily tugging away at the leash and producing hoarse, straining sounds as a result of being pulled. Unable to reach the brother, he wrapped himself around the student's legs several times, and when she finally managed to free herself, he began to mouth and nip at her hands. Her pleading only encouraged him further, until at last he began to bark continuously for attention.

The brother finally suggested that it might be best to get Rory settled in his kennel area before proceeding with the interview. The woman agreed, but before handing over the leash, she said, "Wait just a few seconds . . ." Crouching down to gather Rory to herself, she anxiously began hugging and kissing him good-bye. The emotional farewell proved too much for the young puppy. Overwhelmed by the intensity of her affections, Rory squatted helplessly and let go with a minor flood, making the student groan in frustration, "Oh, Rory . . . !" The scene could not have been more predictable.

When the monk returned from placing the pup in the kennel, the student was in tears. She looked up and remarked awkwardly, "I know that all of this must seem rather silly, but I feel absolutely distressed about leaving him. . . . We're very attached and the thought of leaving him for training . . . Well . . . Please, tell me, is the training going to break his spirit?"

In response, the brother walked her over to the window and pointed to the front yard where one of his confreres happened to be working with a seven-month-old Labrador retriever, who was just completing a three-week training course. As the two walked harmoniously around the yard, their pace and rhythm were so measured that their movements seemed choreographed, like a ballet. The unhesitating attentiveness, wagging tail, fixed eye contact, and perfect pace of the dog were utterly captivating. Its responses to the obedience commands were precise, yet not mechanical, and the brother's soft, encouraging praise brought out energy and enthusiasm in the dog's work.

The student watched silently for ten minutes. When the session ended, the brother said to her, "Three weeks ago she was just like Rory. Now look at her. *That* is spirit!"

What Is Training?

Rory arrived at New Skete unruly and dominant, unresponsive to the leash, and unable to focus on anything for more than several seconds. His owner had raised him with the mistaken notion that obedience training should not begin until six months of age, if at all. The result was a puppy out of control and impossible to live with. As we suspected he would, during his initial training sessions with us he consistently tried to dominate his trainer, fighting the leash and bolting in different directions. Had the graduate student witnessed these first training sessions, she might have frantically "rescued" Rory from the kennel and sped off, convinced that the monks were a bunch of sadists. No doubt she would have been upset by the firm, uncompromising leash corrections Rory received in his first lessons. No doubt, also, she would have been disturbed by the under-the-chin hand corrections and firm shakedowns used to correct his periodic attempts at dominance. What she would not have imagined, however, was the rapid transformation that occurred over the following two months, as Rory changed from a willful, spoiled, stubborn puppy, into a calmer, obedient dog. When she returned to pick Rory up, she stared in disbelief as he moved flawlessly through his paces, happy and attentive. After the demonstration she turned to the brother next to her and exclaimed in an astonished voice, "That's not *my* dog . . ."

Happily, Rory responded to the training commendably and the student was able to get a new insight into the value of a properly trained dog. Nevertheless, the whole process could have been so much simpler. By no means does obedience training have to be harsh or disagreeable. Much of the unpleasantness of Rory's first sessions could have been avoided had his owner understood that "training" is much more than a formal set of exercises a dog learns once it reaches a certain age. Six months is a reasonable time to commence *formal* obedience training with regular daily sessions; however, formal obedience will have its greatest value only when it flows naturally from a basic foundation of socialization, puppy conditioning, preliminary obedience exercises, and play that begins early in puppyhood. This broader training naturally disposes a puppy to accept the human leadership so necessary for more advanced training.

Make no mistake about it: *training is never an option.* If you have a new puppy, one way or another your puppy will be trained — either into an unruly, dominant, spoiled dog with real possibilities for serious problem behavior, or into a companion that is friendly, well managed, and obedient. It all depends on you. Had Rory been raised with this type of understanding, his formal training would have begun with much less compulsion and discipline, since it would have flowed naturally from a healthy leader/follower relationship. As we explained in *How to Be Your Dog's Best Friend*, we understand training as a dynamic process that begins at the puppy's birth and continues throughout its life. It enables a dog to reach its full potential as a dog and companion, in a manner completely in harmony with its canine nature.

Training is educating. Significantly, the word "education" comes from the Latin *educare*, which means "to draw out, to call forth what is already present as a possibility." Applied to your dog, this is not limited to the mastering of five basic commands; it is an ongoing process. We have seen this understanding of puppy development prove itself as we have watched litter after litter grow and learn, conscious of our own role in that process. From the perspective of theory and experience, training is a way of relating to your dog that involves your whole life with it, not simply ten-minute sessions in the morning or evening, as essential as these may be. Many new owners fail to perceive that their puppy begins its training with them the day it arrives home, and not three to four months later, when it reaches that magical age of six months. It is not in a state of suspended animation till then. Rather, it is reacting, responding, learning, and forming habits, if only by default.

Me? A Trainer?

Since your dog is always learning, for better or for worse, it is to your advantage as an owner to give direction to the training process in a manner that enhances your life together. Only by taking a deliberate, active role in training your pup will you have the opportunity to develop a smooth and enjoyable relationship.

However, let us emphasize that you must do this with sensitivity, intelligence, and thoughtfulness. All the good intentions in the world are of little value if the way you treat your pup is unsuited to its immature stage of development. A young puppy's emotional system and physical structure have not matured enough to handle the stress brought on by less-than-thoughtful compulsory obedience training. For example, some dog owners, knowing they must be the boss in their puppy's eyes, go to the opposite extreme of Rory's owner. They make the mistake of being overbearing, misusing dominance in a heavy-handed, stressful way. When a puppy makes a mistake, they deal with it severely, convinced that punishment is the best way for him to learn. This mistaken approach can create a pup that is passively submissive and fearful, lacking any self-confidence. A more patient, guiding, and correcting approach to training, one stressing encouragement and praise, is much more effective in preparing a puppy for a future of companionship and learning. Remember, a pup *must* develop confidence in adolescence.

Puppy training, therefore, is different in tone from traditional formal obedience training. Very young puppies (7–10 weeks of age) have no innate impressions of training; their slates are basically "clean." With brain waves already at their adult levels, they lack only experience. This is the ideal time for them to acquire positive attitudes about life and about training, since there are no bad habits to undo. In puppy training we are less concerned with demanding precise responses to obedience commands than with nurturing basic character traits in your pup: respect for leadership, attentiveness, curiosity, playfulness, and an enthusiastic attitude toward your relationship. The emphasis here is on fun. Puppies learn best in the context of play, just as young wolves and young humans do. By keeping the focus of early sessions positive and pleasant, with lots of play, you can lay a solid behavioral foundation that will prepare your puppy for advanced training later on and serve it throughout its life. It is amazing how formal obedience and advanced training change in character and expression when they come after a program of puppy training in which the emphasis has been on making training interesting and fun.

You can do this, but first you must be aware of how dogs do and do not learn, how they communicate, and what attitudes in yourself draw out the best qualities in your dog.

We remember one client who came to us for advice on his four-month-old Rottweiler puppy, who was starting to growl at strangers. When we went out to meet the client and his dog, they were sitting on a bench in our front yard. As we approached, the pup started to growl in a low, threatening voice, at which the owner quickly tried to reassure him with a soothing voice, saying, "It's okay, boy, it's oooh-kay. . . . Gooood boy, gooood boy, eeeeasy, . . ." gently rubbing him on his side as he did so. Naturally, the growling only grew worse, and the man looked up helplessly, wondering what to do. Fortunately, we were able to settle the puppy down by taking a short walk with him, and after several minutes he became very accepting and friendly. The owner then complained, "I don't understand it, he's such a good pup, and yet he has this thing about growling . . ." We explained to the baffled owner that the pup was merely doing what he was told. Reviewing with him his reactions during the incident, we showed him that he was unintentionally rewarding the puppy's growling by his soft praise and petting. The only message the puppy was receiving was "this is the way to act."

There is no way we can say that this pup was "disobedient." Instead, we can see that the owner showed a misunderstanding of what he was communicating and an ignorance of how to communicate his true intent in a clear, authoritative way.

To Obey Is to Hear

In dog training, most people conceive of obedience simply as something the dog does in response to his handler: the dog is the one who is obedient or not. This is only half of what real obedience is. "Obedience" comes from the Latin word "oboedire," which in turn is cognate to "ob-audire," meaning "to listen, to hear"; by extension, this always implies *acting* on what is heard. Contrary to popular thought, obedience is as much your responsibility as it is your dog's — even more so, since you are responsible for shaping your dog's behavior to fit your living circumstances. The problem with many dog owners is that they fail to listen and respond to the real needs of their dogs; unknowingly, they are disobedient.

To be a good companion to your dog, *you* must be obedient, that is, fully alert and focused on your dog, flexible enough to adapt your approach instantly to his needs. As odd as it may sound, your dog does not know what is best for him; you do, but only by being truly obedient to him.

Brother Thomas, who was the driving force behind founding the training program here at New Skete until he died in a tragic automobile accident in 1973, had this insight into obedience:

> Learning the value of silence is learning to listen to, instead of screaming at, reality: opening your mind enough to find what the end of someone else's sentence sounds like, or listening to a dog until you discover what is needed instead of imposing yourself in the name of training.

This kind of obedience comes only with time, practice, and study, by learning different techniques and methods of training and using them in different circumstances and, if possible, with different types of dogs. Because dogs are individuals, not all respond in the same way to particular types of training. Remember Anka's litter: were we to train Yola in the same way as Sunny, we would probably only compound her submissive, shy personality. In education, teachers discover from working with different children that they must be flexible, adapting a variety of teaching methods to individual students. A rigorous, highly structured program that is effective with one child may be disastrous with another. The same is true in dog training. Part of training means your becoming a student of your dog and employing an approach that will bring out the best in him.

In discussing training, we will not present you with one absolute method of training your pup. We will try, instead, to point out to you some general principles that are important cornerstones for all good training and then show you how these can be applied to different dogs. This will help you perceive and deal with the particular requirements of your own puppy. Working with dogs of all sizes, breeds, temperaments and personalities, we have learned that it is a serious mistake to limit yourself to one particular method of training. Trainers who insist that only one method of training works (their own) betray their own ignorance and pride and close themselves off from a real understanding of dogs.

One last observation, especially for those who have never owned a dog before. Novices in training often experience feelings of awkwardness and uncertainty at the prospect of training their pup. This can discourage them from even beginning. Intimidated by a lack of understanding of training techniques and canine behavior, they often fear that their effort will only manifest their own incompetency and lack of coordination while it ruins their puppy. You will be surprised, however, what hidden talents come to the surface if you approach training honestly. Your attitude is what is crucial. Take advantage of the opportunity to learn as much as you can about it, and then practice regularly with your pup, initially starting with very short sessions in keeping with his short attention span, then gradually working up to more structured ones. Get involved with a local obedience club or K.P.T. class in your area for some hands-on experience, and listen to the insights that more accomplished handlers offer you. Do not be afraid to ask serious questions. Good trainers are usually very generous with their knowledge. Their advice and encouragement can give practical support to the different ideas you come across in your study.

More importantly, never be satisfied with mediocrity; work hard to bring out the best in your pup by striving each day to make your training something more alive than the day before, something more than a mere mastery of techniques. Our culture is obsessed with technique, and technique *is* essential in training; however, if it is to deepen your relationship with your dog it must be wedded to intuition. The point of practicing regularly and faithfully is not to create a robot. It is to strive toward a level of freedom and understanding with your dog that speaks of true companionship. When that occurs, training reaches the frontiers of art.

CHAPTER THIRTEEN

Reading Your Dog

Though dogs have no capacity to communicate with words, they do have a rich language of their own that uses sight, sound, and smell to eloquently express their intentions and emotional states. Your ability to understand this language and its particular social setting is the cornerstone of a good relationship with your dog. The apt expression "reading your dog" means really understanding what she is saying to you and not just what you think that might be. By taking into account the dynamic interaction of various forms of body language, you can avoid the harm that occurs in the human/dog relationship when owners misinterpret their dogs' intentions and moods.

For example, one of the complaints we receive from puppy owners involves submissive urination, demonstrated by a puppy who runs up to her mistress and excitedly greets her by urinating on the floor. This behavior is common in puppies, a natural outgrowth from when their mothers cleaned them by rolling them over to lick their genitals and anus. As puppies mature, it becomes a reflexive sign of their acceptance of dominance and authority. If you observe a young pup greeting an older, more dominant dog in a similar manner (crouching low, its wagging tail tucked under, and excitedly licking at the elder's muzzle as it leaves several drops of urine on the ground), you will *never* see the older dog punish the pup. The expression of submission is received gracefully, with an attitude of dominant composure by the older dog as she stands erect, holding her tail high. She understands the sign completely.

Unfortunately, many owners misunderstand its significance and treat it as either a behavioral disorder or a house-breaking problem. We recall one frustrated owner who asked us, "Is she just a sadistic puppy, doesn't she understand? Every time I come home she piddles at my feet. I spank her, tell her how naughty she is, that she's to do this outside, but it only gets worse. Now all I have to do is enter the house and she pees. Why doesn't she understand?"

The man did not understand what his pup's behavior expressed. By misinterpreting submissive urination as neurotic, cowardly behavior, and by punishing her with scolding and spanking, he had set the stage for a serious, long-lasting behavior problem. Punishment was the *worst* possible response he could have made to her behavior; it deepened the problem by making her even more submissive, since her body language had already acknowledged his authority. The proper response to this problem is outlined in chapter sixteen.

Expecting your dog to rise to the level of human communication and thinking will only lead to frustration. Instead, learn to read her by taking what we know about dogs and stepping into her world, trying to view life from her perspective. This requires a different way of thinking than you are accustomed to.

Try a simple exercise. Imagine looking out of the eyes of your ten-week-old puppy. Do not attempt to verbalize, simply imagine being the puppy. Now look up at the big human being next to you (yourself). With the increasing abilities you have as a dog to interpret human body language, what do you "read," how do you react? Look closely at the eyes, the face, the body. Is the stance imposing and towering, or inviting? Consider the voice; you do not understand the words — what is the tone of the voice? Is it cheerful and pleasant, or harsh and abrupt? Does it sound whiny or anemic? Now look around the room from that level. Observe the pair of leather shoes by the door, the large potted plant, the various pieces of furniture, and the inviting electrical cords plugged into the floor sockets at puppy eye level. With olfactory powers of great sensitivity, what is of greatest interest?

The point of this "pup's-eye-view" exercise is to till the soil of your imagination responsibly, to help you sense, in some small way, what things are like from a pup's perspective. A good companion and trainer can enter imaginatively into the dog's reality, interpret it correctly, and then adjust various handling procedures to fit that knowledge. Captain Max Von Stephanitz, the founding father of the German shepherd dog breed, was very perceptive in this regard:

Tranquil domestic scene? Not with a puppy around. Pick up shoes and socks, electric cords, books and magazines, poisonous plants, candy, and anything else your pup could get into.

The trainer must himself be a psychologist; he must learn to read the soul of the dog, *and his own too*. He must observe himself closely so that he shall not only be prevented from underestimating the dog in human arrogance, but also that he may be able to give the dog suggestions and help in an intelligent way. Whoever can find the answer to the question "How shall I say this to my dog?" has won the game and can develop from his animal whatever he likes.

When you approach your dog in this way, the experience is surprisingly multidimensional. Not only does your dog become trained, but you become skilled, as well, and the ongoing knowledge you acquire from your dog's behavior

Inseeing is being conscious of how your pup sees the world. To your pup, shoes and hands will appear much larger than you imagine, even frightening.

has the potential to teach you as much about yourself as it does about your dog. An often neglected aspect of the training process is how your dog becomes a mirror, reflecting you back to yourself, helping you achieve greater self-awareness by drawing out of you greater degrees of patience, sensitivity, and emotional self-control. This is the heart of training.

In *How to Be Your Dog's Best Friend*, we spoke of "inseeing" and its importance in your relationship with your dog. Inseeing is standing inside your dog's psyche, putting yourself at her center, where she is a unique, individual creature, and understanding her from that perspective. This is possible only when you want to understand what your dog is *genuinely* saying. To get inside a dog's head, to understand her from her point of view, you must continually watch, look, and listen, since a dog communicates what is in her mind through her body movements and vocalizations. Inseeing is not a romantic projection of human thoughts and feelings; it takes into account the whole dog by reading what the major centers of communication are saying: ears, eyes, mouth, tail, and body carriage.

In what follows, we will examine the significance of these various centers of communication and the different meanings associated with various gestures. Your friendship with your dog will mature into real and compassionate understanding when you learn to blend intuition with science in a serious grasp of canine communication and behavior.

Canine Communication

Besides becoming a keen observer of domestic dogs, a good way to acquire an authentic sensitivity to a dog's language is to pay careful attention to the lessons available from a natural tutor: the wolf and its pack. The best scientific evidence available strongly suggests that domestic dogs are closely related to wolves, either being directly descended from several species of wolves, or by being cousins, possessing a common ancestry in some earlier, unknown canid that is now extinct. Either way, the studies performed on communication and social behavior in wolves are enormously illuminating for what they teach us about dogs, since the meaning of various postures and vocalizations are generally consistent throughout the canine family. Despite the fact that artificial selection and domestication have emphasized certain characteristics while suppressing others (for example, by promoting pendulous ears or by the unfortunate practice of tail docking and ear cropping in some breeds), all of the behavior patterns we observe in dogs are also present in wolves. Thus, in the following discussion, we gratefully acknowledge the research done in canine communication and behavior by wildlife biologists, ethologists, and animal behaviorists, and we include references to wolves where relevant.

Communication, simply stated, is the passing of information from one individual to another. In canines, this involves hearing, vision, and smell. As we have seen, puppies are born with inherited reflexes that are the basis of instincts, natural behavior patterns that are the means of communication. In the initial phases of life, a young puppy is limited both physically and behaviorally in how she expresses herself. As the brain develops and the pup has the opportunity of interacting with her mother and littermates, however, she becomes more and more capable of expressing a variety of different moods and emotions. These abilities continue to develop long into adulthood.

Vocal Communication

A dog, like a wolf, generally vocalizes in one of several ways, each apparently tied to various body postures that communicate different meanings and moods: whimpering and whining, growling, barking, yelping, and howling, all in a wide variety of tones.

The first vocalizations puppies make are mewing sounds that indicate need; for example, for food or warmth. Pups also make high-pitched grunts and squeaks when they nurse. As they grow older, the mewing sound changes into a whine, which carries over into adulthood as an expression of greeting, submission, or desire. Whining is more characteristic of dogs than of wolves (who only whine when expressing submission), and this is probably due to unintentional reinforcement by owners. Young puppies learn quickly what whining will obtain when their owners continually reinforce this behavior to get them to stop. A classic illustration of this is the puppy that whines the first night she is separated from her littermates. The owner, feeling sorry for her, takes her into bed and lets her sleep there. The puppy learns a fateful lesson in communication, and her whining quickly becomes generalized to any situation of want.

A growl communicates threat and antagonism. It is a warning and may be accompanied with a snarl (i.e., baring of teeth). Young canine puppies growl when they play, thereby learning proper canine etiquette; as they mature, the growl is usually serious. With wolves, it is used by a more dominant wolf over a subordinate and is usually enough to elicit submission. Dogs can use the growl in the same way, and if it is directed toward an owner, it signifies the dog's attempt to assume dominance. An example of this might be an owner getting too close to her pup when she is eating. The puppy may utter a low growl as if to say, "Stay away!" If the owner backs off, the pup easily begins applying this behavior to other situations that challenge the owner's position of authority.

Most domestic dogs bark much more frequently than wolves, probably as a result of selective breeding. Since an early goal of domestication was to have dogs guard and warn, it is clear why they were bred for their barking ability. Wolves, being hunters that do not wish to alert potential prey, bark only in specific situations, such as one wolf's warning to other pack members or to the pups that a stranger is approaching. The bark is a short, quiet "woof" and is generally not repeated.

Domestic dogs bark any time they are excited. Barks are short and sharp, and the tonal quality reflects meaning. High barks are associated with greetings, such as your puppy's excited welcome when you come home, or, when prolonged and frantic, will accompany pain and/or stress and are described as yelps. Warning barks are deeper and alert you that something is up, such as the preliminary bark of the watchdog. The aggressive bark is deeper still and communicates threat. It alternates with growling to send an unmistakable message.

Howling is more common in wolves than in dogs and is their major form of vocalization. It is a prolonged tone, lasting from two to eleven seconds and may fluctuate over a wide range of notes. Each individual wolf's howl is distinct, which seems to suggest that individual wolves can be identified by their howl. Specialists feel that wolves howl for a number of reasons: to reassemble the pack after they have been scattered during a hunt, to advertise territory, or simply as a collective celebratory rite. Wolves howl both alone and in chorus, and when they howl together they avoid unison, apparently preferring chord tones.

Dogs howl much less frequently than wolves, though howling is normal in northern breeds such as huskies and malamutes, as well as in the hounds. In our kennel work, we notice that many huskies and malamutes howl shortly after their owners leave them, presumably as an expression of loneliness, and we have periodically experienced the howling of our shepherds, most frequently while we ourselves are singing. Evidently the harmonies they hear encourage them to join in with their own notes.

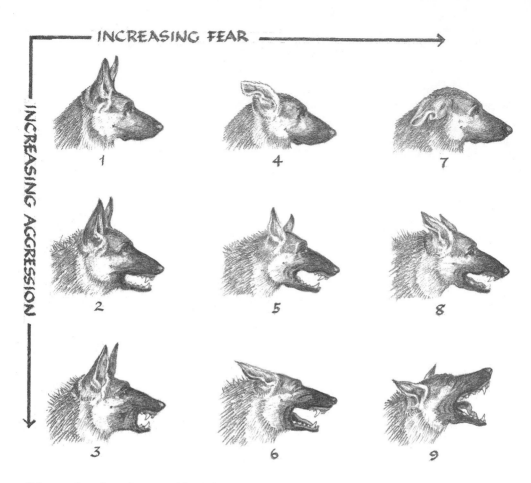

1   4   7

2   5   8

3   6   9

Schema showing nine possible shifts in facial expression of an
adult German shepherd. In 1, 4, and 7, note the increasing fear or
submission, reflected by the ears flattening out against the head
and by the lips forming a submissive grin. In 1, 2, and 3, note the
increase of aggression, with the ears erect, hackles up, and teeth
bared, forming a snarl. In 3, 6, and 9, aggression is mixed with
fear, sending mixed signals. The ears are flattened submissively,
yet the teeth are bared in threat, and the hackles are up. Number 9
is a classic illustration of a fear-biter.

The different types of body language of the dog. In 1 and 2, the
dog becomes alert and attentive. In 3 a play-soliciting gesture is
followed in 4 and 5 by active and passive submissive greetings. In
9 passive submission ends up with the dog rolling over and showing the genital region to the dominant dog or person. The gradual
shift from pure aggression to a mixed fear-aggression posture is
shown in 6–8.

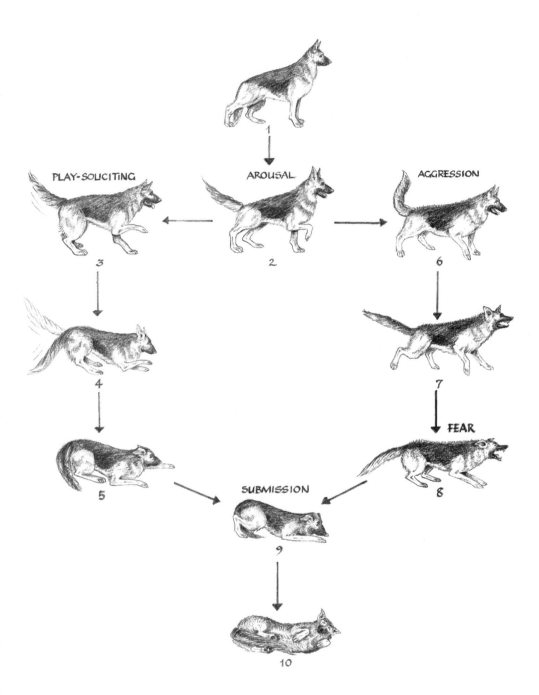

(Adapted from illustrations in Michael Fox's *Understanding Your Dog*.)

Accompanying all vocal communication, and yet also independent of it, are a large variety of postural communications that clarify for us a canine's internal state. Through her gestures, a dog can communicate a great deal without making a sound. Canine body language involves the interaction of facial expression, ear and tail position, and the carriage of the body. Thus, to read a dog you must be aware of all of these elements at the same time.

In a peaceful and relaxed state, a dog holds her ears slightly back and carries her curved tail out at a downward slope, hanging loosely. The body position is the same front and back, and the musculature around the forehead and muzzle is smooth. The mouth may be slightly open with the tongue panting, and the eyes are clear.

As a dog becomes more attentive, her ears prick up in a forward position and her tail rises, wagging slightly. Some dogs lift a front leg slightly, as if in readiness for what is to come. It is common for a dog to express curiosity from this position by cocking her head, holding her ears forward and showing concentration and alertness by the minor skin creases around the eyes.

When a dog tries to solicit play, the front half of the body lowers, with the front paws, elbows, and chest touching the ground, causing the back end to rise high in the air; the tail wags furiously. The ears are raised and the mouth is held open in a relaxed way; the dog may bark spiritedly. A lively bearing in a dog communicates joy and enthusiasm.

With the onset of threat, the body language of the dog changes on the basis of her personality and perception of the situation. When a confident, dominant dog perceives a threat, her posture becomes aggressive; her ears stand erect, pointing forward, and her mouth is open slightly, with the upper lips curled to expose the canine teeth. The facial musculature around the nose and forehead wrinkles and the eyes are dark and piercing, with the eyelids raised. Her tail is raised straight up or slightly over the rear, a sign of dominance, and the tip may be wagging in very quick circles. Her neck and body are erect, with the hackles up to give her an inflated look, akin to a man pulling in his stomach, raising his chest, and flexing his muscles. The dog's legs are stiff, and she may even walk on tiptoe. The whole posture, in

A dramatic example of canine body language in two five-month-old pups.

addition to communicating size and strength, surges and strains toward the threat. The ears, eyes, tail, and body carriage all signal courage and confidence.

As a dog becomes more suspicious and fearful, the signals begin to change markedly. The head drops somewhat, the ears flatten out horizontally or are pulled back against the side of the head, and the tail tucks down between the legs. The mouth may be opened in a grimace combined with the curling of the lips and the eyes become glazed, looking slightly away from the source of the fear. The hackles are still raised, but the body lowers and moves away from the threat. This is the posture of the fear-biter, who signals a potentially confusing mixture of aggressive and submissive body signals.

Purely submissive body language in canines occurs in one of two ways, active or passive, depending on the circumstances. In nonfearful, more *actively* submissive postures, the ears point backward against the side of the head, the mouth is held in a long grin, and the body crouches low to the ground, with the tail tucked under and possibly wagging nervously. Active submission is frequently demonstrated at greetings and may involve the entire group of wolves, as when an alpha wolf (the pack leader) returns to the pack after an absence. In such group ceremonials, the pack gathers around the alpha, posturing submissively while affectionately licking at its muzzle. This communicates friendliness, loyalty, and allegiance.

Passive submission is a more extreme form that communi-

Younger pups show active submission and respect to older dogs by licking at their mouths.

cates helplessness and vulnerability and does not carry as much of the friendly enthusiasm present in active submission. It is manifested by a subordinate in the face of threat and self-assertion by one more dominant. When posturing, the passively submissive dog lies down on the ground and rolls over on its side, exposing her genitals and abdomen, and the front legs are bent at the elbows. The tail is tucked under tightly and wags only slightly, if at all. The ears are plastered backward against the side of the head, and eye contact with the source of dominance is avoided. This posture of total trust and homage is an attempt to make the dog look much smaller than she really is. This gesture of humility placates the dominant self-assertion of the other dog or wolf.

Olfactory Communication

Because a human's sense of smell is so limited in comparison with that of a dog's, it is especially difficult for us to know exactly how dogs communicate using their olfactory sense. Though scientists are convinced that this sense gives canines more information about the world than any of their other senses, it is the least understood component of canine com-

A young puppy displaying passive submission to a dominant adult.

munication. We can only observe various behaviors associated with scent and then conjecture at their meaning.

In the wild, scent seems to define territory, with the alpha wolf generally urinating on objects above ground that will preserve the scent. This seems important for several reasons. First, it clearly defines territory for the resident pack, especially for the younger, inexperienced wolves, who are able to form mental maps of the territory from the scent markings. Secondly, scent communicates to other neighboring packs boundary lines that keep them from trespassing into the resident pack's territory. Scent marks are also important when a wolf pack has been separated during a hunt, since they tell an individual wolf whether an area has been recently traveled through by the rest of the pack.

Within the pack itself, smell seems to be intimately connected with canine social life. Dominant male wolves frequently present anal areas to subordinates for inspection (as if to broadcast themselves), and the subordinates respond by withdrawing theirs, apparently an acknowledgement of the other's dominance and a way of saying, "I'm not really here."

The smell of urine also communicates sexual readiness in the female, who marks frequently when she is in season, as if to publish this fact for a potential suitor (generally the alpha male).

The dog possesses approximately 200 million olfactory cells, compared with 5 million in humans. Its power of smell is conservatively estimated to be 100 times more powerful than that of a human being.

We have already alluded to the importance of scent marking in defining territory for dogs (see chapter eleven). Dogs will also try to cover the scent marks of other dogs intruding on their territory. Scent says, "This is me, this is familiar." This explains why, when people move, they often have problems with their dog marking in their new home (particularly leg lifting in males). Apparently this is the canine way of making oneself at home.

Anyone who owns a dog quickly discovers that dogs are most interested in urine and feces. Animal behaviorists tell us that from a drop of urine or a small amount of feces, a dog can determine the sex of an individual dog, whether or not it has been castrated or spayed, how recent the mark is, the direction the dog was going in, and, if it is a female, whether she is in season.

Another interesting behavior visible in domestic dogs is scratching the earth after urination or defecation. Traditional folk wisdom inferred that this was the dog's attempt at covering over the odor. In fact, it appears to be just the opposite: the spreading of the individual scent around a wider area.

When dogs meet in public, their smelling rituals seem to resemble those of wolves, and because they do not take place within the context of a single pack, displays frequently go beyond simple dominance/submission. For example, two male dogs meeting for the first time may both assume postures of dominance and become progressively more threatening, trying to get the other to back down. Each one allows the other to smell the anal area, a sign of confidence and courage, and if the dogs are left on their own, the encounter could result in a fight.

Dogs well acquainted with each other, who acknowledge a certain dominance order, greet each other in a more relaxed way, with the dominant dog thoroughly sniffing the subordinate and then presenting himself to be sniffed, at the same time raising himself "higher" than the other dog.

As with other canines, a female dog in season broadcasts this fact by urinating much more frequently than usual. Local male dogs, extremely sensitive to this, become highly agitated when they catch the scent. We see this when they congregate outside the house of a female in season. This is one reason spaying your pup before her first season may not be a bad idea. Male dogs can be unbelievably persistent in trying to breed a receptive female.

Pack Dynamics

"Dog talk" is easiest to interpret in its natural context: the pack. Dogs are pack animals like wolves, and they respond naturally to the laws of pack existence. Living with a large group of German shepherds here at the monastery gives us a firsthand look at behavior that closely resembles that of wolf packs. It is quite routine — a five-month-old puppy meeting an older female dog, submission and dominance. Or a mother disciplining her pups out on the lawn, teaching them a proper respect for authority. These and many other behaviors point back to a common ancestral past with wolves and help us to understand why dogs behave this way. Just because your puppy does not live in a wild pack does not mean that she will not instinctively adapt these behaviors to her new domestic environment. We assure you she will. Living with your puppy will be much more enjoyable and meaningful if you understand the basic principles of pack life and apply them to your relationship.

Packs do not hold together automatically. Since wolves are carnivores and must hunt to survive, a great deal of

A mother teaching her pups respect for her authority by preparing to playfully pin the pup to the ground.

cooperation must exist for the pack to achieve its food requirements. Most of the wolves' natural prey (moose, elk, caribou, and reindeer) are too large to be brought down by a single wolf and require a strategic, coordinated plan of attack by a number of them. Refined communication, as well as a tight social structure wherein each member knows its proper role, is essential.

This explains why leadership is so important for wolves. Every pack has a pair of leaders, one male and one female. These alphas are dominant over the other members of their particular sex. Generally, though not always, the alpha male is the overall head of the pack and is responsible for governing and directing pack activities such as traveling, hunting, feeding, and sleeping. His firm dominance preserves order by eliciting submission and respect from subordinate pack members, using appropriate deferential body language.

Beneath the alpha wolves, there is a loose dominance hierarchy into which each pack member fits with a particular spot and role. This social structure is dynamic, changing whenever younger wolves mature, older wolves get sick or injured, at the onset of mating season, and so on. Wolves appear instinctively to strive for the highest position within the pack possible, continually "testing" higher ranking wolves until the question of rank is settled. Thus, to preserve or increase one's status in the pack, an individual must constantly assert itself, fending off upstarts or attempting to move up in the pack hierarchy. You might suspect that this kind of social tension would set the stage for many fights, but surprisingly, actual fights among wolves are infrequent. Challenges are usually settled ritually, without a fight, since submissive postures are enough to end the dispute. Should a lesser ranking wolf challenge the alpha, the alpha wolf may threaten the upstart by posturing in an aggressive, dominant manner, growling, and staring directly at the other wolf. By staring down the ambitious subordinate, the alpha is often able to get it to back down without an all-out fight.

Interestingly, it appears that wolf packs are stronger, more secure and smooth-running, to the extent that the alpha is secure and confident in its leadership, for such dominance inspires fewer challenges. It is when there is no clear authority within the pack, as in times of leadership change, that the pack is unstable and may break up. Wolf packs function best when there is clear leadership, and this is just as true in your relationship with your puppy.

Dominance and submission are absolutely central to pack life and are taught to wolf puppies from the very first. As we saw with Anka and her pups, discipline begins naturally at weaning, when the mother growls and snaps at the pups who are trying to nurse. The pups learn to respond with submissive postures and to direct their oral attention toward an adult's mouth, which provokes the regurgitation of food. This behavior then evolves into expressions of active submission given at greetings. The older wolves help rear the pups both by feeding and by disciplining. Correction is kept basically good-natured; the pups do not fear their elders, but always try to stay with them.

This attitude of balance, a blending of leniency and instructive discipline is characteristic of the way wolves raise their pups. Puppies are presumptuous, taking liberties with adults that would never be tolerated in older pack members. They playfully wrestle and grab their elders around the muzzle, mouthing and biting them. Occasionally this provokes a well-timed response of dominance, with the elder grabbing the pup's muzzle and pinning him to the ground. The purpose is only to educate, to guide the pups in the ways of canine etiquette, teaching them the vital art of submission.

During the juvenile phase (12 weeks to sexual maturity), besides learning the basics of communication and social structure, wolf pups are gradually trained in the serious business of survival. Though it is not entirely clear how hunting is taught, it does seem that play games are an important part of the process. Because wolf pups are physically immature, fatigue quickly, and keep their milk teeth until at least five months, they do not hunt until they are nine to eleven months old. Instead, they stay behind at rendezvous sites, or base camps, often with an adult baby-sitter who is the lowest ranking member of the pack, the *omega*. While the rest of the pack hunts, the pups play with each other and practice hunting field mice. These activities slowly develop and coordinate their innate abilities to stalk, pounce, and run. When the pack is not hunting, adult wolves may initiate games of pursuit, teasing the pups into chasing them around and about. This hunting simulation teaches the younger wolves many hunting skills within the context of a game and provides another clue as to how dogs learn naturally. Fun is paramount.

Here at the monastery, in our exercise yard, it is quite common for comparable games to take place. An example: Uli, a mature female, approaches a precocious five-month-old pup named Kali. Uli stares at her for several moments, tail wagging and ears up, then moves her eyes off to the side mischievously. Kali crouches down, gazing back at Uli. Suddenly Uli tears off in the opposite direction and Kali chases after her wildly, following her through quick turns and all-out sprints, and when she finally runs even with her, playfully nips at the side of her neck. This type of game can go on for an hour, engrossing the full attention of both, and it is an important element in Kali's development.

All puppies, wild or domestic, love to play; you can capitalize on this by making play sessions with your pup part of her training. Play conditions your pup to be enthusiastic about learning and to enjoy being with you. By mixing training with games, you can bring out a healthy attitude in your pup that will carry over to conventional obedience work when she is older.

This treatment of canine communication is by no means exhaustive. Much about a dog's language and behavior remains mysterious, and what we do know seems to point to the presence of deeper levels of communication that are still beyond our abilities to recognize and understand. This is why study of your dog is so fascinating: it is open-ended. Learning to read your dog is a process that should continue throughout your life together. By developing more sensitivity to your dog's manner of communicating and fuller understanding of canine behavior, your appreciation and enjoyment of each other will continue to grow.

CHAPTER FOURTEEN

Lessons from the Pack: Becoming Pack Leader

Now we can apply some basic principles of wolf-pack life to the way you handle your puppy. By using certain exercises we can mimic the natural integration of pups into a pack. Remember that puppies learn their proper place in the pack through constant contact with their mothers and the other pack members. Body language, proper physical dominance, and eye contact teach puppies the meaning of leadership and their role as followers. They are happiest when this is clear and consistent. Since every puppy needs a leader, the success of your relationship rests on your being a benevolent alpha figure to your pup. Start right away; leadership is much easier to establish with a twelve-week-old, twenty-five-pound puppy than with a sixty-pound adolescent.

We will concentrate first on physical contact. New owners often try to get pups to behave by *explaining* what is expected, by reasoning with them. They forget that puppies have no verbal skills, and when puppies fail to respond to spoken instructions, they often become impatient and exasperated. Only later, through training, does a pup learn the meaning of specific words and commands. You will be much more effective if you concentrate less on what you say and more on what you do.

The first series of handling exercises we recommend focuses on teaching a puppy to be calm and relaxed when handled. Before advancing to obedience exercises, your pup must first be calm enough to pay attention to you. This may seem self-evident, but the majority of dogs brought to us for obedience training totally lack attentiveness. Their owners cannot get their attention. The dogs arrive unfocused and unruly — dominant — and in human/dog relationships, that always spells trouble. To avoid this, you must train your pup to focus on you right from the start of your relationship. Genuine leadership presumes attention, and when you get it, you will be close to becoming the alpha in your pup's life.

The following exercises are designed to establish you as leader in your puppy's eyes and can be started a week or so after you obtain him. By teaching him to be calm and to hold still while you are handling him, you will show him that you are the dominant figure in the relationship, and that you are a benevolent leader, worthy of his trust.*

Exercise One: Restraint

First, sit down on the ground or floor with your pup comfortably placed between your knees or legs, facing away from you. Put your right hand over his chest and your left hand under his muzzle. This is a basic exercise in restraint. If he accepts this handling calmly, praise him in a soft, reassuring voice and gently massage him. If he squirms and fights to get free, hold him firmly and put him right back in position, saying in a firm voice, "No, stay!" As soon as he settles, resume massaging him with your hands, gently petting him from the top of his head down the back of his neck. Any more struggling can be handled in the same way, with a quick shake which, though startling, does not hurt him. Make sure that your hold is firm, since the message you want to give your pup is one of control, with no indecision. Do this for several minutes per session. We find that most puppies come to accept this handling during the first or second session and to see it as very pleasant. This also forms the basis for the "Stay" command later on.

*In the following discussion, we are highly indebted to the insights of Jeanne Carlson, a trainer/behaviorist from Seattle, Washington, and author of the commonsense video "Good Puppy!" available from Sound Dog Productions, P.O. Box 27488, Seattle, WA 98125-2488.

A basic exercise in restraint. Put your right hand over his chest and your left hand under his muzzle and begin massaging him gently.

Exercise Two: Examining Mouth and Ears

When you are able to restrain your pup in a calm, relaxed manner, move on to the second exercise, which includes examining his mouth and ears. Throughout his life, it will be necessary at times to give your pup medicine, take inappropriate objects out of his mouth, clean his ears, and check his teeth. Puppies who do not become used to this when they are young can grow very defensive about being examined

Once your pup is comfortable, massage the top of his head and neck and manipulate his head from side to side.

when they are older and may even bite. To prevent this from happening, you need to familiarize him with these examinations now, while he is still easy to handle.

Begin by practicing the calming exercise we have described. Allow your pup to relax his head in your hand as you massage him and then gently begin wrapping your right hand around his muzzle from underneath, gradually getting him used to having his muzzle held. This may take a little time, so there is no need to rush things. Be gentle, and when he accepts it, praise him encouragingly as you manipulate his head around from side to side. If he becomes restless, go right back to the calming exercise to settle him.

Once he allows you to hold his muzzle and move his head around in a calm and relaxed way, you are ready to open his mouth and take a quick look inside. To do this, put your right

Placing your right hand under his muzzle and your left hand over it, carefully pull his jaws apart, taking a quick peek into his mouth.

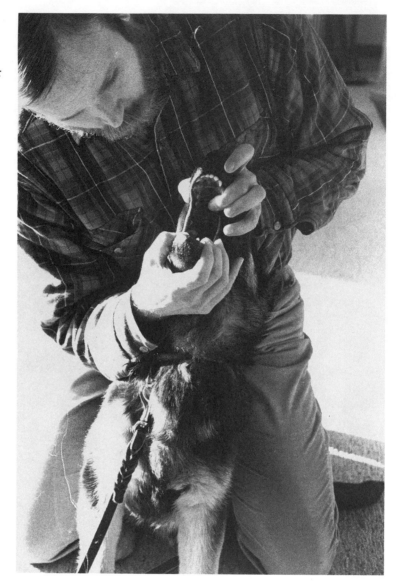

hand under his muzzle and your left hand over it and lift his lip briefly. Praise him and pet him. Then, to open his mouth fully, place the fingers of each hand between his jaws and carefully pull them apart. Take a quick peek and then release, giving him plenty of praise. Be brief at first, since your pup will not be used to this maneuver and may initially dislike it. After several episodes, however, he will accept it without protest. If you find your pup tries to mouth or nip at your hand, clasp his muzzle lightly and give him a swift shake, accompanying this with a firm "No!" Open your palm for him to lick and if he does so, praise him cheerfully. This exercise is particularly useful for gaining control over your pup's mouth and inhibiting the oral, nippy behavior common in puppies.

With your pup still relaxed, begin to examine the ears, first by massaging around the base with your fingers, then working over the surface of the ears themselves. This conditions your pup to having his ears touched and is invaluable for weekly grooming sessions. Puppies should have their ears thoroughly cleaned once a week to prevent infections from starting.

Exercise Three: Full-Body Massage and Repositioning

The third handling exercise, a logical extension of the previous two, involves examining your puppy's whole body and moving him safely when he is in a reclining position. This is valuable to be able to do should your dog be injured or should you need to move him while he is resting. We know of a number of biting incidents that happened when an owner tried to get his dog to move while the dog was sleeping. Conditioning your puppy ahead of time is a sensible way of preventing such accidents.

Start in the relaxed position of exercise one. To make your pup lie down, grasp both front legs with your hands and move them out from under him, gently moving him into a down position as you praise him. Move your hands around his neck and back, massaging him in a soothing manner, making sure that he is totally relaxed before proceeding any further.

When you sense he is completely at ease, kneel beside him, roll him over so he is lying on his side, and continue with your massage. Talk to him in a calm, reassuring way. If he starts to struggle, get him back down with your hand by pushing firmly against his shoulder as you say, "No, stay!" then follow immediately with praise when he settles. At most, correction should be a quick, gentle shake by the scruff, enough to let him know that you are in control. Continue lightly massaging his entire body with your fingers, paying particular attention to the feet and tail areas, which

With your puppy on his side, work your hands in a soothing, relaxed manner over his entire body.

will help accustom your pup to having his nails clipped and temperature taken. Use eye contact to reinforce the connection with your pup, giving a firm glance when he is restless, and a kind, affectionate look when he is relaxed and accepting.

While he is relaxed and comfortable, grab both sets of paws and calmly roll him over, continuing to stroke and pet him, then roll him back, praising him as you make eye contact. Finally, slide him around, as if you were moving him out of the way. Conclude the session with an "Okay" and his name, plus plenty of praise.

We have long known the benefits of canine body massage and described our approach to it at length in *How to Be Your Dog's Best Friend*. Massage is a valuable bonding technique that helps both owner and dog relax in each other's presence. Aside from using it as a relationship-enhancing exercise with older dogs, however, we also use it here as a preliminary training exercise with young puppies to develop their sense of trust and confidence in a human leader. A puppy that will allow you to handle, examine, manipulate, and groom him is one that trusts you and accepts you as leader. He acknowledges your dominance as he experiences your kindness, and becomes comfortable with giving you attentive, responsive eye contact.

These preliminary exercises are invaluable foundations to the training process. They can be started shortly after you obtain

While your pup is relaxed and comfortable, take hold of both sets of paws and gently roll him over.

your puppy and can continue on indefinitely, since they will become mutually relaxing exercises that both of you will look forward to. They communicate dominance and leadership to your pup in a relaxed, nontraumatic way, and establish a level of trust between you that will make formal obedience a smoother process than you ever dreamed.

One last observation: these exercises are suitable for most puppies; occasionally a puppy will be unusually touch sensitive and may react poorly to the handling. If this should happen and you experience extreme reactions of trauma, biting and/or agitation, *stop,* and seek the advice of a trained professional. Such a pup may require special types of handling and training that go beyond the scope of this book.

CHAPTER FIFTEEN

Basic Training for Puppies

Retreatants at New Skete often comment on how impressed they are with the behavior of our dogs and the gentle way in which the dogs receive them. Since we include our shepherds in as many daily activities as possible, they are a highly visible part of our life, and guests encounter them frequently throughout the day. Such contact makes it imperative for the dogs to be friendly and obedient, totally lacking in aggressive outbursts or skittish, freaky behavior. The best way to develop this behavioral soundness is by constantly exposing the dogs to everyday situations in a controlled manner, using basic training and starting this process early on.

A typical example: at dinner there are often a half-dozen dogs calmly on down-stays around the dining room table, not begging for food, simply happy to be around. During the meal, they either watch quietly or fall asleep, and it is often the case that you even forget they are there. If, occasionally, one dog should break her down-stay when her master gets up to collect dishes or serve food, the brother quietly corrects her and puts the dog back where she was originally told to stay. Rarely is anything more required.

In this type of atmosphere, even a young pup can learn to stay for an entire meal. Initially, to prevent her from wandering around, her master simply keeps her on leash next to himself, with one foot on the leash. If the pup tries to get up during the meal, the brother corrects her gently by pushing her back down with a quick "No." Experiencing this consistently over a period of several days and seeing the example of the older dogs, most pups quickly learn to relax and not fight the tether. Then, in the following months, they can gradually learn the down-stay away from the table.

At the conclusion of the meal, the dogs wait for grace to be sung and an "Okay" that releases them from their down-stays before they walk over to their masters. Then an affectionate pat on the head and some soft, reassuring praise is the usual response of each brother.

Apparently, guests see something remarkable in all of this. On one recent occasion, a retreatant remarked, "Brothers, how do you get them to do it? What's your secret? I have only one dog, and Max would never be able to lie still for an entire meal. I'm amazed . . ."

Anka and two four-and-a-half-month-old pups on down-stays during lunch.

An Overview of Puppy Training at New Skete

There is no secret about how our dogs are able to stay so relaxed during meals and other community functions: quite simply, we train them, steadily and progressively. Since monasteries are by nature quiet reflective spots, the chaos brought on by an unruly pack of dogs would be completely out of place. For a group of dogs to fit into this environment, they must be properly *trained*. This process is most successful when it begins early, as soon as a puppy starts living in the monastery. An eight-week-old puppy has had little chance to develop bad habits.

Initially, besides house-training and the preliminary handling procedures, we begin a gentle introduction to basic obedience exercises, Sit, Stay, Come, Heel, and Down (see chapters eleven and fourteen) that gradually becomes more structured and challenging as the months go on. When we start working with a pup, we keep the two to three daily sessions very brief, under five minutes each. The tone of each lesson is intentionally relaxed and pleasant. There is no fixed timetable for the puppy to "succeed," no pressure on the pup (or handler) to get everything right all at once. Our goal is to introduce each exercise in as simple and natural a way as possible. To avoid unnecessary stress, we begin with noncompulsive methods that condition the pups to respond correctly to the commands. For example, we raise our fingers from the pup's eye level to above her head to "shape" the sit, or we pass the pup's favorite toy from eye level to the ground to get her to follow willingly into a down (see chapter eleven). Repeating these exercises several times and rewarding the correct behavior with reassuring praise quickly makes the pup comfortable with moving into these positions, making it relatively easy for her to learn the more structured commands later on. During each session, we keep our gestures animated and lively to maintain the pup's interest, and we break up the various exercises with short moments of eye contact. We always conclude training with a short play session that is fun for the puppy.

Over the course of a month, these daily sessions prepare the puppy for more disciplined training as she enters the juvenile stage, the phase when she starts "testing her wings." By now, the pup is responding positively to quick, attention-getting leash corrections and the training sessions become more structured and challenging. Though being careful to keep the training enjoyable and the pup highly motivated, we leave no room for doubt as to who the alpha figure is; if a correction must be made, it is done swiftly, with *just enough force as is necessary* to change the behavior. Then, we immediately reinforce the correct behavior with sincere praise. Eventually, using ten- to fifteen-minute training sessions, we work briefly on each of the five obedience exercises. By quickly shifting from one exercise to another, we maintain the pup's attention and avoid boredom, the chief malady of all obedience training.

As the puppy displays a growing understanding of each

exercise, we use it repeatedly in practical situations through-out the day — down-stays in the living and dining rooms, sit-stays to greet guests, long down-stay at night in bedroom, and so on. Training needs this practical focus and enables the pup to spend greater blocks of time with the monk who is caring for her.

When puppy training is combined with proper management — daily exercise, frequent socializing, balanced diet, and regular grooming, it allows the pup to fit smoothly into the life of our community. The easiest way to lose enthusiasm for a puppy would be to fail to provide her with the practical skills necessary to mature into a friend and companion. If a puppy is not taught how to behave in a calm, relaxed manner, she inevitably becomes an energy drain, a burden, and it is likely that her master would end up spending less and less time with her. The real point of obedience training is to allow the young dog to be with her master often, naturally and in control. Pups are always happiest when they are able to be with those who have the responsibility of caring for them.

This brief description provides a general outline of how we raise our puppies. Following this program, by six months of age our puppies are well socialized, have a solid foundation in the basic obedience exercises, and perform them happily and reliably in everyday life. What is more, there is nothing extraordinary or exceptional about this.

Training Your Puppy in Basic Obedience

There is no reason this same sort of program cannot be applied successfully to your relationship with your puppy. Though training is not "easy," it is within the capabilities of puppy owners who set their minds to it. You must combine behaviorally sound principles and actual training of your pup in regular practice, preferably both at home *and* at a weekly Kindergarten Puppy Training (K.P.T.) class. If one is available in your area, we strongly recommend it (usually they begin at fourteen to sixteen weeks of age) in addition to following the guidelines described in this book. Our methods coincide with most K.P.T. programs, and the benefits are well worth it. Besides basic puppy obedience and valuable socializing experiences with other pups and people, these classes will give you important feedback on how you are handling your pup. An experienced trainer can spot mistakes in the way you are training that you might not be aware of. Also, seeing other owners work with their pups, exchanging ideas and experiences, is a great way to gain a proper perspective on your pup's behavior. It is very good for morale.

If a K.P.T. class is not available in your area, take the program described in the following sections and begin working twice a day, ten to fifteen minutes each session. Before you start, read through the exercises *several* times and mentally visualize them in sequence. You *cannot* train your pup with a leash in one hand and a book in the other. Imagine the session beforehand; think about the brisk pace, the animated tone of your voice, the attention-getting pops on the leash, the sincere praise you offer when your pup responds to you correctly. If you are not confident how to proceed *prior* to the actual training session, you will project indecision and awkwardness — cues for the puppy to start acting unruly and unfocused, heightening your sense of frustration. When you clearly understand what you are going to do beforehand and anticipate mistakes the pup might make as well as your responses to them, you will communicate a greater sense of presence and leadership that will help to focus your pup.

In the following sections, we assume that you have worked with your pup for several weeks in the preliminary exercises described in chapters eleven and fourteen, and that she is now comfortable walking on a leash. The exercises below are intended for puppies between three and five months of age. They serve as a preliminary introduction to the training that we have already described at length in *How to Be Your Dog's Best Friend.*

Training as an Art

Good training is concerned with more than simple obedience. The central issue in all puppy training should be how to teach the particular obedience skills in a way that draws out the best elements of the pup's personality. This is why training is an art — it is the process of drawing out, evoking from your pup behavior that will allow her to live peacefully with you. A puppy's knowledge of the basic commands, "Sit," "Stay," "Come," "Heel," and "Down" is no guarantee that the training process has been successful. A six-month-old puppy may indeed be able to execute the commands;

however, if in doing them she shakes fearfully and cowers, has her tail tucked under and ears flattened, shows no animation or enthusiasm, at what price has the training come?

Therefore, good training includes not only the precision of a dog's performance, but the attitude she displays in working. When a dog is animated and happy in her exercises, she also projects nobility, self-confidence, and a sincere desire to please. This does not happen automatically. *It is learned by experience.* Despite what most people assume, dogs do not have an innate desire to please their master or mistress. This popularized bit of wisdom is simply not true. Your dog has a natural desire to please herself, to receive pleasant sensations, and she is quite capable of learning how to bring those about. In the training process, she must be taught to *associate* pleasing you with something pleasant, with receiving praise and affection. This inspires her to work diligently for that reward.

The reverse is also true. When your dog associates an action of hers with something unpleasant or uncomfortable, she will try to avoid it. In puppy training, a minor leash correction simultaneous with a clipped, firm "No" is unpleasant enough to get her attention without harm.

This is the basis of all dog training, both for puppies and older dogs; with puppies the unpleasant sensations are kept deliberately at mild, nonstressful levels. When your pup does the right thing, praise her *immediately*, in an encouraging, animated tone of voice. Properly timed praise is essential; your pup needs to know that she has done what you want as soon as the behavior occurs so that she makes the proper association between the two.

Similarly, corrections must be well timed, at the very moment of the infraction. When your pup makes a mistake, an immediate pop on the leash with a clipped "No" will get her attention, giving you the chance to repeat the command and reinforce her compliance with praise. Remember, correction is not punishment; it is communication between you and your pup. It carries with it no anger, and it is just unpleasant enough to help her change her behavior. Once that occurs, it is over, forgotten. In this work, you are the initiator, the leader, and as each day passes your leadership will express itself by clearly and consistently applying the rhythm of praise and correction to let your pup know what is and is not desired. This must become second nature to you.

This type of attitude may take an emotional adjustment on your part. To train effectively, you must learn to be at ease with giving corrections, thinking of them as helpful guidance and information you are giving your pup to make her life easier. It is perfectly okay for your pup to make mistakes. Puppies learn by trial and error; hence, mistakes are simply opportunities for them to learn. When your pup makes mistakes, you have the chance to show her what you are asking her to do. She will make the proper connection between the two — as long as when the mistake occurs, your correction is properly timed. Then, as her behavior changes, your encouraging praise pleasantly reinforces her obedience. By repeatedly strengthening the behavior you wish from your pup with praise and affection, while discouraging unwanted behavior with appropriate corrections, you can, with repetition and consistency, teach the obedience exercises humanely and gradually shape your pup's behavior to fit in smoothly with your domestic requirements.

Learning How to Correct

For the sake of your relationship with your pup, you must learn how to make leash corrections properly. People who do not know how to use a leash invariably have major problems with training, since the pups never learn to pay attention to them. A leash used correctly gets your pup's undivided attention and enables her to respond to your request. But be careful! It is not sufficient to simply pull on the leash and expect your pup to respond to you. That usually results in a tug-of-war and confuses the issue of leadership. A *combination* of related elements must all work together:

- a properly-fitted training collar that is put on correctly
- a leash that is held so that there is always some slack between you and your pup
- a three-step correction consisting of a "No" with leash pop, repetition of command, and immediate praise upon compliance.

Let us look at each of these elements.

The Training Collar Once your puppy shifts from a flat nylon or leather buckle collar to a training (slip) collar during his first month with you, it is important that the training collar fit properly. Often a new owner purchases a collar many times too large for her puppy, and it hangs like an Olympic medal at the base of the pup's neck. Two problems result from this mistake. First, the leash correction is not immediate, since it takes longer for the pop to be felt by the puppy. Second, a low-hanging collar is positioned at the least sensitive part of the pup's neck, where the muscles attach to the rest of her body. Thus, for a correction to be felt, the owner will have to *overcorrect*, using much more force than would be necessary were the collar positioned higher on the neck.

That is why for most breeds we recommend using a soft braided nylon training collar that is snug going over the pup's head and which rests comfortably high on her neck. Because nylon collars are lightweight and flexible, they do not tend to slide down to the bottom of the pup's neck as many steel collars do, so you can make easier, more effective corrections. An exception to this would be training a long-coated breed like a bearded collie or Old English sheepdog, whose long hair tends to tangle easily in the nylon collar. For these cases, we suggest steel training collars with small links that are pounded flat, not rounded, so that the collar moves through the ring cleanly when pulled. In such cases, make sure that the pup's hair is tucked underneath the collar so that it stays high up on the neck. For most pups, you can anticipate two inches of slack when the collar is pulled tight.*

Putting the Collar on Correctly There is only one correct way to put the training collar on your pup. One of the most common mistakes new owners make is to put the training collar on upside down. When this happens, the collar does not release when it is pulled, the pup resists and chokes, and the training collar loses its value and causes your pup unnecessary discomfort.

Here is how to put on the training collar correctly every time.

1. Hold the collar out in front of you horizontally, holding a ring in the forefinger and thumb of each hand.

2. Thread the nylon through the left (inactive) ring, pulling the cord through with your left hand. Let the resulting loop hang freely. Notice that it drops naturally into the letter P.

3. With your pup on your left (you are both facing in the same direction), slip the collar over your pup's head.

---

*A flexible, braided nylon training collar is the best. Collars come in two-inch increments and are flexible enough for a knot to be tied to shorten it, should a more precise fit be necessary.

The correct way to put on a training collar. Notice how the collar falls naturally into the letter **P**.

Clip the leash to the live ring that is now coming over the back of your pup's neck, through the inactive ring, and is next to your side. Pull the leash and then let it slacken: the collar should immediately release.

It is easy, but incorrect, to put the training collar on upside down. Check the photograph in this section to make sure your pup's collar is on right. If you notice that your correction is not releasing properly after a leash pop, immediately check the collar. Chances are you have the collar on backward.

How to Hold the Leash   When you are working with your pup on the leash, hold the leash in a comfortable, relaxed

The starting position, showing the correct way to hold the leash.

manner that gives your pup enough slack to make a mistake. This will probably feel awkward at first, going against your instincts, since most people are inclined to hold the leash taut so that they can maintain some sort of control over their pup. In reality, however, this only accomplishes the opposite. When the leash is taut, the constant pressure on the pup's neck causes the pup to resist, resulting in more straining and pulling. There is something Zen-like in this — in training, more "control" proceeds from less "control."

Basic Training for Puppies | 175

We suggest holding the leash in the following manner:

1. Put your right thumb through the loop of the leash, letting the leash lie across the open palm of your right hand.
2. Close your right hand into a fist.
3. Lift the first two fingers and use them to grab the leash a quarter of the way down, resting your right hand against your right thigh.
4. Grasp the other end of the leash with your left hand, knuckles facing forward, letting it rest on your left thigh.
5. This is your starting position. Whenever you walk with your pup, keep your hands below your waist and leave your pup some slack with the leash.

The Three-Step Correction   Effective corrections communicate information to your pup, guiding her into desirable behavior. The quicker you become familiar with the sequence of a proper leash correction, the more success you will have training your pup, and the quicker she will fit into your life. Here is what we mean by this. The corrections we are speaking of have nothing to do with crass, "yank-'n'-spank" techniques that force a puppy to obey. When puppies are jerked repeatedly this way and that, out of incorrect and into correct positions, the whole training process becomes forced and unpleasant and the pup's attitude suffers.

With a constructive correction, the focus is different, clarifying what you want, as well as motivating and conditioning your pup to respond correctly to you. The emphasis here is positive, on getting your pup to look willingly to you for leadership. When your pup consistently looks to you for guidance, then you can draw her best out of her.

To begin the correction, get her attention by giving your quick "pop" with the leash, then immediately releasing the tension on the collar by allowing the leash to slacken. A clipped "No" should coincide with the pop. Never maintain constant pressure on the collar, since this will only cause your pup to resist and pull away from you. The quick pop/ "No" is meant only to interrupt the unwanted behavior and get your pup's attention. When that happens, give the positive command immediately, following with cheerful, encouraging praise as the pup responds.

Initially, you may feel awkward popping and releasing the leash. With practice, however, this sequence of pop-command-praise will become spontaneous and natural and you will use it continually as a means of communicating with

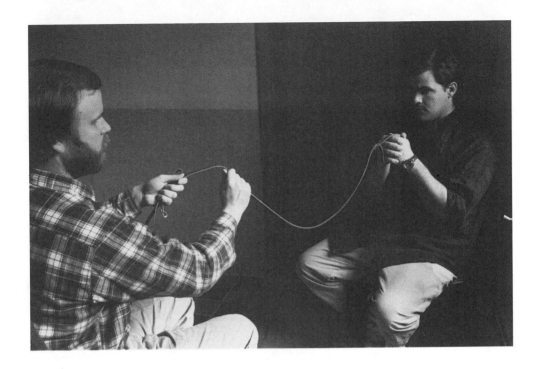

your puppy. It will get your pup's attention and establish you as the leader figure in her life. The following exercise, which simulates the pulling of a puppy on a leash, will help accustom you to the movement of the leash pop before you actually begin using it on your puppy. Spend several sessions practicing this with a helper until you are comfortable with the movement. Then you can gently introduce it to your pup.

Practice leash corrections with a human helper before attempting them with your pup.

1. Have your helper sit in a chair facing you, at a distance of one leash length.

2. Have him put his right hand through the loop of the leash, and then clasp both of his hands firmly together. The loop should be positioned around the right wrist.

3. Take the other end of the leash and hold it out straight. Grasp the leash a foot from the clip with your left hand (knuckles on top), and with your right hand hold on to the clip. Now make a quarter turn sideways to the right.

4. Instruct your helper to try to prevent you from pulling his hands toward you. Now, without jerking the leash, try pulling his hands toward you with your left hand. Do you feel the tension and resistance? The harder you pull, the more he tends to pull away from you. This

simulates the pulling a dog makes on a taut leash and the futility of trying to force him into obedience. Relax.

5. Have your helper begin putting tension on the leash again. This time, instead of pulling the leash straight back, in one continuous motion with your left hand, slacken the leash, "pop" it, and immediately release it again. His hands should jerk forward in your direction, and he should feel the effectiveness of the pop. It is attention-getting. Remember, strength is not the issue here. A snappy "pop" is all that you are looking for. Now synchronize the "No" with the pop. Repeat this at least a dozen times per session.

Using Your Voice Correctly   Before continuing on to the obedience exercises themselves, there remains one more preliminary point that needs to be emphasized. *Clear communication with your pup requires the proper use of your voice.* Particularly in the beginning stages of your life together, your puppy will be much more conscious of your tone of voice rather than the specific words that you use. Because of this, you must learn to vary your voice pitch in accord with the specific meaning you intend. Remember the primary canine sounds that your puppy was conditioned to in her litter. When necessary, her mother communicated her authority in low, guttural growls that all of the pups learned quickly to respect and obey. Higher tones were associated with the sounds of her littermates, and elicited enthusiasm and playfulness. The general rule to draw from this is to use lower voice tones with correction, discipline, and the stationary obedience exercises (Sit, Stay, and Down), and higher tones (though not silly) with praise, encouragement, and the active obedience exercises (Heel and Come). When your pup experiences marked contrasts in the tone of your voice, she will respond more readily to your true intent, resulting in less frustration and irritation for you.

These general principles of sound and voice border on two related areas of pet/human communication that often cause problems for owners: whining and nagging. Please, in your daily life with your pup, as well as in training sessions, avoid any kind of whining or nagging. These only undermine your leadership, communicating weakness and indecisiveness that result in your pup's learning to ignore you. The command is not "Sitsitsitsit . . ." or "Pleeeze siiiiit. . . ." It is "Sit." Give your command clearly once. If your pup does not respond, use the three-step correction. This communicates a clear set of expectations to your pup — you mean what you say and you are willing to back it up with action. Also, keep the volume of voice calm and controlled, and avoid the temptation to yell or shout at your pup. The cardinal rule in puppy training is never to lose your temper. Aside from emotionally unsettling you, it may prove harmful to your pup. Besides, it is totally unnecessary. Your pup has very sharp hearing and will respond well to a curt "No." Save your loud, bellowing voice for a real emergency.

The Basic Exercises

Following the approach described in this book, by the time you begin working with your pup formally during the juvenile stage (after three months of age), she should be able to walk on leash in a fairly relaxed manner and be accustomed to having a training collar around her neck. Further, you will have already introduced her in a very general way to Sit, Down, and Come exercises, and you will have spent ample time familiarizing her with being handled and touched. With this foundation to build on, the more structured obedience sessions can now follow naturally, without a great deal of stress.

Readers will undoubtedly notice that we do not use treats in our method of puppy training unlike many other trainers. This is a deliberate choice. Our experience in breeding, raising, and training puppies has been that treats are neither necessary nor as helpful to long-term training as is an approach based solely on praise. While it is indeed possible to train puppies using food rewards, these are often misused by owners and have the effect of focusing the pup's attention on the food instead of on the owner. Sincere praise focuses the puppy's attention on the owner, motivating the pup to work out of a more personal connection, thus strengthening the relationship.

Because our approach to training emphasizes companionship, not competitive obedience, it uses the puppy's name with the commands more often than other techniques do. We find that doing this helps focus a pup's attention and prepares her to do something. The only command we do not use the pup's name with is "Stay," in which the idea is to do nothing.

When we begin the first formal training sessions with one of our own pups, we start off with some informal leash work using the "Let's go" command (chapter eleven) and then the "Sit" command. This serves as a bridge from the preliminary puppy exercises to the formal commands by introducing the pup to the general idea of walking at the handler's side, receiving light corrections, and sitting when she stops. Demanding the precision of a formal heel during the first sessions would most likely involve too many corrections. After several days of loose leash work, as the pup's attention becomes more focused on the handler and she begins walking closer to his side, we are able to begin teaching the formal heel. No session should ever last more than fifteen minutes.

Heel The object in heeling your puppy is to teach her to walk next to you on your left side, at your pace, with a loose leash. Heeling has importance independent of making walks enjoyable and pleasant for you. When a pup is out in front pulling on the leash, the message she receives is that she is the alpha, the leader, and as she makes the decisions on the walk, deciding where to go and at what pace to move, so she will generalize that tendency to your entire relationship. The result will be an unruly puppy who fails to pay attention to you. On the other hand, the pup who learns how to walk by your side at your own pace is following your lead, paying attention to you. This sets a healthy tone for your relationship.

First, choose a quiet area to work in, with few distractions and with enough space to move around. Backyards are usually suitable. If you live in a big city, start by practicing inside your apartment, since you do not want to be competing for your pup's attention with the sights and sounds of city life. Begin by getting your pup to stand or sit next to you on your left side. Make sure her collar is on correctly and assume the starting position with the leash, being careful to keep some slack. You are now ready to proceed. In a pleasant tone of voice, say your pup's name with the command "Heel," immediately moving forward with your left foot, the one closest to your pup. Do not wait for the pup to begin walking. Simply move forward, tapping your left leg enthusiastically with your left hand. Since she is familiar with the leash, your pup should begin following right away. Cheerfully praise her. If she should fail to move, give a quick pop/"No" (releasing the pressure on the leash immediately), repeat the command, and praise her as she begins to move forward. Be animated. It is important for your pup to sense your enthusiasm and encouragement as she is following you.

As you proceed in the same direction, it is probable that

The puppy heeling correctly at the handler's side.

your pup will soon trot past you and begin pulling on the leash. *Do not pull or jerk the puppy back to your side.* Instead, give a quick pop/"No" correction and immediately reverse your direction 180 degrees, tapping your leg reassuringly as you say "Heel" again. Praise her warmly as she follows after you. Remember, the pop is merely attention-getting, and the "No" is free of any anger or frustration. You are merely introducing your pup to walking next to your side. Keep your hands low and your leash loose. By going back and forth, using little pop–release corrections when necessary, your pup will quickly begin looking to you as leader, watching to see when you are going to turn. By praising her enthusiastically, you will be conditioning your pup to focus on you throughout the session.

As you and your pup become more proficient at walking on leash, vary your routine, practicing left- and right-hand turns, figure eights and circle patterns. With puppies, it is

Basic Training for Puppies | 181

You can also correct minor forging by turning left, into your pup, moving your left hand out over her head.

important for you to prepare them sufficiently for the turns. Several steps before you turn, say your pup's name as you bend over slightly and slap your leg, getting her full attention. Then say "Heel," turning as you allow her to follow with you. If she scoots off in another direction, give the three-step correction and continue encouraging her, slapping your leg vigorously as you move along. When you do this consistently over several months, you will be amazed how quickly your pup learns to follow you, and equally how that response reflects her perception of you as her leader. In time, vary the pace of your walk, going from quick to slow to normal speeds. This breaks up the monotony of a constant pace and helps keep your pup tuned to you.

Sit By the time you start formal sessions with your pup, she will have already been introduced to the sit through the noncoercive methods we described in chapter eleven, so this

Teaching the sit from a stationary position.

will be a command she should already have some familiarity with. What you must do now is link the command with her ability to walk on leash, allowing the sit to flow smoothly from the heel. In time, your goal will be the automatic sit; your pup will sit automatically every time you come to a stop. At this stage, however, any thought of that is premature; all you should concentrate on now is getting your pup to respond to your "Sit" command on leash.

Some pups are able to make the connection from the noncoercive sit to the regular sit on leash with little difficulty, while others require some help and preparation. It just depends on the individual puppy. The following are two methods of teaching the sit that we have found quite effective for pups, one starting from a stationary position, the other used in conjunction with the heel.

To teach sit from a stationary position, have your pup standing next to you on your left side, facing in the same direction you are. You can either stand or crouch, depending on the size of your pup and how jumpy she is. Take your

As you walk with your pup at heel, move your right hand out in front of her so that she can see it. Then raise your hand straight up in front of her as you say, "Kora, sit," and glide to a stop.

right hand and position it between her collar and neck so that you can hold her still. Gently put your left hand on your pup's withers, and in a continuous stroking motion, move down the length of her back, over her tail to the hocks. As you tuck her into the sit position, lift up on the collar with your right hand and say "Sit." Praise her verbally as you hold her in this position for several seconds, then release her with an "Okay." Repeat this procedure over the course of several sessions until your pup appears completely at ease and relaxed with it.

Preconditioned puppies can often make the transition from heel to sit without having to spend separate sessions learning the stationary sit. As you are walking with your pup at heel preparing to sit, move your right hand out in front of your pup's path where she can see it. (This will require that you bend forward somewhat as you walk.) Raise your hand straight up in front of her as you say "Kali, sit" and glide to a stop. Your pup will follow the movement of your hand

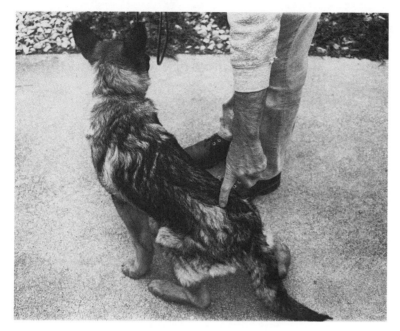

If your pup still does not sit after the first correction, repeat the leash pop and touch her rear lightly with your left index finger.

with her head, causing her rear to sink naturally into a sit position. Praise her cheerfully, and immediately move into heel again, repeating the process often throughout the session. A helpful way to condition your pup to sit in a straight, forward fashion early on is to move into the sit position from a 180-degree turn. When your pup moves around you to follow your turn, it is natural for her to move into straight sit position when the command is given. Even so, do not be concerned with perfectly straight sits early on in puppy training. Pups tend to be a little clumsy, and that can be refined as the training continues later on. For now, the focus should be on getting your pup to sit when you ask her to.

If your pup ignores your sit command when you come to a stop, give her the quick pop/"No," repeat the command firmly, and praise her when she corrects herself. Do not jerk the leash and repeat the command simultaneously. "No" is your corrective word. You do not want your pup associating the word "Sit" (or any other command) with a correction. If your pup still does not go into the sit after the first leash pop, repeat the correction, and as you give her the command once again, touch her rear quarters with your left index finger and pull up slightly on the leash with your right hand. Pause momentarily, then begin with heel again and repeat the sit sequence.

The intention behind this heeling and sitting is to get your pup under control right away during the early phases of training. Pups tend to need movement to focus their attention. By alternating heel and sit throughout the first several lessons, and by striving to keep the climate of the training light and encouraging, your pup will quickly learn to follow your lead willingly, making the teaching of the other commands much easier. This will also make your daily walks must less of a struggle as you establish a consistent pattern of behavior that your pup becomes accustomed to.

Stay   Stay is a control exercise to use with either the "Sit" or "Down" commands. In puppy training, we begin to teach it as soon as the pup has learned to sit reliably. The object of the exercise is simple and direct: the pup is not to move out of the position she was commanded to stay in.

Begin in the heel position, with your pup sitting next to you on your right. Put the leash in your left hand and hold it vertically over your pup's head, making sure that there is a slight amount of tension on the leash. With your palm open, fingers together, bring your right hand in front of your pup's face and say "Stay" in a firm, deep voice. Remain beside your pup for a few seconds to make sure that she is set, then step in front of her, continuing to hold the leash taut. If your pup starts to move with you and breaks the stay, give an immediate leash pop straight up with a "No" and repeat the exercise. Initially, keep the time you expect your pup to stay very brief, five to ten seconds, and then return to the heel position. After several more seconds, praise her warmly.

When your pup begins to be able to stay in this preliminary manner, make things a bit more challenging. While you are standing in front of her, reinforce the stay command with your hand signal and walk halfway around your pup. Then return to your starting position and move halfway around her in the other direction. Practice until you are able to walk around her in a full circle. If she should break position, correct her immediately with the three-step correction, reinforcing the command with the hand signal.

Anticipation is the key to teaching the sit-stay. *Watch your pup like a hawk;* the moment she breaks, give her a leash correction with a "No" and repeat the exercise. If your timing proves to be off and she ends up out of position, simply heel her back to her original position and start over again, making sure to watch more closely the next time for any signs that she is about to break the command. With consistent practice, your pup will soon come to understand what you are asking

The hand signal for "Stay," once your pup understands the command. At this point, the leash need not be held directly over the pup's head. However, make sure your right hand gives the signal at your pup's eye level.

for, allowing you to loosen the leash and step farther away from her without her breaking.

Once your pup understands the sit-stay, it is important to apply it to common, everyday occurrences in your home. For example, dogs love to bolt through open doors. To avoid this potential problem, practice making your pup hold the sit-stay each time you lead her up to a closed door. After parking her in the stay, open the door, making her wait for your permission before proceeding through the doorway. Consistently practicing this each day is a sensible way of training your pup to move with you in a controlled manner, and one day it might save her life by preventing her from bolting out into the street.

Another practical application of the sit-stay is to use it for introducing your pup to guests as well as to people you may meet outside. Often pups get into the bad habit of jumping up on people because their owners do not practice bringing them up to people on the leash and making them sit-stay. This results in puppy unruliness that will make friends avoid coming to your house. We will address separately the problem of jumping up; nevertheless, the foundation for proper control of introductions is the sit-stay. Prepare your pup for more challenging introductions by first bringing her up to members of your household during relaxed moments and making her hold the sit-stay. By practicing this in a progressive, controlled way, you can show your pup how to meet people.

Eye Contact   Throughout this book we have stressed the point that your puppy must learn to look to you as the leader in your relationship. One of the primary means of developing this relationship is to include structured eye-contact exercises in your daily training sessions with your pup, to build on the moments of spontaneous eye contact mentioned before. Just as the alpha wolf maintains order in the pack by utilizing eye contact in many different situations, so must you with your pup. A puppy who learns to make eye contact with you willingly early on will not only acknowledge your leadership, she will also bond with you more deeply.

With your pup facing you in a sit-stay, snap your fingers in front of her face and draw her attention up to your eyes. As you do this, say in an animated, cheerful voice, "Kali, watch me now, watch." Do not bend over to look at her or go through all sorts of verbal gymnastics to get her attention. The object is to get her to look up at you. If she is distracted, it may be necessary to give a little upward flick on the leash to get her attention. However, when you do, hold the eye contact only for several seconds at the start, since direct stares can be intimidating to dogs. When she looks up at you, praise her warmly for several seconds and then return to her side.

You can easily practice making eye contact during training sessions as well as in more relaxed moments with your pup. The point is to do it naturally and frequently. As you and your pup progress, the moments of eye contact will spontaneously become longer and more regular, and you will experience the profound effect it has on the quality of your relationship.

Come   We dislike labeling one exercise as being more important than any of the others. In obedience training, all of the exercises are interrelated, fitting and working together as a

Work on achieving regular eye contact with your pup. As she faces you on a sit-stay, snap your fingers in front of her face and draw her attention up to your eyes.

whole to help you develop control of your pup in a wide variety of circumstances. Each has its proper place. Your puppy needs to achieve a knowledge of each of the five basic obedience skills, not just one or two.

Unfortunately, many owners single out the recall as the most important exercise to the exclusion of the others. Certainly the recall is a crucial exercise. By far the most persistent complaint we receive concerns the inability to get adult dogs to come when called, which inevitably has dire consequences. However, the solution is not some sort of "shortcut." It is totally unrealistic to teach "just" the recall, for reliable recalls require the connectedness and consistency the other exercises foster. Owners who take the attitude, "I don't care about all this training, all I want from my puppy is for

Basic Training for Puppies | 189

him to come when I call," use this self-deceptive smoke-screen to avoid the time and responsibility necessary for developing a trained and well-adjusted companion. In our experience, rarely does a pup learn "just to come." The most effective way to teach come is through the early puppy conditioning we have described in chapter eleven, then to follow that up with a structured training program that covers *all* the exercises.

The goal in teaching the recall is to train your dog to come to you reliably and willingly, whenever and wherever you call. If this sounds impossible, it is only because so many owners often make serious training errors that have precisely the opposite effect on a puppy: they *teach* her *not* to come. Before considering a positive approach to the recall, let us first examine several of these common mistakes and describe the effect they have on puppies.

The most basic error affecting the recall is when owners allow their pups to be off leash in uncontrolled situations before they are prepared for it. A fundamental rule in training is for the handler to always be in a position to either prevent or correct a dog's error. Pups learn very quickly that they do not *have* to come when they are put in circumstances in which their owners have no control over them. With common attitudes such as "It is a nuisance to walk my pup on leash," or "Dogs were meant to be able to wander freely," they are begging for trouble. They are actually placing the pup in the position of leader, since she decides on her own whether she wishes to come to the owner or not. This fosters an attitude that is counterproductive to training.

A second error, often flowing out of the first, occurs when owners get into the habit of repeating the come command over and over. Yelling "Come, come, come," at your pup, without backing up the first command with some form of controlled correction, only conditions your pup to ignore you. She learns that she does not have to come.

Finally, there is the mistake of calling a puppy over to discipline her. Never, under any circumstances, call your pup to yourself to punish her. Never. Not for house-soiling, destructiveness, overbarking, roughhousing, or anything else. If you do, your pup will associate the punishment with the act of coming, not with what she is being disciplined for, and the next time you call her to come to you, the real message she received will be painfully obvious. If you must discipline your pup, or subject her to something unpleasant (a shot, medicine, etc.), go get her. In this manner, you will always preserve positive associations with the recall.

After your pup has been initially conditioned to coming through the jingling of keys, informal round-robin recalls, or simple retrieve play sessions, teach a more structured recall using the following three-step process that keeps the tone of the exercise happy and at the same time gives you control over your pup at all times.

Step One: Leash-Length Recall   The first step in the recall is to make sure that your pup understands what the word "Come" means. Start by putting your pup into the sit-stay. Step out in front of her at leash length and make her hold that position for several more seconds. Then, in a pleasant voice say, "Kali, come," crouching over slightly and opening your arms wide. Make sure that your body language is open and inviting. If she comes, praise her enthusiastically, guiding her gently into a sit as you soften up on the praise. Use good judgment here; too much praise can end up distracting your pup and switching her into a play mode. Keep her focused on the session. If she does not respond to your command, give her a slight tug on the leash (remember to release the pressure immediately) and repeat. At this short distance, most puppies learn the meaning of "Come" very quickly, allowing you to move on to the next step.

Step Two: Moving Backward with Puppy Following   The purpose of this exercise is to teach your puppy to keep the person she is coming to always in front of her. One of the most frustrating scenes owners can be involved in is having their dogs race toward them when they call, only to veer off at the last second and go flying by, always just out of reach. Dogs can make a great game out of this and may keep you occupied for a long time. You avoid this by training your pup always to come toward you.

Begin by moving your pup into the sit-stay position as you stand in front of her. Call your pup to you as in step one, only now begin to trot backward, keeping the leash a little slackened and your pup always a few feet in front of you. Praise her in an encouraging tone as you move, keeping her focused on coming to you. If she should start to go wide, as if to go past you, simply turn the other way, give a slight tug on the leash, and continue to trot backward. You can keep this up through several turns until you finally funnel the

To condition a young pup to come, jingle the keys as you trot backward, encouraging the pup to follow you.

puppy into a sit. Puppies think that this exercise is great fun and usually respond to it with zest and animation.

Step Three: Recall with Long Line Attach a fifteen- to twenty-foot nylon cord to your pup's collar and casually let her explore around the yard. Pretend not to pay any attention to her. When she is the length of the cord away from you and occupied with some smell, crouch down to the ground with your arms wide and call cheerfully, "Kali, come," clapping your hands together several times. If she does not respond immediately, give a quick pop on the cord and continue encouraging her, keeping the tone of your voice pleasant. Do not reel your pup in like a fish; tug and release. The purpose of the tug is simply to focus her attention and get her moving voluntarily toward you. Your voice and body language will then help her to form a positive association with the recall — a come is for love and praise.

You can do a variation of this during training sessions by putting your pup into a sit-stay and clipping the leash to the outstretched cord. Reinforce the stay with a firm hand signal and begin walking away from your pup toward the end of the line, watching over your shoulder to make sure that she does not break. If she holds, turn around when you reach the end of the cord and call her as above, crouching to the ground, with your arms wide. Stand up when she is halfway to you and funnel her into a sit once she reaches you, praising her happily. If she breaks the stay as you walk away from her, quietly go back to her and reposition her; then try again at a shorter distance.

In each of these exercises, your pup always has the initial option of not responding to your command. What makes her quickly correct herself, however, is the attention-getting pop immediately accompanied by encouraging praise. When you practice consistently, the recall becomes deeply ingrained in your pup, so that there is never a time when she will not come. You never have to get angry. Furthermore, by always keeping the recall positive and upbeat, you can gradually work on increasing the distance from which your pup will come reliably and willingly.

If a Mistake Happens   Occasionally, accidents do happen — house or apartment doors are left open, kids let go of the pup's leash, or you simply get careless and assume that your pup will come to you in the park. Suddenly you find yourself with your puppy off leash and not responding to your command. In such unforeseen circumstances, there are several emergency measures you can take. First, if it can be avoided, do not chase after her. After four months of age pups become much quicker and can usually avoid a single person out in the open by running around and making a great game of things. Instead, try moving quickly in the opposite direction. Dogs have a predatory instinct that manifests itself when something runs away from them, and often you can trigger this by pretending to "escape" from your pup. When she catches up with you, simply reach down and take hold of his collar. *Do not discipline her in any way.* Kneel down next to her and settle her quietly for several seconds, then clip on the leash and work with her briefly, taking her through some zippy heel, sit, and come sequences on leash.

If running away from her is not successful, try turning your back to her and sitting down on the ground, acting very casual. Sometimes it is even helpful to lie down all the way on your back. This often provokes curiosity that will bring the pup toward you to investigate. As she approaches, praise her quietly, but stay very still. When she is next to you, sniffing, gently put your hand on her collar and attach the leash, praising her softly. Again, follow up the episode with some brief obedience exercises.

To avoid accidents during your pup's first six months, we suggest you put the issue of off-leash recalls when out of doors on a back burner. Instead, work on making sure that the foundation you are laying for the recall is consistent and positive, and simulate off-leash situations in such a manner that you always have a chance to correct. Then, as your pup matures, you will have the basis to expect more.

Down The final exercise, down, often gives owners lots of trouble because it requires a puppy to move into a controlled, submissive posture that implicitly acknowledges your authority. If you have a strong-willed puppy, this can unleash a leadership struggle that results in some yipping and resistance. This is why we begin getting our puppies accustomed to moving into the down position voluntarily during the first weeks after adoption by conditioning them with noncoercive methods described in chapter eleven. It defuses the potential resistance the pup may make to being placed in the down, so that when we come to work on the down formally later on, the pup is already used to moving into the position. Even if your pup has not had the benefit of such early conditioning, it is essential for you to work firmly and patiently until she learns to accept it, for once a pup knows down, the length of time she can spend with you in a controlled manner increases dramatically, and again, helps solidify the bond that is developing between you.

The best way to begin teaching down is to work on a comfortable surface, either carpeting or grass. Start by kneeling beside your pup while she is positioned in a sit-stay. Steady your left hand on the back of her shoulders as you pass your right hand under her front legs, clasping her left leg just below the elbow. As you gently lift her front legs up and out, say "Kali, down." At the same time apply mild pressure on her shoulders with your left hand. Ease her into the down position, praising her reassuringly as soon as she is lying down. Make sure that when you do this, you avoid pulling her legs out from under her, since this could easily frighten her. Once she is down, keep your left hand stroking her shoulders to ensure that she does not immediately bounce back up, then release her with an "Okay" and praise after she is in the position for five to ten seconds. Keep the down very brief to start off with. If she tries to get up, correct her immediately with a "No, down" as you apply downward pressure to her back with your hand, then praise her as she holds.

Clasping both forelegs, lift up her legs gently and ease her into a down.

A variation of this exercise for a mellow puppy is to kneel beside her while she is sitting, as before, only now place your right hand behind her right foreleg at the same time as you drape your left arm around her withers, placing your left hand behind her left foreleg. Lift up her legs and ease her into the down, saying "Kali, down" as above, following this with praise.

Practicing this guided down several times a day will quickly accustom your pup to the position, allowing you to begin weaning her from being *placed* into the down to moving into the down herself. To make this transition, stand next to your pup in the heel position with her sitting next to you. Fold your leash into your left hand and rest it where the leash and training collar meet, underneath your pup's right ear. Now turn left 90 degrees so that you are facing your pup's right side. In one continuous, graceful motion, pass

In one continuous, graceful motion, pass your right hand down in front of your pup and say in a firm, deep voice, "Kora, down." Be sure to bend at your waist.

your right hand palm down in front of your pup as you say in a firm, deepened voice, "Kali, down," making sure to bend over at the waist. Many pups will follow the movement of your hand straight to the ground and move into the down easily. If this is the case, follow immediately with a "Stay" (using the hand signal as well) and praise her reassuringly. After several seconds, release her with an "Okay." If your pup does not follow your hand movement down, your left hand is in perfect position to give a quick, forward pop with the leash as you say "No, down." *Do not force her down; pop the leash and release.* If she corrects herself, praise her. If not, place her into the down manually.

A point to remember with this exercise is that sometimes when puppies go into the down position, they roll over on their backs and begin acting playful. If this should occur, stand up straight at once. By not feeding into the play mode, you will project a positive tone of dominance, and most pups will respond by straightening themselves up and focusing on the command.

Working toward a Down-Stay Once your pup understands the down and is able to move into it on her own, gradually extend the length of time that she is able to hold the position.

Down achieves its true goal only when it matures into a sustained down-stay, because that is what enables your pup to remain calmly in your presence without becoming an annoying bundle of unfocused energy.

Be patient with this process. Because pups have short attention spans, initially they are able to stay down only for short periods of time. You need to work methodically, step by step, to increase the potential, without putting too much pressure on your pup. We suggest two approaches. First, during training sessions, gradually increase the length of the down-stay from ten to twenty to thirty seconds and up, keeping your left hand over her back to start with, so that you can correct her swiftly should she break. When she is comfortable with this, make the exercise more challenging by standing erect, then moving around her in a circle. If she breaks, calmly use the three-step correction and try again. Being introduced to mild distractions and receiving gentle corrections for the errors they provoke will teach your pup to hold the down-stay for longer and longer periods of time, allowing you to be more imaginative with distractions. For example, try stepping over her as she holds the position, or

Practicing the down-stay. At first, keep your left hand over her back so you can correct her quickly if necessary.

Once your pup is holding a down-stay, make things more challenging by jumping over her.

clapping your hands together as you walk around her, or tossing a stone on the ground several feet in front of her. These kinds of distractions make the down-stay more reliable, teaching her to hold the position in spite of the temptation.

The second approach is to look for natural opportunities to put your pup into the down-stay when she will be disposed to holding the position for longer periods of time, such as after walks and play sessions, when she is likely to be tired. Put her into down-stay and then sit down and relax, reading the newspaper or watching television. Do not be concerned if she falls asleep; the point is to get her accustomed to remaining in one position for an extended period of time. If she should break the stay without permission, get up and correct her without making a big fuss about it, then return to what you were doing. Consistency on your part will show her that you are serious about the stay and habituate her to accepting the position. Finally, whenever you release her after a successful long down-stay, always be sure to give her plenty of praise.

Concluding the Session: Enjoying Your Pup

All work and no play can make for a rigid and dull relationship with your pup that lacks the mutual enjoyment so necessary for creating a quality bond. Because successful obedience training always involves constant repetition and practice, it is important to balance the more technical side of training with time set aside simply for fun and play. The end of each training period is an ideal time to do this. Concluding the session with play enables several things to occur. First, it creates a very positive "aftertaste" to the lesson for both you and your pup. Play is relaxing and enjoyable; finishing the training period with five or ten minutes of fetch, Frisbee, tag, or some other similar game, connects the training with something that both of you enjoy. When play is a regular part of each session, you create a strong incentive for your pup to focus and pay attention to you; she will look forward to training, since she knows the play period will soon follow.

Second, play is a vital ingredient in psychological health for all puppies. As we have seen, young pups learn how to interact with each other in the litter by playing, spontaneously creating games that teach them how to be dogs. This should not stop when they join their new pack. Regular play periods with their owners contribute to the emotional adjustment all pups must make if they are to live normal, happy lives.

Most importantly, play deepens the bond of friendship between you and your dog and helps avoid problems that might otherwise develop. By spending time together that is mutually enjoyable, you and your pup will grow in respect and appreciation for each other. Thus, as an important part of the training process, play helps the owner/dog relationship reach its full potential, maturing into something that is genuinely life-giving for dog and owner alike.

Looking Back

Throughout this book we have continually highlighted the importance of becoming the alpha figure, or pack leader, in your puppy's life, and we have presented positive elements involved in achieving that. All puppies require the consistent, responsible guidance of their owners in order to mature into balanced, well-adjusted companion dogs. What makes the training process such a necessary part of a healthy dog/owner relationship is that it confirms your position as leader at the same time that it provides your pup with the practical skills necessary to live happily with you. *Training is a humane form of dominance.* In following your directives, your pup implicitly recognizes and submits to your leadership. This goes a long way toward preventing problems before they have the chance to develop.

CHAPTER SIXTEEN

Discipline and Common Puppy Problems

No matter how well-behaved your puppy is, it is entirely normal for there to be occasions when discipline is necessary to correct bad behavior. Much like children, and aside from simply not knowing any better, pups go through bratty episodes when they vie with you for leadership, testing you to see just how far they can assert themselves. In such circumstances, you must respond correctly as a convincing pack leader, letting your puppy know without confusion the error of his ways. Too often new owners let bad behavior go unchecked, unintentionally allowing it to evolve into something more serious. This is usually because they are uncertain as to what constitutes legitimate discipline for a pup and are afraid of being abusive in any way. The unfortunate result is a spoiled, self-willed puppy.

It is also possible to err in the opposite direction. When owners administer discipline incorrectly, such as disciplining a puppy long after the fact (as commonly occurs in episodes of house-soiling or chewing, when the pup does not understand the reason for the correction), or by using ill-advised techniques such as a rolled-up newspaper or a harsh slap across the rear, puppies can end up manifesting shy, skittish behavior.

Especially with puppies, discipline must always walk the fine line between too much and too little. What makes discipline such a difficult topic to address is that it varies according to the circumstances. No book can tell you the precise correction to use in each particular situation; we can only

A firm scruff
shake for a
younger puppy.

offer guidelines, which you must then apply to your own puppy. As we have emphasized, each pup is an individual, and what may be appropriate for one pup may be excessive for another. The real starting point for discussing discipline is for you to know your puppy, to be able to "read" his body language and get a feel for how he responds to correction. Then you can proceed intelligently, using only as much force as is necessary to make your point and without losing your own self-control.

This is why we recommend disciplinary techniques that mimic those your pup would receive in a natural setting, particularly from his mother or a senior pack member. These harmonize with his nature as a canine while effectively communicating your displeasure. For example, you will discover from your eye-contact sessions that your pup becomes highly sensitive to the message you send to him with your eyes. Usually this will be kind and encouraging; however, there will be instances when your assertive glare will stop his behavior cold, particularly when it is accompanied with a deep, barklike "No!" We draw from the example of the alpha wolf, who regularly maintains pack order through a threatening growl and stare.

There are also times when a puppy merits stronger correction than simply a penetrating look or a strong verbal rebuke. Particularly if you have a puppy who is dominant and headstrong, you may find that he is unaffected by eye contact and voice tone. For your pup to get the point, you must express your authority with physical discipline that immediately fol-

The shakedown. Grab the scruff of the neck with both hands, make eye contact, then follow with several quick, firm shakes as you say, "No!"

lows his bad behavior. For these occasions, we prefer using the shakedown method, which resembles what the mother does to her pups to keep order in the litter. If the pup is quite young (8–12 weeks), grab the scruff on the back of his neck and shake it firmly with a "No!" If the pup is older, grab the scruff of the neck with both hands and lift him off his two front feet, making eye contact, then follow with several quick firm shakes as you say "No!" If your pup has advanced to the point in his obedience work where he understands the down, follow up your discipline immediately with a down-stay, since that position expresses submission and effectively reinforces your dominance.

Discipline and Common Puppy Problems | 203

Ordinarily, these disciplinary techniques are quite effective for puppies raised within a well-rounded program of conditioning and training. When applied correctly, they communicate your authority in a humane and convincing way that generally avoids the need for sterner techniques later on when the puppy is older. However, one word of caution: occasionally a five- or six-month-old puppy from one of the more dominant breeds (German shepherd, Rottweiler, Akita, or Doberman pinscher) may misbehave in a manner that merits stronger measures. For example, out of the blue your self-confident, five-month-old male German shepherd may growl at a guest you have invited into your house. In a situation like this, involving either the threat or actual manifestation of aggression, you should seriously consider using a firm cuff underneath the chin with your opened hand. We believe this because we have seen only too frequently the results of ineffective corrections involving aggression — the aggression escalates and then real problems occur. Better to nip it in the bud.

To make this correction effectively, your dog must be anchored in a sitting position with your left hand holding on to his collar. As you make eye contact with your dog, cuff the underside of his mouth with your opened right hand, rapping him sharply several times as you say "NO!" The discipline should be firm enough to elicit a short yelp, and it is best to follow it up immediately with an obedience command that reinforces your authority. After that, over the course of several weeks, stage "mock" situations that give your pup the chance to learn how he is supposed to act in such situations. By reinforcing correct behavior with generous praise, you establish a healthy pattern for him to follow that curtails aggressive displays.

Remember, use this correction with an older puppy only in the rarest of circumstances, and only when the puppy is emotionally strong enough to handle it.

Finally, there are a number of specific problems common to puppyhood that all new owners must learn to deal with. All puppies make "mistakes." No amount of preventive thinking can possibly cover all the potential problems involved in raising your pup. Because he is still young and immature, your puppy will, at times, behave in ways that annoy and irritate you. When these inevitable occasions occur, you must be careful to respond with understanding and balance, avoiding either a passive, "he'll eventually grow out of it" attitude, or the "put the baby to sleep with a sledgehammer" type of solution. Both of these extremes only make matters worse. Instead, by steering a more moderate course, blending prevention with correction, you can change unwanted behavior in a manner that is properly suited to your puppy's young age.

Here it is important to distinguish puppy problems from the more serious behavior problems characteristic of older dogs. Unlike deeply ingrained, neurotic behavior that requires professional help to treat, most puppy problems are entirely normal. That is, they are the result of your puppy being a young canine and acting inappropriately within a domestic context. For example, it is perfectly natural for a dog to bark, chew, bite, play, dig, jump, and urinate — being a dog means doing these things. The difficulty comes about when these activities are not channeled to fit our domestic situation. Your pup has no innate idea how to behave in your home; he will simply do what comes naturally. Since it is you who introduced your puppy into your home, it is also your responsibility to train and teach him how to act and to help him learn from his experiences. This is much easier to do while he is a puppy, before problems have the chance to become something more serious. In what follows, we will consider a number of typical puppy problems and offer you some practical suggestions for resolving them that are both effective and humane.

Mouthing

As we have seen, puppies use their mouths to explore and investigate everything, especially each other. Should you watch a six-week-old litter of pups playing, you would observe them mouthing and nipping each other continually, chomping on ears, neck, muzzle, legs, or tail, learning how hard they can bite down before their playmate protests. Such behavior becomes a natural way for them to communicate and express themselves. With this background, it is easy to understand why your pup would direct this same sort of behavior toward you once he arrives home. Separated from his littermates, you are now the main focus of his attention, so it is only logical for him to express this by mouthing your fingers, arms, feet. At first this might seem like cute, harmless behavior, but his sharp milk teeth will quickly convince you otherwise. Furthermore, should you try ignoring it, his mouthing will only get worse, becoming a normal way of behavior toward friends and visitors, as well. Before this becomes a bad habit, here is how to stop it.

1. When he starts to mouth you, quickly clasp your hand around his muzzle and shake it quickly as you say "No!" He should whine in displeasure. Then open your palm for him to lick. If he does so, praise him — licking is allowed. If he tries to mouth or nip at you again, repeat the correction.

2. Another technique that discourages mouthing is to let him experience an unpleasant result from it without any show of anger on your part. Begin by petting your pup around his neck and chest. As he begins to mouth your hand, *gently* put your index finger down his throat, just enough to elicit a gag reflex. (Anyone with long fingernails should not attempt this.) When your pup gags, remove your finger and open your hand for him to lick, praising him if he does so. If you do this consistently, your pup will quickly associate the unpleasant gagging with the mouthing of your hand and the behavior will stop.

3. The massage/dominance exercises we discussed in chapter thirteen are also helpful in teaching your pup to accept being handled and manipulated without responding orally. For corrections, use either a quick scruff shake or one of the two techniques described above.

4. Finally, avoid all tug-of-war games with your pup. They condition him to be mouth-oriented and unrestrained in his bite.

Chewing

Puppy chewing is the flip side of mouthing, in which your pup focuses his oral attention on all manner of household objects and personal items, gladly chewing whatever is within his reach. Puppies are amazingly resourceful; if something can be chewed, your pup will chew it, and there are several very good reasons for this. Puppies have a physical need to chew that is associated with the teething process. This begins around three months, with the permanent teeth pushing up underneath the puppy teeth, and peaks between six and ten months of age, when the permanent teeth are set solidly in the jaw. During this period, if your pup does not have something to chew on, he will actively try to find something. Chewing also occupies your pup's attention, relieving boredom and normal puppy tensions. A puppy can keep himself occupied for hours at a time if he has something to gnaw on. Hence, rather than waiting for a full-scale problem to develop, control your pup's natural inclination to chew by following these guidelines:

1. The first priority in controlling destructive chewing is prevention. Use common sense. Before you even bring your new pup home, make sure that shoes, socks, books, and other personal items are picked up off the floor, and store valuable objects up and away where they cannot be damaged. Check to make sure that electric cords are safely out of reach and tape over electric outlets you are not using.

2. Once you have your pup, always be aware of where he is and what he is doing. Take the same attitude you would if you were caring for a baby.

3. Whenever you leave him unattended for any reason, short or long absences alike, confine him safely in a crate or a "puppy-proofed" area. It is astonishing how many complaints about puppy chewing come from clients who insist on giving their pups free rein in the house while they are away. This is foolish, sentimental thinking. It is completely unrealistic to expect a young puppy not to chew if he is left alone in the house unconfined.

4. There should be nothing in the confined area that could be easily chewed on, except for *one* permissible object that is his. Make this object the focus of all his chewing. To get him accustomed to it, use it right from the start for play sessions, as well as a replacement object after he has been corrected for chewing on something inappropriate (see below). We prefer meat-scented nylon bones because they are long-lasting, safe, and nonabrasive to the teeth, as are all natural hard bones. While pups love rawhide bones and squeak toys, these are too easy to destroy and older pups occasionally ingest large pieces of them, which can be quite dangerous. Also avoid traditional favorites such as old shoes or knotted-up socks. Once pups learn that chewing on leather or cotton is acceptable, they are unable to distinguish old articles from new ones. To your pup, a shoe is a shoe.

5. Before leaving your pup alone for an extended period of time, roll the nylon bone between your palms

for several minutes so that your scent is firmly on it, then present it to your pup as you leave. Keep your departure low-key and nondemonstrative, since highly emotional farewells can lead to separation anxiety that your pup will try to relieve in any way he can — through destructive behavior if that is a possibility, or by nonstop barking and whining. Leaving a radio set to a classical music station can also be a calming influence.

6. Beyond mere prevention, you should also begin actively conditioning him to ignore forbidden objects and to focus his chewing solely on the nylon bone. Initially this means using a quick shakedown whenever you catch him chewing on something inappropriate, always presenting him with the nylon bone instead. Follow with encouraging praise if he accepts it.

7. As your pup grows, concoct situations in which he must learn to ignore different objects placed temptingly on the floor while you are in the same room. Make sure his nylon bone is one of the objects. After you put your pup in a down-stay, pretend to read the newspaper, keeping a close watch on him out of the corner of your eye. If he starts to edge over to one of the forbidden items, wait until he actually starts to put his mouth on it, then correct him with a firm "No!" pointing out his bone instead. If he repeats the mistake, give him a brief shakedown and present him with his bone again. Several such sessions should bring him to the point where he will ignore the various articles and play only with the bone *while you are in the room.* At that stage you can begin practicing leaving the room for very short intervals, so that should he go back to chewing on a forbidden object, your quick return can catch him in the act, the only justifiable occasion for a correction. The object of this exercise is to gradually prepare your pup for the day when he will be able to be trusted alone in the house while you are away.

8. Make sure your puppy receives plenty of exercise each day. Proper exercise helps to curtail boredom and high energy levels, two significant factors in destructive behavior.

9. A final, practical point: if you ever have to forcibly remove an object from your pup's mouth, place your hand across the top of his muzzle behind the teeth, thumb on one side and fingers on the other, while your other hand pulls down the bottom jaw. Praise the pup as he releases the object.

Most puppies have the annoying habit of greeting people by jumping up on them, which is actually an attempt to reach the individual's face. For puppies, the facial area of both dogs and humans is the chief point of contact, the primary reference point in all social encounters. This stems from behavior learned around the time of weaning; recall how wolf pups jump up and lick at the muzzles of older pack members to solicit food, which the adults then regurgitate for them. After weaning, this face licking continues with a more generalized meaning, becoming the ordinary way subordinate wolves greet those of higher rank.

Regardless of how natural this behavior is, however, when it occurs in human society, it quickly becomes an annoying and potentially dangerous habit. While a small pup jumping up might seem harmless enough, it becomes something more serious once that pup is fully grown. Furthermore, most visitors to your house will not appreciate your pup's paws on their clothing, and pups in the habit of jumping can easily frighten young children or knock over an unprepared elderly person. Our advice is to stop the behavior as soon as it begins, following these guidelines:

1. Resolve to discourage all occasions of jumping up. It is not fair to your pup to allow him to jump up on you, then to correct him for jumping up on others. This is bound to confuse him. Keep your expectations consistent.

2. Whenever your pup attempts to jump up on you, simply grasp both of his front paws securely, holding them up long enough for him to become uncomfortable with the position. Show no anger. Most pups like to be up for only a very short time; when he starts to protest, continue holding on to him for several more seconds, allowing him to become very uncomfortable. Then put him down gently, helping him into a sit. When he experiences this response consistently, he will avoid jumping up on you.

3. Another possibility is to put the palm of your hand flat out in front of your pup's face when you sense he is about to jump. This blocks the jump and disposes him to respond to a sit command.

Whenever your pup jumps up, grasp both paws securely, holding them up long enough for him to become uncomfortable.

4. Since jumping up usually occurs during greetings, teach your pup an alternative manner of greeting both yourself and other people. We recommend crouching down to his level when he comes to greet you, then guiding him into a sit and petting him calmly for several seconds. For greeting guests, practice bringing him up to people on leash, leading him into a sit-stay several feet before he reaches the person. Have the individual then approach. If your pup tries to jump toward the person, give a quick leash correction sideways as you move to the right. Circle him around on heel and repeat. When he allows the individual to pet him without jumping off the ground, praise him cheerfully.

When puppies start eating food and playing with toys, around four weeks of age, it is quite common for them to show the first signs of possessive behavior. For example, as the litter eats from a common dish, a dominant pup may suddenly growl and snap at his neighbor, trying to scare him away from his share of the food. Often, the other pup will growl right back, learning that he must stand his ground if he is to get his own portion. The same dynamics occur during play sessions: a puppy might be playing with a particular toy when another littermate tries to take it away from him. The first pup growls threateningly, and if he happens to scare the challenger off, he learns an important lesson about dominance and pack life. Thus, what we call possessive behavior begins quite early as a normal part of puppy development.

As a pup grows older, however, the situation changes radically; possessiveness can easily evolve into a serious problem leading to aggression if it is not checked right from the start. Never procrastinate with this. Having your full-grown dog growl menacingly at you because you approached him too closely while he was eating, or because you were trying to take something away from him, is a very unsettling experience. By training your pup to let you pick up his food, or take any object out of his mouth, you assert your alpha stature in a healthy way before the behavior has a chance to develop into something serious. Here are three simple steps to follow with your pup to condition him away from possessive behavior.

1. At his feeding time, instruct him to sit. Place the dish down in front of him and let him begin his meal. After several seconds, pick up the dish and command him to sit again. Treat any growling with a decisive shakedown. After any correction, make sure you do not give him back the food until you have made him sit.

2. Teach your pup to take part of a biscuit gently from your hand. First instruct him to sit. After praising him, offer him a small piece of dog biscuit, making sure he takes it gently. This simple exercise teaches a pup self-control around food.

3. Each day, practice giving him the nylon bone, then

taking it away from him, praising him as you do so. If he resists, utter a clipped "No, leave it," praising him if he releases it. If he still does not let go, give him a brief scruff-shake with a verbal reprimand, then repeat the process. Then let him play with it.

Submissive Urination

We have noted how puppies, having been originally cleansed by their mothers while they are on their backs, subsequently demonstrate submission to adults by moving into a similar position, involuntarily releasing a small amount of urine as they do so. In canine terms, this reflexive act acknowledges authority and has a placating effect on the higher ranking wolf or dog, defusing possible aggression.

Because of its deep, instinctive roots, it is not surprising that this same behavior is often transferred into a puppy's new pack. In a domestic situation, submissive urination reflects the same recognition, only now it is directed toward a human alpha, and it can also occur during moments of extreme excitement. Needless to say, if the behavior happens repeatedly, it becomes an unwelcome problem that must be handled with sensitivity and understanding if it is not to grow worse.

1. Submissive urination must be clearly distinguished from house-soiling. The puppy does not intend to urinate, only to show submission; therefore he must never be reprimanded for this behavior. Punishment will only encourage a more pronounced display of submission.

2. It is vital to teach a submissive puppy the obedience commands in a positive, confidence-building manner. Whenever possible, use noncoercive techniques that avoid triggering submission by dominating physical contact (see chapter eleven). The pup needs to experience praise and encouragement in a manner that draws him out of himself.

3. Avoid highly emotional greetings, as well as situations in which you tower over your pup. Whenever you arrive home, ignore your pup for five minutes. Then, when you do greet him, crouch down to his level, guiding him into a sit. If possible, do this on a noncarpeted

surface such as grass, tile, or linoleum in case a mistake does occur.

4. Stage controlled introductions to other people by bringing your pup up to them *on leash* and making him sit in front of them. It is difficult for a pup to urinate while sitting and the position is ideal for controlling excitement.

Carsickness

When a dog is able to ride well in the car, it significantly increases the time he is able to spend with his owner, making for a more flexible and enjoyable relationship. By conditioning your puppy to ride in your car at an early age, you avoid the headache of carsickness later on. Neglecting to work with a pup on car etiquette makes practical matters like trips to the veterinarian a major project, not to mention ordinary outings for recreation and exercise. Start taking your pup for daily rides in the car soon after he comes home, following these general guidelines:

1. Your pup should learn to ride in the back of the car. For safety purposes, use a crate, safety harness, or car barrier, to protect you and him from sudden stops.

2. Begin the conditioning process by taking your pup on a very short trip (up and down the block, for example) every day for a week. Make sure it has been two to four hours since your pup last ate, and avoid a route with curves. Keep the trip upbeat and happy, and follow up the excursion with a play session, so that your pup associates the car with something he likes.

3. Do not scold the pup for whining, and ignore any vomiting. Clean it up when you get back home, and try again the next day, making the trip even shorter. If necessary, limit the trip to going up and down the driveway.

4. When your pup shows no signs of nausea, begin increasing the distance of the ride. Always be sure to praise your pup at the end of the trip.

5. Though it is fine to leave the rear windows open a crack for ventilation, do not allow your pup to put his head out the window. This common behavior is dangerous, since your pup could be hit by a flying pebble or

other foreign objects. Also, be sure *never* to leave a pup or adult dog unattended in a car out in the sun, since they are more sensitive to heat prostration and death from heat than we are.

Stool Eating

Coprophagy, or stool eating, is one of the more distasteful habits a young puppy can engage in. Though it is utterly incomprehensible to most owners, there are usually very specific reasons for the behavior which, when addressed quickly, can be resolved before they become chronic. There is no need for panic if you observe your pup doing this. Treated sensibly, most pups will overcome the problem without a lot of difficulty.

To understand why stool eating occurs at all, it is helpful to recall a pup's first experiences in the litter. Puppies are naturally inquisitive. When they are with their littermates before weaning, their mother consumes all of their waste material. This is natural maternal behavior, essential for keeping the litter healthy. After weaning, much like little children, pups naturally investigate their own feces, smelling, licking, and even consuming them. This is why breeders and owners must be diligent about picking up stools. Keeping floors and yards clean helps control the problem right from the start.

Once a puppy is in his new home, stool eating can indicate one of several things. Often it points to a dietary deficiency. The pup is not digesting his food properly and subsequently smells undigested protein in the stools. This can be caused by poor food or an internal problem requiring the attention of a veterinarian. It can also be related to boredom. If a puppy is alone in a fenced-in backyard, for example, he may entertain himself with old stools. This is especially the case in colder weather, when frozen stools seem to be an object of particular fascination.

To treat coprophagy effectively, follow several specific points:

1. Make sure that the food you are feeding your pup is a high-quality brand, one that is both palatable and nutritious. Be on the watch for signs of poor digestion — large

stool content or stools that are loose. You may wish to consult your veterinarian about this.

2. Be conscientious about picking up your pup's stools. While some professionals recommend mixing digestive enzymes or meat tenderizer with your pup's food (they supposedly give the stool an unappetizing scent), or spraying Listerine or Tabasco sauce on an old stool (same idea), it is just as easy to take away the source of the problem. If your pup has a yard to play in, pick up stools regularly, or, if possible, as soon as he eliminates when he first goes out.

3. When you are walking with your pup in the neighborhood, do so on leash and do not let him smell the droppings of other animals. Give him a quick leash pop to direct his attention elsewhere. With consistent corrections, you will find that he will learn to ignore them.

CHAPTER SEVENTEEN

General Care of Your Puppy

Throughout this book, we have emphasized that raising a puppy involves much more than good intentions and sentimental feelings. Because your pup is entirely dependent upon you for its welfare, you must learn to see your role comprehensively, in every aspect of her life. Real companionship presumes a commitment to care for all of your pup's physical and social needs. Thus, in addition to her basic training and upbringing, you are responsible for her physical condition as well, for providing proper diet, conscientious grooming, and regular, vigorous exercise. Since these are essential to a pup's health and well-being, we will discuss each of these topics in the following sections.

Feeding Your Puppy Properly

With all of the advertising hype surrounding pet foods and an abundance of commercial brands available from which to choose, it is little wonder many a new puppy owner is confused about how and what to feed her pup. Though it is outside the scope of this book to discuss specific brands of puppy food, there are some basic principles about diet and feeding that all puppy owners should understand so they can make responsible choices for their pups. We will try to illustrate these principles by answering some common questions that many new owners have.

What Is Puppy Food?   Because puppyhood is a time of rapid growth and intensive development, puppies require approximately *double* the daily amount of nutrients per pound of body weight that fully grown dogs need. In addition, their need for specific nutrients differs from adults': these cannot be obtained from adult food no matter how much they eat. Thus, it is harmful to feed puppies the same type of food as adult dogs. To meet a pup's special nutritional needs, many dog-food manufacturers produce specially formulated puppy foods for the first year of a pup's life. These are nutritionally complete and balanced to give a puppy the ideal amounts of protein (usually between 28 and 30 percent), and the vitamins and minerals especially required for proper bone development. Normally, they make it unnecessary for you to supplement your pup's diet.

How Long Should My Pup Stay on Puppy Food?   Manufacturers generally recommend puppy food for the entire first year of a pup's life, but some pups may have to switch to adult food earlier. A pup who is growing too quickly can possibly develop panosteosis (long-bone disease). For this reason, always double-check your pup's diet with your veterinarian.

What Type of Puppy Food Should I Use?   There are three basic forms of commercially produced dog foods available: moist (canned), semimoist (sealed pack), and dry kibble, and each form has its pros and cons. Our preference is to feed as the major part of a pup's diet a premium dry puppy food that has a meat protein source as one of its first two ingredients. Dry food is economical, convenient, good for keeping your pup's teeth clean, and relatively digestible and palatable.

Canned dog food is highly digestible and palatable; however, it is expensive. It contains 75 percent water, meaning your pup will have to eat much more of it to get the same amount of nutritional value that she would with kibble. Because it is soft, it also lacks the dental benefits of kibble. Instead of relying exclusively on a diet of canned dog food, we recommend using small amounts as a mix with dry kibble to enhance the kibble's palatability. Also, some companies market very high quality, balanced raw-meat foods for dogs in frozen packs. This can be used along with kibble instead of canned food.

Semimoist foods are also highly digestible and palatable and very convenient. They come in premeasured portions and do not require refrigeration. Like canned meat, they are expensive and lack the dental benefits of kibble. Also, since they contain large amounts of sugar, salt, and preservatives, they can lead to problems with hyperactivity and obesity. We advise you not to use them regularly.

How Do I Select a Particular Brand? When considering particular brands, look for a puppy food from a company with a serious background in research and testing, whose labels meet or exceed the standards established by the National Research Council (NRC) and the Association of American Feed Control Officials (AAFCO). Avoid generic or store-brand pet foods: though inexpensive, they may prove costlier in the long run because of the medical problems associated with poor diet. Veterinary studies have shown these products to be of inconsistent quality and low digestibility or food value. Instead, consult your breeder and veterinarian for several possibilities and stick with one food that your pup finds palatable. You may have to purchase the food at a feed or pet-supply store where the higher quality dry foods are usually sold. Supermarkets carry good canned foods.

How Often Should I Feed My Pup? For the first four to six months a puppy should get three meals a day of puppy chow. Eventually she will be able to consume more food at each feeding, so she can then be cut down to two meals a day. For most dogs, it is preferable to continue this twice-daily feeding throughout adulthood since it is healthier for them to digest two smaller meals than one larger one. If your pup is home alone during the day, whoever walks the pup at midday should feed her beforehand.

What Other General Feeding Recommendations Would You Offer? Feed your pup either in her crate or in a quiet, undistracting area at the same time every day. Serve the kibble with a small amount of canned or fresh-frozen thawed meat for dogs, moistened with warm water. In place of meat you may use cottage cheese or a cooked egg, and twice a week you could include a tablespoon of yogurt, which helps to restore intestinal flora. Give your pup fifteen minutes to finish her food; if she is not interested in it, pick it up without a fuss and refrigerate it. Later, warm up the leftover meal and use it for her next meal. Cold food can cause diarrhea.

Feeding should be a fairly straightforward process, one in which you train your pup, and not vice versa. If your puppy goes on a hunger strike for a meal or two, wait her out. Many owners make the mistake of adding sizable amounts of meat and people-food to get their pups to eat. Aside from disrupting the nutritional balance of the meal, this also produces puppies that are spoiled, finicky eaters. They learn to continually hold out for something better. Keep your feeding consistent — a premium, balanced kibble with a little canned meat is quite sufficient in most circumstances. Naturally, if your pup is acting sick or does not eat for several days, take her to your veterinarian for an examination.

One other suggestion: never feed your pup from the table. Aside from becoming a nuisance, puppies fed from the table tend to lose interest in their own food. Before you have your dinner, make sure your pup has already eaten and then train her to hold a down-stay away from the dinner table while you eat.

How Much Should I Feed My Pup?   This will vary according to the particular breed and the individual dog. The recommendations on the bag or can are only general averages and must be adjusted by your own observation and understanding of your pup. However, beware of overfeeding; it is always better to keep your pup on the lean side rather than to let her get too heavy, since excessive weight in puppies can lead to serious health problems as they get older. Conversely, if you can see her ribs, either she needs more body fat and her food should be increased, or you should have a fecal sample checked for possible parasites.

Should My Pup Always Have Water Available?   While puppies need lots of water, we find it is preferable to offer it to them frequently rather than allowing them unlimited access to it. Puppies tend to gulp large amounts of water at once, causing house-training problems. Later, as the puppy gets bigger and is reliably house-trained, water can be kept available at all times.

Grooming Your Puppy

Grooming is more than keeping your dog clean and attractive. It is an overall monitoring of your dog's physical health and appearance, and an aid in teaching her to be handled. Though many long-haired breeds require more time for brushing and caring for their coats than their short-haired counterparts, even tight-coated breeds require some brushing. Besides removing dead hair, dandruff, and dirt, brushing stimulates natural oils in a dog's hair and spreads them throughout her coat, giving it a healthy, well-cared-for sheen. All dogs benefit from brushing.

In addition to coat care, however, regular grooming allows you to check for fleas and ticks, dry or irritated skin, dirty ears that can easily become infected, eyes inflamed or irritated by foreign particles, tooth problems, and toenails in need of trimming. By examining these areas regularly, you will spot problems before they have a chance to develop into something more serious. This helps keep your dog alert and healthy and saves veterinary bills.

Starting Early   Without doubt, it is best to start grooming your pup as soon as you get her: people who delay acquainting their pups with grooming often find it difficult later on, particularly nail clipping and ear cleaning. We begin routine grooming sessions as early as three weeks of age, so that by the time the puppies go off to their new homes they are fully acquainted with it. This makes subsequent grooming by the owner a relatively simple procedure, one the pup learns to enjoy.

Brushing and Coat Care   Because of the wide differences in grooming techniques for different breeds, check with your breeder or local professional groomer for specific tips on how to groom your puppy. Some breeds with long hair or dense, wiry coats require complex grooming procedures, and owners of these breeds should not attempt to clip or groom before they have received specific instruction. In general, however, most owners need a grooming brush appropriate to their pup's coat type and a metal comb. For example, short-coated dogs (Doberman, beagle, boxer, Great Dane) need to be brushed with a bristle brush; breeds with double-textured coats (German shepherd, husky, chow chow) should be brushed with both a grooming rake and slicker brush; breeds with long hair (Afghan, Shih Tzu, Maltese, Yorkshire terrier) do best with a combination of slicker and pin brushes, as well as a comb for final feathering.

We recommend daily brushing for a puppy, with sessions kept short and pleasant. Brush her either on the floor or on a steady table, as you prefer, and use a nonskid grooming mat or carpet to help keep her in position. Place the puppy on her side or in a sit and begin brushing gently. If the pup starts to struggle and give you a hard time, a firm shake with

The technique for brushing depends in part upon your pup's coat type. For most breeds, start brushing hair from the opposite direction. Note the hand keeping the pup safely in position.

a "No, stay!" will help get her under control; follow immediately with praise.

The technique for brushing depends in part upon the coat type. In general, start brushing the hair in the opposite direction first before concluding by brushing in the direction of the growth. If you own a pup with long hair, be sure to ask your breeder about the best technique for that breed.

As you brush, speak to your pup in a soft, reassuring manner, and be sure to praise her when you finish. One bit of caution: if you use a grooming table, make sure you never leave your pup unattended. She might get curious and fall off the table, breaking her leg or hurting herself in some other way. Keep one hand on her at all times.

Clipping Nails A dog's nails should be kept short by regular trimming. When nails are too long they cause the toes to

Your pup's nails should be kept short. Clip just the tips once a week.

spread and put unnecessary stress on the pasterns (wrist joints), making it difficult to walk. Also, long nails easily scratch people, furniture, and floors.

Though many owners are reluctant to try clipping nails themselves, if you start when you first get your pup and initially clip off only the tips, your pup will become comfortable with having this done, and you will acquire more confidence in your own skill. You may want to have your veterinarian or groomer show you the procedure firsthand.

We recommend clipping the nails once a week using professional nail clippers made for this purpose. Start off with two people, one to hold the puppy in place while the other does the clipping. After several sessions, the pup will become used to the procedure and only one person will be necessary.

To clip the nail, hold the paw with your hand and steady each toe individually by grasping it with your thumb and

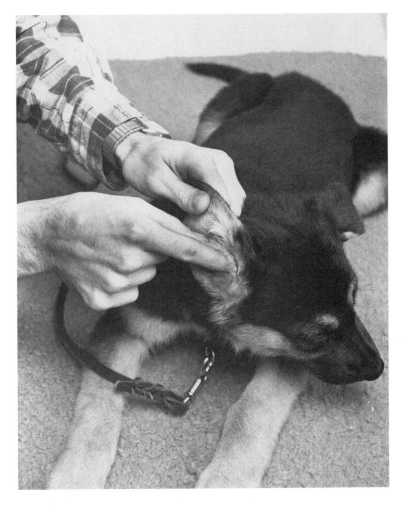

After applying a generous amount of otic cleanser into each ear, allow the pup to shake it out, then wipe around the visible portion of the ear with a cotton ball.

index finger. This allows you to control how much of the nail you take off with the nail clipper in the other hand. Try not to cut into the "quick," the vein that runs partway up the nail. The quick is easy to see if your pup's nails are translucent, allowing you to clip just in front of it. However, if the nails are dark, the quick will be hidden and you must be more careful. This is why we suggest clipping off just the tips once a week. If you should accidently clip the quick and cause a little bleeding, do not panic. Simply use a little styptic powder or alum to stop the bleeding.

Cleaning Ears and Eyes   We clean our dogs' ears once a week, using an otic cleanser, such as Ear-Rite, obtainable from a veterinarian or local pet-supply store. Apply a gener-

Giving a puppy a pill. Hold the upper jaw with one hand, open the mouth and put the pill on the back of the pup's tongue with the other hand, close the mouth, and caress the throat. This is easy if you have done the preliminary handling exercises described in chapter fourteen.

ous amount liberally into each ear, then massage the base of the ears for thirty seconds. After letting your pup shake the solution out, carefully wipe the visible portion of the ear around the canal with a cotton ball to remove residual wax. Do not probe too deeply into the ear canal, and avoid using Q-tips. A gentle swabbing is sufficient. If you notice your puppy shaking her head violently, scratching at her ears repeatedly, or having a foul smell coming from the ear, consult your veterinarian.

It is easy to check your pup's eyes every day for routine buildup of mucus and foreign particles that collect on the

inside corners. When there is a buildup, take a small cotton ball moistened with warm water and dab the eye corners, freeing the discharge. Never dab the cotton over the eyes, since cotton fibers can scratch the eyeball. A recurring buildup of yellowish mucus or crusty foreign matter may indicate an infection and should be checked by your veterinarian.

Bathing How often should you bathe your dog? It is generally not necessary to bathe most dogs on a regular basis, since dogs do not perspire as we do, and frequent bathing washes away natural oils that keep their hair shiny. Unless a dog is filthy or has rolled in something noxious, a bath twice a year is usually adequate. On those occasions, make sure to groom your dog before the bath and remove any tangles or mats. For shampoo, we suggest a pH-balanced shampoo for dogs instead of human hair products. Since dogs have a more alkaline skin than humans, human shampoos can cause itching or scaling of their skin. After the bath, make sure you thoroughly rinse out all of the shampoo, let her shake herself several times, and when you are finished toweling her off, keep her out of drafts until she is completely dry.

Exercise How much exercise does a dog need? All dogs require some daily, vigorous exercise for good health and sound behavior. How much depends on the individual dog's breed. For example, daily exercise requirements for an Irish setter are entirely different from those of a pug. Before you get a new puppy, make sure you have a realistic grasp of the amount of daily exercise needed for her breed. High-energy dogs that do not get enough exercise often develop problem behavior and give their owners nightmares.

In general, a four-month-old puppy should be tired out from exercise twice a day. Be creative and responsible in this: exercise involves more than walks for elimination. Within your circumstances, schedule two daily sessions long enough to tire her. Do not exercise your pup by allowing her to run free throughout the neighborhood, a sure recipe for problems. Along with long walks and hikes, play fetch or Frisbee with her in a fenced-in yard or an enclosed area near your home. If you jog, however, beware of taking your pup with you at too early an age, since the stress on her joints might lead to problems. Wait at least until she is six months of age. Swimming is another great exercise for dogs; when you provide this for them when they are young, they learn to enjoy it immensely.

Also, daily obedience training is important exercise for a pup; the energy and concentration demanded in a training session help tire her out. Keep the sessions snappy and interesting, and strive to keep her focused on you. In short, there are many different ways to responsibly provide your pup with exercise, and the bonus is that they improve the quality of life for you and your dog together.

CHAPTER EIGHTEEN

Troika: When the Relationship Transforms

Dogs began a life of domestication as slaves rather than allies, and the warm relationship that has since developed — and indeed was in existence in early dynastic times in Egypt — developed gradually, together with mutual understanding and regard. It is a truism to say that the dog is largely what his master makes of him: he can be savage and dangerous, untrustworthy, cringing, and fearful; or he can be faithful and loyal, courageous, and the best of companions and allies.

— R. Fiennes and A. Fiennes, *The Natural History of the Dog*

If we have gone to some length throughout this book to explore the various elements of a successful relationship with a puppy, it is because *your* effort is crucial in the relationship. When you take the time and energy necessary to raise a puppy correctly, wonderful things happen. The dog becomes a friend.

In what follows, we present three stories (a *troika*) to exemplify what we have been talking about. The stories involve German shepherds only because we are breeders of shepherds and are most familiar with them; similarly inspiring examples can be found from any breed. The intention of the stories is solely to encourage you, to illustrate what any conscientious breeder knows: that given sound breeding, when owners take their dogs seriously as companions, when they take the time to raise them with intelligence, love, and effort, friendships develop that are unique and transforming. Such relationships take the dog/human bond beyond the boundaries of what most people expect and significantly raise the quality of human life.

Buck

In his classic story *The Call of the Wild*, Jack London immortalized an unforgettable mixed-breed dog named Buck, crafting a tale that chronicles Buck's theft from a California household, his journey to Alaska and baptism into pack existence, and his eventual succession to lead sled dog on a team during the Klondike gold rush of 1897. In the story, after passing through the hands of several mean-spirited owners, Buck finally falls into the possession of the kind and noble John Thornton, who rescues him from an abusive trio of greedy prospectors and wins Buck's undying loyalty. The rest of the story is London's account of their relationship and the adventures they share.

Though a work of fiction, the story's power comes from London's uncanny powers of observation, his empathic understanding of canine behavior, and his ability to relate these in a fascinating tale of companionship and adventure. What makes his narrative even more compelling is that he based Buck on a real dog by the same name, whom he had come to know well when he lived in the Yukon. This makes his portrait ring true. Although the story occasionally lapses into sentimentality and romanticism, it is remarkably successful in evoking the mysterious, elusive nature of the dog.

In one of the more moving passages of the book, London describes Buck's "attitude" toward Thornton:

> For the most part, however, Buck's love was expressed in adoration. While he went wild with happiness when Thornton touched him or spoke to him, he did not seek these tokens. . . . Buck was content to adore at a distance. He would lie by the hour, eager, alert at Thornton's feet, looking up to his face, dwelling upon it, studying it, following with keenest interest each fleeting expression, every movement or change of feature. Or, as chance might have it, he would lie farther away, to the side or rear, watching the outlines of the man and the occasional movements of the body. And often,

Buck.

such was the communion in which they lived, the strength of Buck's gaze would draw John Thornton's head around, and he would return the gaze, without speech, his heart shining out of his eyes as Buck's heart shone out.

London captures the deep exchange of feeling possible in a relationship with a dog when the dog is a companion in the fullest sense, a friend of unparalleled loyalty and devotion. This is not hyperbole. When people experience the profound dedication and love that a dog can give, bonds develop that are often quite exceptional. For example, dramatic and inspiring illustrations of this come from the various service-dog organizations for the blind and handicapped — The Seeing Eye, Guide Dogs for the Blind, Fidelco, and Therapy Dogs International, to name only a few — whose specially trained service dogs enable individuals to live self-sufficient, meaningful lives. Because of the profound needs of the people they serve, these dogs often manifest a deeper side of the canine nature, one that is not sufficiently appreciated by the general public. Such a dog (coincidentally named Buck as well) lives with Len and Betty Cohen of Therapy Dogs International, and since the Cohens obtained Buck as a young puppy from New Skete, we have had the opportunity to watch their relationship develop over the years. It is an instructive example of the remarkable versatility and spirit of the dog, and of the bonds that can develop in a dog/human relationship.

Len and Betty Cohen first visited New Skete in 1981, to obtain a replacement puppy for their first therapy dog, a German shepherd named Thunder, who had recently died at fourteen years of age. They came with very special needs: both have been disabled from birth; Betty is without arms, while Len has only one. Since Len works five days a week as a salesman, it was important for Betty to have a dog who could offer not only companionship but also much-needed help with household chores and daily tasks.

As they described to us their situation, they also emphasized how their first dog, Thunder, had been much more than just a "working" dog: he had been a vital part of both of their lives, providing unfailing companionship, support, and service for them from the time they first obtained him at two years of age. Since service organizations for the handicapped were not yet in existence when they first obtained Thunder, they had trained him themselves, and throughout his adult life he gave them a measure of independence, protection, and freedom that would have been unthinkable beforehand. Now they wanted to extend that legacy with another dog.

It took us two tries. The first pup we placed with them, Samson, sadly developed physical problems that made him unsuitable for therapy work. However, when Len contacted us with the disappointing news about Samson, we immediately found another puppy. A promising litter that had been whelped six weeks earlier was just in the process of being evaluated for proper placement. The puppies, six males and one female, were out of a breeding of two particularly intelligent New Skete shepherds, Pascha and Reggie, and they had already shown signs of being precocious. For example, they were unusually playful and curious about the toys we provided for them, and when we took them on brief outings into the woods nearby, they showed little fear and lots of inquisitive behavior. But of all the pups, one had especially caught our eye: the red-collared male, a handsome black-and-tan puppy who seemed particularly intelligent and poised and who also showed a strong orientation to people.

When Len and Betty came to evaluate the pup's potential, the moment the energetic little puppy entered the conference room the match seemed just right. He was friendly and self-confident, and the Cohens were very much at ease with his spunk and playfulness. After thinking the matter over, they left that afternoon with the puppy they named "Buck," and over the years since that first meeting, Buck has confirmed repeatedly the wisdom of that decision. While Len and Betty have conscientiously done their part by socializing, managing, and training Buck throughout the past seven years, Buck has responded beyond their expectations. Not only has he matured into a remarkable therapy dog, he has become a telling example of what the expression "total dog" means. We saw this recently when the Cohens brought Buck to visit us at New Skete.

*   *   *

The brown-and-tan van eased past our church and bell tower and slowed to a stop beside the long row of Austrian pines bordering our driveway. It was a beautiful June afternoon, and several tourists were strolling around the front of the monastery, talking quietly and taking pictures of the domed church. As the door to the van opened, a large German shepherd hopped out onto the driveway. He paused for a moment to stretch, lowering his chest and forelegs to the ground as if bowing toward the church, after which he straightened himself out and started leisurely sniffing the ground, wagging his tail gently. He was stocky and masculine in appearance, with a big head and a lightly colored black-and-tan saddle; a three-foot leather leash hung loosely to the ground from his collar. Edging over toward the stone wall circling the church, he started to sniff the stones more intently, poking his nose into the gaps along the wall to scent each one carefully. Nothing. He placed his front paw atop one of the stones and leaned his head forward to investigate the base of a large Canadian hemlock; when that yielded nothing either, he resumed sniffing the wall. Finally, he settled on a spot. Lifting his right rear leg, he marked the wall generously, and with a satisfied look on his face, he sauntered over toward Len and Betty Cohen, who by now were standing next to the bell tower talking with the tourists.

"He's a therapy dog," explained Len, who then asked the visitors if they would like to meet Buck. They required no encouragement. "Come on over here, Buck," said Len. "Come say hello."

Buck walked over in a relaxed manner and stood in front of the people, who petted him down the length of his back several times while they spoke to Len and Betty admiringly. Buck was perfectly at ease with the attention and seemed to know instinctively how much was enough. After several moments he casually moved over to a shady spot and sat peacefully, panting quietly from the hot day.

Later on in the afternoon, we talked with Len and Betty in the same conference room where they had first met Buck as a puppy. Buck remained on a down-stay in one corner of the room, positioned so that he could keep an eye on Len and Betty at all times, as he did the entire visit, except for several brief respites when Len called Buck over to praise and pet him. Buck was entirely relaxed, yet always aware of what Len and Betty were doing. This quality of watchfulness was dominant in him. He did not show off unnecessarily or beg for attention: he just watched quietly as we talked, occasionally letting out a long sigh, or at most, cocking his head quizzically when we spoke about him.

When we pointed this out, Len smiled and told us how Buck had grown naturally into this role. "As a puppy, he was unusually bright and very willing to please. He always wanted to learn, and so we were able to start training him soon after we got him. Since then, I've been able to keep working with him, and the training has progressed steadily, without a lot of difficulties . . ." As Len paused, Betty was quick to add, "And he's at the point where he's almost always able to anticipate my needs before I tell him, which is so important because, in a very real way, he is my hands!"

When we asked what this meant, Len offered to take Buck through some of his routine exercises in our dining room and kitchen.

"Will the fact that he's in an unfamiliar environment make any difference?" inquired one of the brothers.

"I don't think so," said Len. He turned to Buck and asked in an animated tone, "Buck, you want to work a little bit?"

Immediately Buck's ears perked up. Getting up from the floor quickly, he wagged his tail enthusiastically and whined excitedly, pacing back and forth in anticipation. Following us into the dining room, he trotted around the room, sniffing the floor, while Len set a dinner plate, cup, salad bowl, and silverware on the dining room table. After filling the kitchen sink with water, Len called out to Buck, "Okay, Buck, get the

Buck picking up a dish from the dining room table.

dish." Buck paced quickly by the table setting several times and then hopped up, putting his two front paws on the edge of the table. Fixing his eyes on the salad bowl, he carefully clamped down on the dish with his jaws and then hopped back down to the floor with it in his mouth.

"Good boy, Buck!" said Len, walking over toward the sink. "Bring it to the sink, Buck. Come on, you can do it."

Buck trotted over to the sink, where Betty had positioned herself, and placing his two front paws on the edge again, he gently dropped the dish into the sink.

"Atta boy, Buck! Now go get the other dishes."

Buck trotted back into the dining room as if hunting for quarry. While Len pointed to the remaining dishes, Buck circled the table once and then picked up the plate, then the cup, and then the silverware, each time eagerly taking them to Betty at the sink. The session was punctuated with Len's constant praise and encouragement. After the dishes were properly carried to the sink, Len put a plastic laundry basket filled with towels on the floor. Looking at Buck, he said, "Get the basket. Come on."

Buck looked down at the basket and then back to Len, who repeated the command. "Come on, Buck, bring the basket." After pausing several seconds, Buck clamped down on the side of the basket and lifted it up, followed Len into the laundry room, and set it beside the washing machine. Immediately Len patted the top of Buck's head appreciatively and Buck barked happily in response.

We watched in amazement. There was nothing of the

Buck bringing in
the laundry
basket.

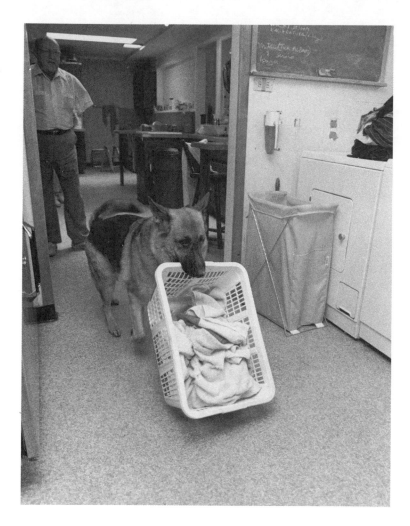

butler in Buck's attitude: it was clear that he was responding
out of a real sense of love and connectedness and that Len
and Betty had given the same back to him. Devotion was the
real motivator. As we returned to the conference room, Len
put Buck in a down-stay and explained that such simple exercises have been of immense help to Betty when she is alone
at home.

In fact, his description was too modest. On a videotape
made of Buck for New Jersey television, we saw an even
fuller picture — Buck opening and closing doors, turning
light switches on and off, picking coins up off the floor, and
answering the telephone. The video also allowed us to see
Buck helping Betty with ordinary tasks in town. For example,
one segment showed how Buck makes bank deposits and

picks up the mail for Betty. As Buck entered the local post office ahead of Betty, he carried a small package to be mailed in his mouth. Trotting over to a vacant window, he jumped up to the counter and gave the package to the postal clerk, who in turn gave Buck Len and Betty's mail. Chore completed, Buck walked out of the post office at Betty's side, having eloquently demonstrated how Betty is able to accomplish many common tasks that would be otherwise impossible for her. With Buck's help and assistance, she is an example of being *handi-capable* (Len's and Betty's expression), and her life has been the richer for it.

As we talked, however, Len and Betty were quick to point out that Buck's conscientiousness is not limited to household chores. It especially manifests itself in events that happen suddenly and without warning. Controlling the emotion in her voice, Betty told us the story of how Buck responded to an automobile accident they had been involved in during the previous year, in Vermont. After the accident, Len and Buck were able to get out of the truck, but Betty was pinned inside, unable to move. Knowing Betty was in pain, Buck stayed right beside her, licking her face and guarding her until help came. When the rescue squad finally arrived, Buck would not allow them to approach Betty until Len called him off; he did not harm them, he merely growled until he was certain they meant no harm. Betty continued, "And that whole day [after the accident] when I didn't come home, Buck was out of sorts. He didn't want his supper that night. And the next day, when Len brought him along to visit me in the hospital, Buck immediately jumped up on my bed and lay down on the bed with me. Then he kissed me, gave a big sigh, and went right to sleep, as if he hadn't slept since he last saw me." Betty looked down at Buck with an amused look on her face: he was sleeping then, as well.

Beyond what Buck is able to "do," however, there is always the broader picture, the dog in his wholeness. One of the more moving segments of the video showed how Len and Betty have been able to share Buck with others in a variety of community services. Because of Buck's friendliness with people, he has been taken to nursing homes to visit elderly and afflicted residents. This contact has been of immense value to these people, often lonely and forgotten, who find such joy in the simple act of petting a dog. For example, at one point on the tape, an elderly woman in a wheelchair was petting Buck hesitantly, uncertain what his reaction would be. Buck simply moved next to her in a very gentle manner, and the woman looked up at the camera with a big smile on her face. Buck's poise was disarming, demonstrating why such vulnerable people are often able to trust a dog much more readily than other humans. In these situations, the dog can become a vital, loving instrument of therapy and care.

Buck has also visited over ten thousand schoolchildren, with whom he has been used to foster awareness about the handicapped and their particular needs. At the same time, this contact has given children a firsthand experience of the wonderful things that are possible with a dog when he or she is trained properly and treated with love and respect.

Betty summed it all up quite simply. "It's easy to focus on Buck as a helper, giving us more freedom to live independent lives, but the real story is in his being a companion, a real pal . . ." She then reached over with her foot and caressed Buck's head, and Buck looked up affectionately, as though nothing else really mattered.

Sam

Why do pets, especially dogs, matter so much to children? Standard images of American life have always included children and their dogs. From Norman Rockwell paintings to high-profile dog-food commercials, pictures of children with their dogs are commonplace and quite natural. We simply expect dogs to be part of the normal landscape of childhood. Parents often purchase dogs to be companions for their children, and even if they cannot fully articulate why, most have a vague understanding that such relationships are more than just a good idea. They bring a stability and constancy to the child's life that helps balance the many changes children experience.

Child psychologists and therapists emphasize that dogs can in fact have a profound effect on human development, helping children integrate such fundamental human values as love and friendship, loyalty, respect for nature, responsibility, and basic self-awareness. In their own inimitable way, dogs often give children a sense of companionship and unconditional love that can sometimes be obscured or totally missing in their relationships with parents and peers.

Part of what makes this possible is the simplicity both children and animals intuitively bring to life. It is the good fortune of children to be able to form relationships with animals directly, without interpretation, naturally applying a rich tapestry of imagination to their various encounters. To children, animals talk and listen; they possess a vast array of emotions and feelings that are vital in reflecting the child's world back to the child. Because animals are not perceived as adults, they have the capacity of being allies, confidants, peers — friends in the best sense of that term. Through the eyes of animals, life is presented in ways a child can understand and learn from. This is why they play such an important role in nursery rhymes, fairy tales, Saturday-morning cartoons, animated motion pictures, and comic books.

As suggestive as these ideas may be, however, it is only when we see them exemplified in real life that we can appreciate precisely how a dog can make a difference in the life of a child. We have experienced this in a moving way with Robert Mauser, a boy who had to fight a cancerous brain tumor at the age of eleven. Among the many who supported and encouraged Rob in his recovery was a German shepherd named Sam (Samantha), whom Rob's parents had obtained as a puppy from New Skete. Shortly after Rob finished his final treatment of chemotherapy and while he was well on his way to recovery, the Mausers spent several days at New Skete, allowing us a glimpse of a remarkable story.

*　　*　　*

"Stay, Sam, staaaay . . ."

The young teenager glides the grooming tool down the back of the German shepherd's soft, sleek coat several times, carefully making sure he covers the whole area, while he holds her still with his other hand. It is a mild July morning at the monastery, and Rob Mauser is receiving a lesson in dog grooming from one of the monks. As he continues brushing her, Sam endures the session patiently, holding her ears back somewhat, occasionally looking up at him with her large, chestnut-colored eyes. The brush collects only a small amount of shedding hair.

"Okay, Rob; now stroke the grooming rake in the opposite direction several times," says Brother Christopher, and as Rob does so, the hair on Sam's back stands up slightly, causing Sam to whine for a moment and begin panting.

"Good girl, Sam, staaaay," says Rob, and after several passes, he reverses the direction and smooths the hair back down again. Sam's coat is in beautiful condition: there is no flaky dandruff, and the hair is soft and full, with a nice sheen.

Rob, Michele, Mandy, and Sam with Brother Christopher.

"Do her tail, too, Rob," says fifteen-year-old Michele, Rob's sister, who is helping with the grooming.

"Okay, but could you hold her collar for a minute?" replies Rob, and as Michele positions herself next to Sam's head, Rob lifts Sam's tail and starts to groom it gently.

"Hey, look at this," says Rob, pointing to some blood spots on the back of Sam's hocks. The blood is fresh, and as we check the source, we discover more blood, which confirms that she is in season. Sam turns her head around and tucks her tail under, as if embarrassed by the attention, and Rob smiles and says to her, "Don't worry, Sam, we won't let you have any puppies . . . " As Rob finishes brushing Sam's tail, Michele takes a small ball of cotton, dips it in some otic cleanser, and starts cleaning Sam's ears, gently easing the cotton deeper down into the canal. Sam groans uncomforta-

Rob tossing a ball for Sam.

bly in response and shifts her head to the other side, letting Michele know that this is a part of the process she does not enjoy. Still, she tolerates it, though when Michele finishes, Sam shakes her head several times to get out any remaining cleanser.

"Okay, Sam, sit for a minute," says Rob, and as Sam moves into a sit, Rob takes each one of her paws in his hand and checks her nails, with Brother Christopher's guidance.

"They look pretty good, Rob. I think we can let them go for now," judges Brother Christopher, so Rob and Michelle conclude the grooming session by offering Sam plenty of approval and praise. Naturally Sam relishes this, becoming progressively more excited and playfully dancing around the two of them. Suddenly, however, she spots her tennis ball

Troika: When the Relationship Transforms | 239

on the ground nearby. Trotting over eagerly, she stands directly over it and looks up at Rob, then back to the ball, then back to Rob.

"Oh, so you want to play ball, huh, Sam?" Rob laughs, and as he moves toward the ball, Sam starts wagging her tail wildly with excitement. Rob picks up the ball and holds it high in the air, playfully moving it back and forth several times. Sam's eyes follow it without wavering, until finally she barks once impatiently.

"Okay, Sam, go get it!" and Rob tosses the ball toward the other side of the yard. Sam is after it in a flash, and a simple game of boy playing fetch with his dog follows for the next ten minutes. But this game is quite special; to appreciate it, we have to go back a little to the beginning of the story.

Three years previously, Rob's parents, Bob and Corrine Mauser, had obtained a seven-and-a-half-week-old New Skete pup for Rob and Michele, who were then ten and twelve respectively. We gave plenty of consideration to the choice of this particular puppy, since it would have to live in a very busy household with six children and one other dog, a year-old, ten-pound Shih Tzu named Mandy. Experience has taught us that not just any puppy adapts well to a family with lots of children. Puppies with extremely dominant, pushy personalities, who are competitive and active, can be headaches in family settings because they tend to resist human leadership and often start dominating the children, treating them as littermates. Pups that are very shy are equally problematic; one of the natural roles a pet dog assumes in a family setting is that of playmate. Children include pets in games with neighborhood friends, and the Mausers knew that Rob and Michele would not be exceptions. Because of this, their pup needed to be outgoing and friendly, yet gentle enough to be in constant contact with children; it would also have to get along with Mandy.

With these factors in mind, we selected a promising puppy out of a breeding between a lively, intelligent New Skete shepherd named Megan, and Sunny (Ch. Brentaryl's Grayson), a champion stud from Caralon Kennels in St. Louis, Missouri. The pup, a female whom the Mausers named Samantha, came from a litter of ten and was outgoing and friendly with people but not especially dominant with her littermates. Most of her scores on the Puppy Aptitude Test were three's and four's (see chapters five, six, and appendix), indicating to us that she would be a good choice for a family with children.

From the day Sam became part of the Mauser's household she made a smooth transition, becoming fast friends with Mandy and easily adjusting to the rest of the family. Rob and Michele were quick to divide up the daily responsibilities for Sam, making sure that she was walked, fed, and played with. Also, since the Mausers had a steady stream of visitors coming to the house every day, Sam received plenty of early socialization and training. Because of this, it is quite understandable that Sam developed steadily into a pleasant, well-adjusted dog, bonding solidly with the family and being good-natured to their guests.

Then the unexpected happened. When Sam was a year and a half old, an event occurred in the family that would have a profound effect on Sam's relationship with Rob and on Rob's relationship with her. Rob became ill with symptoms resembling flu: double vision, severe headaches, and pain behind the eyes. The "flu," however, did not go away. As Rob's condition worsened, his parents took him to the hospital on three separate occasions to find out what was wrong. Finally, doctors diagnosed the problem: Rob had a rare form of brain cancer.

In the operation that followed, doctors removed a large tumor, beginning a long ordeal. After the operation, Rob had to undergo a drastic experimental chemotherapy, involving seven weeks of daily radiation treatments, then more periodic chemotherapy. After each round of chemotherapy, Rob was sick beyond words, and he understandably had to battle against discouragement and depression. Unable to attend school for a year and a half, cut off to a large degree from his friends, Rob's struggle was not solely with the cancer; it was also with boredom and loneliness. It was in this context that Sam became a vital source of comfort to Rob, helping to alleviate his sense of isolation by her constant presence. A typical example illustrates: during his convalescence, when Rob would come home from the hospital totally drained and exhausted, Sam would spend entire days with him, staying in his room, watching television with him, simply being with him. She had an intuitive awareness of his need and expressed that by lying close to him.

Another facet of that companionship addresses a subtler issue. One of the most difficult aspects of an illness such as Rob's is the effect it can have on a child's self-esteem. Loss of hair and body weight can easily make a child feel completely alienated, a stranger in his or her own body. To Sam, however, the changes in Rob were entirely beside the point. When she would come up beside the bed and spontaneously lick Rob's face, or put her paw on the bed to ask for a pat, *it was Rob she saw,* not a stranger, and her way of interacting with him remained entirely natural throughout his illness. She never treated him as if he were somebody different, an untouchable, and this experience had an extremely positive effect in maintaining Rob's self-image.

Rob's parents have also noticed something else at work: because Rob has become largely responsible for Sam, taking care of her daily chores when he is well enough, he experiences *her* need for him each day; Sam depends on him, and she lets him know this in unmistakable ways. For example, when it is time for her dinner she comes over to Rob and nudges him with her nose, whining softly. The gesture hardly requires translation. Routine occurrences such as this helped Rob preserve a healthy self-respect that has been essential in keeping his spirits up.

When Rob was well enough, the two of them took regular walks in the woods just by themselves, and throughout the day, Sam stayed continually with Rob, frequently brushing up against him, asking to be petted, always taking Rob outside of himself. No doubt this was an important factor in helping Rob both to cope with his illness and to work through the long period of recovery. Happily, the medical signs are now quite positive. With the final treatment of chemotherapy finished, and Rob beginning to feel consistently better, he has been able to return to school. Interestingly enough, before that, Sam was instrumental in helping him meet the challenge. By going with him on daily walks to school and back, she helped Rob regain his strength, getting him to the point where he was able to be up long enough to attend school. Referring to those walks, Rob mentioned to us with an amused twinkle in his eye that Sam has always walked quite well with him on leash, "unless she sees a squirrel. Then I have to hold on for dear life!"

Ten minutes of fetch have passed and Rob finally calls out across the yard, "Okay, Sam, that's enough. Come on back and bring the ball."

Looking at him from the opposite side of the yard with the ball in her mouth, Sam starts to trot back obediently, and by the time Rob flops down on a garden chair near the rest of us, Sam lies down next to him and puts the wet tennis ball between her two front paws. She pants noisily, and Rob strokes the side of her neck several times to calm her down, perhaps his way of telling Sam that he is temporarily out of energy.

As we speak casually about Sam, Rob looks at her affectionately and remarks, "One of the things I like most about Sam is her curiosity, how she cocks her head whenever I make different noises at her, as if she is trying to figure out what I mean."

"That's something I've really noticed about Sam," adds Rob's mother, Corrine, "and about Mandy, too, for that matter. Dogs are so sensitive. Though they haven't treated Rob any differently, the two of them have shown an intuitive awareness of his illness that I would say is real empathy. I remember this one day when Rob was particularly down and the two of us had to sit and talk things out. Sam and Mandy were also there, and when the conversation got pretty emotional, Mandy started to whine and cry, while Sam crept close to Rob and looked up at him with her deep, sorrowful eyes. Then she buried her head in his lap. It was as if they understood everything he was going through."

Sam whines briefly for a moment and then gets up and walks over toward Mandy, who is sleeping nearby in the shade. She sniffs her gently, and when Mandy stands up, the two of them start mouthing each other playfully. Rob laughs at them and then calls them over, petting both of them briskly. As he does so, the look in his eyes says much: it is lively, the simple joy of playing with a dog on a day that has become truly a gift.

Runge

The front door of the country house opens slowly and a massive, richly colored German shepherd bolts across the front lawn toward the driveway, vigorously barking out his alarm. Despite the light layer of crystallized snow on the ground, his gait is swift and sure, and as he pulls up effortlessly ten feet in front of us, his deep barking echoes from the ash, sugar maple, and locust trees that surround the property.

He stands tall, imposing.

His tail is erect, wagging ever so slightly, and his hackles are raised; his ears are straight and confident. He holds his position ten feet from us and continues to bark.

We try to appear calm and relaxed. We call his name, crouch low, and beckon him to come over. *"Runge, don't you remember?"* He ignores our greetings, absorbed as he is in a more important task: letting his master know that we have arrived.

A voice from the house calls out, "It's okay, Runge; they're friends."

Runge's loud barking gradually stops as his master, the artist Maurice Sendak, emerges from the house. While Maurice follows the front walkway down to greet us, Runge waits patiently, continuing to eye us keenly and sniffing deeply with his nose in the air. His hackles subside. After several moments his tail begins to wag in a more relaxed manner, betraying the first signs of recognition. It has been over two years since Runge last saw us at New Skete, so his initial lack of recognition is perfectly understandable. Two years is a long time in canine chronology.

When Maurice finally reaches us, all trace of territorial posturing in Runge vanishes. Acting as though he is embarrassed by his former bravado, he joins fully in Maurice's warm greeting, circling around the four of us happily, wagging his elegant, bushy tail back and forth. Mercifully, he does not jump. Instead, he leans affectionately into us with his side and rump, enticing us to pet him.

"He's beautiful, isn't he?" says Maurice, vigorously rubbing the top of Runge's large head. As Maurice's hand passes gently down the neck and top line, Runge stands still. He is beautifully proportioned, almost regal. He is a deep black-and-tan shepherd, big-boned, with a lush, full coat that makes him appear even larger than he is. Gray hairs surround the top of his muzzle, complementing his mature bearing.

For several moments, Maurice massages his fingers into the croup area above the tail, causing Runge to groan in pleasure. Twisting his head upward to meet Maurice's eyes, he holds eye contact for several seconds, then playfully dances off to the side as if encouraging us to follow him. "Come, come," says Maurice, ushering us toward the house. As Runge prances enthusiastically back and forth ahead of us, we follow him admiringly up the front walkway.

At five and a half years of age and ninety-eight pounds, Runge is a long way from the lively, twelve-week-old puppy Maurice came to get at New Skete. His poise, balance, and spirit confirm what was then only a promise, and watching him fully grown rekindles a sense of wonder at life's beauteous progression: nature melding with human care and responsibility. The fruit of that marriage is what now commands our respect and admiration. But that requires some background.

*   *   *

Maurice is no stranger to dogs. As anyone knows who is familiar with his many illustrated books for children and adults, he has always had a profound interest in animals, dogs in particular. Indeed, a number of the dogs he has cared for throughout his adult life have appeared prominently in his books: Jennie, the spunky Sealyham terrier who appears in *Where the Wild Things Are* and who is the central character in *Higglety, Pigglety, Pop;* Io, a golden retriever featured in *Some Swell Pup* and *Dear Mili;* and Erda, Aggie, and Runge, the German shepherds seen in *Outside Over There* and *Dear Mili.* His fascination and love particularly for German shepherds developed after reading J. R. Ackerley's deceptively charming tale *My Dog Tulip.* The story of Ackerley's extraordinary relationship with his German shepherd, Tulip (in real life, Evie), moved Maurice so deeply that it prompted him to get his first shepherd, Erda. Years later, after his first two shepherds, Erda and Aggie, had died, he contacted New Skete about the possibility of getting a new puppy. Enter Runge.

Runge was born the morning of August 6, 1984, the Feast of the Transfiguration on our church calendar. He was the third of eight puppies from a breeding of New Skete's Natasha and Ch. Brimhall's Supercharger. From the first day, he was the largest in the litter, a very masculine puppy with a calm, confident temperament that never showed a lot of stress, but quite playful. The early notes we made on him at five weeks of age focused on his balance and affection. "Though the biggest puppy in the litter, purple-collar male [Runge] does not bully and interacts well with the other pups. Approaches people readily, as well. . . ." On the puppy tests given at seven weeks of age, he manifested intelligence, curiosity, and sociability, and throughout the "fear period" (8–10 weeks) we noted no obvious personality change. Basically he was an unflappable puppy, inquisitive, yet not hyperactive. Because of that stability, we decided to place him with Maurice, believing that he would be able to fit into the fairly quiet, solitary lifestyle of an artist and still hold his own on social occasions.

Their first meeting was somewhat prophetic. Runge was already twelve weeks old when Maurice was finally able to come and get him. Prior work commitments abroad had made it impossible for Maurice to arrive any sooner, so Runge had to spend a month more than was usual in the puppy kennel. As we anticipated, he handled the month without difficulty, showing no signs of shyness, which might have been the case with some pups. In fact, when we finally brought him into our dining room to meet Maurice for the first time, he confidently marched right up to him and began playing and pawing at Maurice's pants leg and hands — a bit of the "you did not choose me; I chose you" syndrome. Later, after they had been playing together for a while, Maurice had to leave the room briefly to get something from his car. As he stepped over the puppy gate we had set up to block off the room, Runge tried valiantly to follow him. He put his front paws up on top of the divider and started whining impatiently, as if to say "What about me?" The gesture captivated Maurice. He had asked for a pup showing poise and self-confidence, with a balanced temperament that could harmonize with his life as an artist. Since he was a bachelor who lived and worked at home, they would be spending lots of time together, and Runge would need to adapt to a carefully structured, disciplined way of life. This seemed like a good start.

Over the years since that day, Maurice has kept in close touch with us, periodically spending several days at the monastery for retreat and bringing Runge with him whenever possible. He also enrolled him in our three-week training program when Runge was eight months old, and was quite conscientious and disciplined about reinforcing that schooling afterward. This contact has given us the chance to observe Runge's development firsthand, over a long period of time, to work together on various dimensions of the whole relationship: training, handling, and management. We have seen not only the steady maturing of the dog, but the maturing of a rich relationship as well. Maurice approaches Runge with the sensitivity of an artist, of one trained to see beneath the surface of things, and so brings a unique perspective to the dog/human dynamic. His is a vision in which the dog becomes muse not only to his creative work as an artist but to his self-understanding, as well. We had come to speak to him about this at his home in Connecticut.

We are brought into a spacious, naturally lit living room that is comfortably reflective of Maurice's work and interests. Mickey Mouse artifacts, children's toys, and stuffed *Wild Things* are placed throughout the room on chairs, desks, and shelves, mingling naturally with beautiful posters by Toulouse-Lautrec and Winsor McCay. Books on art and music fill the bookshelves, and on the desk there is a haunting picture of Maurice walking down a nearby road with three dogs from his past: Erda, Io, and Aggie. A leather leash

Maurice Sendak and Runge.

hangs on a doorknob of a set of doors that open out into a rolling backyard. While we chat informally, Runge stares attentively out the window at a group of mourning doves feeding in the backyard. His eyes blink repeatedly and his nostrils flare as he scrupulously studies them hopping around the ground for seed. He seems familiar with them, which is why he does not bark; nevertheless, they completely absorb his interest. His attentiveness befits his namesake, the German artist Philipp Otto Runge, a visionary painter of the early nineteenth century, who, Maurice explains, blended an intense observation of nature with an intuitive awareness of the divine presence within it.

We call Runge away from his gazing, and he hops up onto the couch next to one of the brothers, who shoots a quizzical look at Maurice.

"It's okay; in this house, couches are for dogs." Maurice chuckles, and almost simultaneously Runge leans his head affectionately into the brother with a pleased grin on his face. He knew. Rolling over on his back playfully, he paws at the brother, who returns the playful gesture with a couple of teasing pats of his own and Runge begins to make a game out of it. He is totally at ease. After a while, Maurice goes into the kitchen to check on the coffee, and Runge quickly rights himself and follows him, returning just as quickly when Maurice reenters with the coffee. While we sit down around the table to talk, Runge hops back on the couch and props his head on one of the cushions to watch us. He listens attentively, almost as if to witness that everything we talk about is true. He need not worry. In the ensuing conversation, Maurice becomes the real witness, continually pointing to a relationship that has grown and developed in many different ways.

Maurice, you speak of Runge as if he were not only a friend, but a teacher as well. Most people don't think of their dogs this way. Why has this been the case for you?

"Well, it's been a combination of things. Runge is the latest so far in a long line of dogs I've had, and I've been learning and getting better with each one. I've been best with him. I learned on Jennie, she suffered a lot, and then on Erda, and Io, and on Aggie. Each of these have been relationships that are privately intense, unlike relationships with most friends. You wouldn't dare reveal to your friends what you reveal to your dog. With our dogs, we wear no masks. A dog is so ruthlessly and unashamedly honest in the demands it makes of you; it is entirely dependent, and that need can provoke some surprisingly strong reactions from us. And so, in seeing myself through him, I see how many unpleasant aspects of my nature have to be repressed simply because I love him. Because of the way he has developed, I've had to try to give up certain bad habits, out of real respect for him. It would be totally inappropriate to behave in those ways. And of course, I benefit from that repression or self-discipline."

When you say, "It would be totally inappropriate to behave in those ways. . . ." In what ways?

"Well, losing my temper, for example, which is only too easy for me. I have a violent temper that, at times, I've taken out on him. Yet, in spite of this, he's been the healthiest dog I've ever had. My anger doesn't really faze him, and because of his strength and loyalty, I've come to see how inappropriate such behavior is."

His stability prompts you to change?

"To work on that and to change myself, yes, absolutely. It seems to me that the way you relate to your dog is a subtext to the way you relate to everything and everybody. Since dogs are so transparent, they mirror you back to yourself, and the challenge for us is to take that seriously. Unless you're totally crazy, you can't use the reflection to make a case against the dog. It has to be you. . . . So the value of the dog that is balanced and well-trained is that it helps you develop as a human being."

So the relationship with your dogs has been the fertile ground for a new level of consciousness?

"Precisely. To put it almost too simplistically, it is like reliving your childhood with each dog — each time slightly improving because you see the mistakes you've made with each pup. When you see the dog cowering away from you, just as you likely did with your own parents, it forces you to look at yourself. Runge doesn't shrink away from me because I simply could not bear that. So I've had to learn to prevent that from happening. That means repressing all sorts of feelings inside yourself. It's as though you have a blueprint inside, not a good one either, and you tend to act out unconsciously on that blueprint. But with each dog, as you improve, the dog improves, because your self-training is better. You're emotionally calmer, more conscious. So in that sense, Runge has benefited from all the other dogs."

What you're really saying is that the dog speaks the truth to us about ourselves. Yet most of us don't want to face that. Why haven't you been able to ignore it?

"First, because I don't know how to — but, luckily, as an artist, that is a gold mine. Despite the fact that these experiences can be extremely painful emotionally, personally they are the pure gold I mine in all my work. Which is why in another way, he's the miner, he digs for me, unwittingly. He brings up the ore that I use in my work. By living with him I experience these very primitive feelings in myself all the time, and either I use them against him when I'm bad or repress them and deal with them when I'm good or, best of all, I get them on paper, which is why he's in the picture. He's the miner, he's the digger; he brings it up. Nobody else does in the same way. People can't, because socially I can control those situations. Most of us can. We don't reveal that deeper side to each other. We talk about it . . . but when you are alone with the animal, I tell you, like I suspect happens with mothers and their babies, things happen which are quite uncontrollable and terrifying. Socially unacceptable behavior occurs because you are now dealing with a nonverbal creature and reliving, perhaps, a nonverbal moment from your own past."

The dog can't tell anyone!

"The dog can't tell. And a baby can't tell. Babbling won't help and barking won't make a bit of difference. Language is terrible in the way it is contrived to mislead you. Runge doesn't have language, and so he can't deceive. A baby can't either. A baby, if you hold it the wrong way, will scream because it knows it is in danger and it screams to be put in arms that are safe. The mother takes it and it is immediately pacified. Why? Because it is now safe and knows how to tell you directly and emphatically. So does the dog. I mean the dog that flinches from you . . . that hurts. It's no joke."

Runge moves off the couch and saunters over to Maurice, who brushes his hand along his neck for a few moments. He then quietly says to Runge, "Okay, that's a good boy, go on back to the couch." Runge obeys without complaining, and giving a long yawn, settles his head on the cushion once more as Maurice continues. "But when you face that side of yourself honestly, there is a purification that can occur if you let it, one that helps free you from yourself. He doesn't know it, but he's helped me grow tremendously. Through this relationship I've lost some impediments in my life, and I have to assume that I've lost them in my other relationships as well. But this is the one I see it in most."

The effect is transfiguring?

"Absolutely. I mean I'm happier now than I've ever been. It's true. A lot of it is him, maybe most of it is him, but I've been growing up and freeing myself of these shadows. The significance of Runge is that I see how I'm freeing myself through him. I don't see how I'm doing that in any other way because the relationship I share with him is incredibly intense and basic. He shares my room, he shares my bed, he shares my every thought. So much so that it's obvious to me when things change in him for better or for worse, and it's been that way with every animal I've ever had. No doubt I've profited by his being a solid citizen, 'cause if he were a nervous dog we would have had a terrible time. Yet you knew when I got him that he was a tough little bugger. It is his toughness of spirit that has really made me learn. I'll never get over it: I've never intimidated him. Only once or twice when I really got upset at him did he worry, but in general, no. And yet in five years there was only once when he didn't come when he was called."

Would you say that it is the most important relationship you have?

"In a very particular sense, yes, I would say so."

Perhaps because you connect with him in a very unique way?

"I connect with him in a most crucial way that I don't with other people. It has to do with infant intimacy. Since I'm an artist who really thrives on early memory, whose main talent is to mine this thing we've been speaking about, and to handle it quite honestly, without softening it or holding it up in a rosy light. . . . That isn't a subject you can discuss with most people. It's not what concerns them. . . . But that's what concerns *me!* My life, after all, is devoted to being an artist and the best artist I know how, and I have no grandiose concepts of my talent. I have one subject, which is childhood, and I have one intention before I kick the bucket and that's to mine it as much as I can, to really dig down to where the subsoil is. And Runge is my most intimate companion in this project, because I relate to him in this nonverbal way. We journey together."

The doorbell interrupts the conversation. Runge springs from the couch immediately and starts barking as he moves toward the door, while Maurice follows him. A U.P.S. delivery. When Maurice tells him it's okay, Runge stops barking and stands next to Maurice's side, wagging his tail, as Maurice signs the receipt and thanks the delivery man. They return and Runge resumes his watch on the couch.

You were speaking just a moment ago about your work as an artist and the relationship Runge and your other dogs have had with it. When considering your art, one senses the intuitive dimension you bring to it; meanings are thrown in left and right . . . in a sense, the drawings seem to grow out of your life. What has always struck us about your use of dogs and animals in this is how they are not decorative objects at all, but instruments of meaning. They're always there, you never miss them. Yet, it's curious that none of your interpreters have ever picked up on that.

"You're right, in my entire career no one has picked up on the significance animals play in my work. They all see it as 'Oh, isn't that sweet; he puts his dog in his pictures, just like Hitchcock appeared in a cameo in every one of his movies.'. . . That's as much as most people think about what I have done. They have no idea what it means to me. It isn't a conceit that my dogs are there in all my books. Without even being consciously aware of it, or trying to draw a particular lesson, dogs are in my books as a reflection of my behavior all the time, of my advance through life. For example, just as Jennie changed graphically, started to look better as I learned to draw better, I improved as a person as I drew. She was an icon. She had to appear in the books. That's how I registered myself, through my whole relationship with her, with my relationship with the world. So it climaxes in *Some Swell Pup*, that little book, where kids get it and say 'Mommy, that's how you treated me,' 'cause there is no difference between the nature of a human child and the nature of a puppy. Basically, if you're an indifferent person, a callous person, a sadistic person, you will not differentiate. You'll treat the child just as badly."

Then there is your most recent picture book of the recently discovered Grimm tale "Dear Mili," where, in the context of a story about death, of a little girl and her mother's passage into the next world, we observe the presence of your dogs all throughout the book . . .

"That's right. When people say, 'What is that book to you?' I use a word that baffles them, and even me sometimes, but I know it's the correct word, and that is grace, pure grace. *Outside Over There* [an earlier picture book] has the same mother, the same atmosphere, the same mood; however, it is full of strife and it ends in strife. *Dear Mili* ends in a solution, and I don't mean death is a solution. It transcends the mere fact of the girl and her mother dying. There's a grace note in it. So, it is an amalgamation of things; all my dogs are in it: Runge as a pup, Aggie, Io, and Erda when she was old and near death. So I'm painting this picture of my relationships, and I'm coming to a solution to *Outside Over There* in *Dear Mili*. Where in *Outside Over There* the story ends on a truculent note, where this poor kid gets a letter from her father which dumps this problem on her, in *Dear Mili* something is at peace. Me, that's what's at peace. That book is the rounding off of so much of my life that I can't even gather it all up. And the paradox is that it's such a sad story."

Looking back over these past five years with Runge, how has your perspective on raising dogs changed?

"I think of an almost comical thing when I first came to you people: I told you what I had to have. I had to have a dog that would do this, do that. He had to be balanced. But I didn't realize that what I was saying was that the dog was going to have to provide for all the things I didn't have. He had to be the perfectly mature human being that I couldn't be. Right? Now the end of that story is not really the end. Happily I've learned it's me who does all that, and when I do, then I get a dog who's like that. The dog can't deal with all of those things. You've got to give them to the dog, and then, if you do it right, you get back all the things you wish for . . ."

Which is precisely what we've been trying to say throughout our book!

"The dog becomes your dream come true, the very thing you wanted. But, *you* make your dream come true — from hard work and application of principles — then you get the dog you hope for. Most of us don't want to accept that responsibility, accept how upsetting it is to raise a puppy and how much effort you have to go through to get what you want. Hard work, self-examination, disappointment, strain, anxiety . . . all those go into making something happen. And there are no guarantees, either. But with Runge, it's like a miracle because he's exactly the dog I hoped to get from you. The paradox is that I had everything to do with that. Before, you were to provide me with a guaranteed puppy, like those little Japanese flowers you put into water and they grow up in two minutes. You were to provide me with a guaranteed German shepherd puppy who would look beautiful, be perfect, and grow up to be Rin Tin Tin in a matter of two years. You promised, that's the guarantee! That's quite a difference, isn't it?"

Indeed!

"There's one other thing. Perhaps the best thing that's happened with him, because it has been this way with almost every other dog I've ever had, is that the dog was first Philip and Sadie Sendak's baby before it was the dog. Runge is the first dog I've had who has been finally transformed from Philip and Sadie's baby into a dog. He's not me anymore; it's been a long birthing, but he's finally a beautiful German shepherd and no longer a cranky kid. He's a dog. He's stopped being me. He's become this gorgeous animal, and the baby, to make an image of it, has disappeared. He's gone; he can come up in books and always in my work, but finally my vision is focused and I see a dog.

Runge hops off the couch and comes over to Maurice, whining. He butts his nose against Maurice's arm and then paces back and forth several times. It is close to four o'clock in the afternoon and time for his walk. A respectful hint. "Yes, I know, Runge, we'll go out in just a minute." Maurice looks back to us with a smile. "That's just the way he is. He loves the daily routine, the walks, the different timetables. For example, we nap every day — I take a nap at five-thirty. And if it gets a little late, he'll look at me like, 'When are we going to nap? It's twenty-five to six, what's the matter with you?' He's so ritualized, it's wonderful."

We follow Runge out the front door, and immediately he sweeps across the front lawn with his nose riveted to the ground, zigzagging back and forth as if to catalogue all the smells. Gradually he zeroes in on one scent of particular interest at the base of one of the locust trees. Sniffing it thoroughly for several seconds, he licks the bark tentatively with his tongue. Finally, he draws his head up and cocks his rear leg high in the air, dousing the trunk proudly with his mark. He then picks up a stick nearby and trots over to the driveway to say good-bye to us.

Pulling out of the driveway and then proceeding down the main road, the last view we have is of Maurice and Runge crossing the front road into the adjacent field, with Runge leaping up into the air for the stick Maurice holds in his hand.

A New Way of Seeing

To make an end is to make a beginning
The end is where we start from . . .
And the end of all our exploring
Will be to arrive where we started
And know the place for the first time

— T. S. Eliot, *Four Quartets*

There is a story recounted by a seventh-century Christian monk named John Moschus about an old abba [monk] living in an isolated monastery in Palestine with his dog. One day, a monk from another community brings him word of an important monastic gathering that is to take place at the monastery of Besorum, which all of the monks of the region are supposed to attend. After receiving the brother graciously, the old abba assures him that he will be present at the meeting and, thanking him, begins to see the brother off.

At this point, the story takes a curious turn. As he is about to depart, the brother nervously explains to the abba that he still must journey farther into the wilderness to notify the brothers at the distant monastery of Charembe. The trek will be long, and, since he has never been there before, he is afraid of getting lost. He even asks the abba if *he* would be willing to deliver the message, instead, since he knows the way. The old abba smiles and tells him not to worry. Calling his little dog over, he says to him, "Go with this brother as far as the monastery of Charembe, so that he may give them his message." Moschus then concludes the story, "And the

Companionship with a dog is a lifelong process that starts as soon as you get your pup. Through conscientious care, training, and love, the relationship will mature into something far exceeding your expectations.

dog went away with the brother, till he brought him in front of the gate of the monastery."

The story's simplicity lends itself naturally to meditation. First, we feel the connection between the abba and his dog; besides the noteworthy fact that the abba even has a dog (apparently quite rare in monastic tradition), what stands out is the quality of that relationship, the harmony of understanding present between the two. Only insofar as the dog is a companion to the abba is the dog able to guide the other monk.

And what of that monk? What must he have thought as he saw the abba solemnly instructing the dog to take him to Charembe? Moschus is silent about this, leaving it for us to imaginatively reconstruct the details. But given the particularly unsophisticated attitudes toward dogs characteristic of Middle Eastern cultures of the time, the possibilities are quite interesting. The monk's initial reaction was probably a mixture of confusion, disbelief, and anxiety. Follow a dog into the wilderness on the simple word of an abba? On one level this would appear to him madness. Nevertheless, despite his misgivings, the monk would have been challenged to obey, since obedience is the heart of monastic living, the cornerstone of a monk's spiritual life. Thus, with the old abba reassuring him that there is nothing to fear, we can easily imagine the monk walking tentatively into the desert, led only by the confident steps of the abba's dog.

And what happens in the desert? More than simply walking to a distant monastery, one would think. The desert becomes the locus for a deeper journey, one taking place in the monk's heart. As he follows the dog farther into the wilderness, he is forced to listen in an altogether new way, one rooted in the recognition of his own poverty. He is wholly dependent on a dog, a creature to whom in ordinary circumstances he would never give a thought, and the experience changes him forever. With the dog leading him steadily through the desert, he becomes increasingly aware of his presumption, his lack of respect, his insensitivity to its mystery. The dog is now no longer an object, a thing, but a separate creature responsible for his safety. In a culminating moment of insight, he perceives that his view of the dog has been only a reflection of his basic attitude to life, to the created world around him. The result is that he "sees" the dog — and life — for the first time, in a completely new way. The dog *is* different from him, yet even in that difference it embodies a dignity all its own, one he learns to respect on its own terms. Thus, in such a meditation, as we imagine the monk emerging from the desert at the gate of Charembe, we believe him to be both humbler and wiser, now approaching life from a different perspective.

What of ourselves? In a parallel way, the monk's journey is everyone's journey, though in our frenetic world of activity and distraction we often miss the fact that we wander through the desert as well. Who or what leads us? Our age is dangerously out of touch with the nonhuman world around us, leaving our hearts dulled and vision blurred.

Nothing impresses us anymore, and we travel farther into a disharmonious cavern of individualism, with ourselves as our own guides. We arrogantly "process" reality through preconceived notions that are sterile and cold. Our world is stripped of a profound and compelling mystery.

This is blind ignorance. Humankind is in desperate need of recovering its connection with nature, for ultimately it means the recovery of ourselves. We become aware of ourselves by becoming aware of the world around us, a world filled with the presence of God. Without falling into mawkish sentimentality, we must learn to look at nature as an expression of God's goodness and love, a feast of sight and sound that provokes wonder and amazement. This seems to be what the famous nature writer Henry Beston was getting at when he wrote, in *The Outermost House:*

> We need another and a wiser and perhaps more mystical concept of animals. Remote from universal nature, and living by complicated artifice, man in civilization surveys the creature through the glass of his knowledge and sees thereby a feather magnified and the whole image in distortion. We patronize them for their incompleteness, for their tragic fate of having taken form so far below ourselves. And therein we err, and greatly err. For the animal shall not be measured by man. In a world older and more complete than ours they move finished and complete, gifted with extensions of the senses we have lost or never attained, living by voices we shall never hear. They are not brethren, they are not underlings; they are other nations, caught with ourselves in the net of life and time, fellow prisoners of the splendour and travail of the earth.

To see the world in this manner is to have deep respect for nature's astonishing diversity, to be conscious that it is balanced and related in a mysterious unity. We, too, are interrelated. This does not mean being swallowed into some vague, homogenous cosmic order; rather, it is a challenge to participate consciously in a living communion with God through each other and the whole of creation, attentively listening to the vast symphony of life.

The word "symphony" (from the Greek for "sound together") is suggestive here. In the tradition of the Christian East it refers to the idea that all of the individual elements of the created universe are ultimately dependent upon God for their existence as well as being interconnected. To speak metaphorically, they are like countless pieces of a vast orchestra, which when playing together, produce a harmonious melody of beauty and grace. When we hear that "music" with our hearts, we experience life in a new way, as if knowing it for the first time. When that happens, the only proper and true response is reverence and respect. This is precisely what the Russian author Fyodor Dostoyevsky emphasizes when he has the saintly Staretz Zossima exhort his disciples in *The Brothers Karamazov:*

> Brothers, love God's creation, love every atom of it separately, and love it as a whole; love every green leaf, every ray of God's light; love the animals and plants and every inanimate object. If you come to love all things, you will perceive God's mystery inherent in all things; once you have perceived it, you will understand it better and better every day. And finally you will love it with a total, universal love.

For many of us, this love for creation deepens through the relationships we form with our pets, particularly our dogs. By their very nature and need, dogs draw us out of ourselves: they root us in nature, making us more conscious of the mystery of God inherent in all things. When we take the time and energy necessary to raise our puppies correctly, when we learn to truly listen to them, seeing them as they really are and guiding their development accordingly, a deeper part of ourselves is unlocked, a part more compassionate and less arrogant, more willing to share life with another life. And whenever that happens, we know the real meaning of happiness.

Evolution and Interpretation of the Puppy Test

Puppy evaluation was first begun in a systematic and objective way with the Fortunate Fields project in Switzerland in the 1920s and 1930s. This philanthropic organization developed an elaborate system for evaluating German shepherd dogs for various tasks, most notably guiding the blind, and then used these results to develop a successful breeding program.

Important advances occurred later with the research project of Drs. John Fuller and John Paul Scott in Bar Harbor, Maine. As we have already seen, their research into canine behavior, especially the formulation of "critical periods," has had a profound impact on the way puppies are raised and evaluated. The practical consequences of this work are most clearly set forth in Clarence Pfaffenberger's book *The New Knowledge of Dog Behavior,* in which, after drawing heavily on Scott and Fuller's research and personal advice, he presents the system used for breeding and evaluating puppies that boosted the success rate of the Guide Dog program dramatically. When Pfaffenberger began his work in the mid-1940s, only 9 percent of the dogs who started training graduated from the program as responsible guides. When he published his findings in the 1960s, 90 percent of the dogs were graduating from the program as guide dogs.

Pfaffenberger stresses the importance of understanding genetics (breeding only dogs of proven working ability and health) as well as implementing early socialization techniques and puppy evaluations. His testing evaluated puppy responses to such things as new experiences, encounters with strangers, and body sensitivity, as well as their overall problem-solving ability. His work was a significant breakthrough for better breeding because he showed that temperament could be reliably evaluated at a very early age; puppy reactions at eight to twelve weeks of age could predict adult potential. Although the goal of his program was the development of consistently sound guide dogs, his principles have been adapted by breeders for their own needs.

For the general public, the first standardized test for puppies was the Puppy Behavior Test of William Campbell, an animal psychologist, published in his important and innovative work *Behavior Problems in Dogs.* Though the book was initially designed for veterinarians and other professionals as a source of practical answers to behavioral questions frequently asked by clients, the book also included an excellent chapter on puppies that discussed puppy testing and selection, elementary training, and common problems. His puppy test gave breeders and potential puppy owners a consistent and successful way of sizing up puppies and continues to serve as a basis for more recent adaptations.

In our experience, the most successful of these recent tests has been the Puppy Aptitude Test developed by Joachim and Wendy Volhard. The Puppy Aptitude Test took elements from each of its predecessors (Fortunate Fields, Pfaffenberger, and the whole of Campbell's test), and integrated them into one system. The result is a puppy evaluation that reliably measures individual temperament (that is, dominance versus submission, independence versus social attraction), as well as obedience and working potential. (A detailed explanation of this test by Melissa Bartlett, "A Novice Looks at Puppy Aptitude Testing," appeared in the March 1979 issue of the *AKC Gazette.*)

The first five sections of the test, an evaluation of temperament, are based entirely upon the puppy test of William Campbell and reveal a pup's general orientation to people. They indicate the degree of social compatability and how readily a pup will accept human leadership.

PUPPY APTITUDE TEST

puppy (color, sex) _____ litter _____ date _____

The following is a concise chart explaining each test and the scoring, a sample score sheet and an interpretation of the scores:

TEST	PURPOSE	SCORE	1
SOCIAL ATTRACTION: Place puppy in test area. From a few feet away the tester coaxes the pup to her/him by clapping hands gently and kneeling down. Tester must coax in a direction away from the point where it entered the testing area.	Degree of social attraction, confidence or dependence.	Came readily, tail up, jumped, bit at hands.	1
		Came readily, tail up, pawed, licked at hands.	2
		Came readily, tail up.	3
		Came readily, tail down.	4
		Came hesitantly, tail down.	5
		Didn't come at all.	6
FOLLOWING: Stand up and walk away from the pup in a normal manner. Make sure the pup sees you walk away.	Degree of following attraction. Not following indicates independence.	Followed readily, tail up, got underfoot, bit at feet.	1
		Followed readily, tail up, got underfoot.	2
		Followed readily, tail up.	3
		Followed readily, tail down.	4
		Followed hesitantly, tail down.	5
		No follow or went away.	6
RESTRAINT: Crouch down and gently roll the pup on his back and hold it with one hand for a full 30 seconds.	Degree of dominant or submissive tendency. How it accepts stress when socially/physically dominated.	Struggled fiercely, flailed, bit.	1
		Struggled fiercely, flailed.	2
		Settled, struggled, settled with some eye contact.	3
		Struggled then settled.	4
		No struggle.	5
		No struggle, straining to avoid eye contact.	6
SOCIAL DOMINANCE: Let pup stand up and gently stroke him from the head to back while you crouch beside him. Continue stroking until a recognizable behavior is established.	Degree of acceptance of social dominance. Pup may try to dominate by jumping and nipping or is independent and walks away.	Jumped, pawed, bit, growled.	1
		Jumped, pawed.	2
		Cuddles up to testor and tries to lick face.	3
		Squirmed, licked at hands.	4
		Rolled over, licked at hands.	5
		Went away and stayed away.	6
ELEVATION DOMINANCE: Bend over and cradle the pup under its belly, fingers interlaced, palms up and elevate it just off the ground. Hold it there for 30 seconds.	Degree of accepting dominance while in position of no control.	Struggled fiercely, bit, growled.	1
		Struggled fiercely.	2
		No struggle, relaxed.	3
		Struggled, settled, licked.	4
		No struggle, licked at hands.	5
		No struggle, froze.	6

TEST	PURPOSE	SCORE	1
RETRIEVING: Crouch beside pup and attract his attention with crumpled up paper ball. When the pup shows interest and is watching, toss the object 4–6 feet in front of pup.	Degree of willingness to work with a human. High correlation between ability to retrieve and successful guide dogs, obedience dogs, field trial dogs.	Chases object, picks up object and runs away. Chases object, stands over object, does not return. Chases object and returns with object to testor. Chases object and returns without object to testor. Starts to chase object, loses interest. Does not chase object.	1 2 3 4 5 6
TOUCH SENSITIVITY: Take puppy's webbing of one front foot and press between finger and thumb lightly then more firmly till you get a response, while you count slowly to 10. Stop as soon as puppy pulls away, or shows discomfort.	Degree of sensitivity to touch.	8–10 counts before response. 6–7 counts before response. 5–6 counts before response. 2–4 counts before response. 1–2 counts before response.	1 2 3 4 5
SOUND SENSITIVITY: Place pup in the center of area, testor or assistant makes a sharp noise a few feet from the puppy. A large metal spoon struck sharply on a metal pan twice works well.	Degree of sensitivity to sound. (Also can be a rudimentary test for deafness.)	Listens, locates sound, walks toward it barking. Listens, locates sound, barks. Listens, locates sound, shows curiosity and walks toward sound. Listens, locates the sound. Cringes, backs off, hides. Ignores sound, shows no curiosity.	1 2 3 4 5 6
SIGHT SENSITIVITY: Place pup in center of room. Tie a string around a large towel and jerk it across the floor a few feet away from puppy.	Degree of intelligent response to strange object.	Looks, attacks and bites. Looks, barks and tail-up. Looks curiously, attempts to investigate. Looks, barks, tail-tuck. Runs away, hides.	1 2 3 4 5
STRUCTURE: The puppy is gently set in a natural stance and evaluated for structure in the following categories: Straight front Front angulation Straight rear Croup angulation Shoulder Rear angulation layback *(see diagram below)*	Degree of structural soundness. Good structure is necessary.	The puppy is correct in structure. The puppy has a slight fault or deviation. The puppy has an extreme fault or deviation.	good fair poor

(Compiled by and first published in the *AKC Gazette*, March 1979.)

Straight front   Straight rear   Shoulder layback   Front angulation   Croup angulation   Rear angulation

- *Mostly 1's* A puppy that consistently scores a 1 in the temperament section of the test is an extremely dominant, aggressive puppy who can easily be provoked to bite. His dominant nature will attempt to resist human leadership, thus requiring only the most experienced of handlers. This puppy is a poor choice for most individuals and will do best in a working situation as a guard or police dog.
- *Mostly 2's* This pup is dominant and self-assured. He can be provoked to bite; however he readily accepts human leadership that is firm, consistent and knowledgeable. This is not a dog for a tentative, indecisive individual. In the right hands, he has the potential to become a fine working or show dog and could fit into an adult household, provided the owners know what they are doing.
- *Mostly 3's* This pup is outgoing and friendly and will adjust well in situations in which he receives regular training and exercise. He has a flexible temperament that adapts well to different types of environment, provided he is handled correctly. May be too much dog for a family with small children or an elderly couple who are sedentary.
- *Mostly 4's* A pup that scores a majority of 4's is an easily controlled, adaptable puppy whose submissive nature will make him continually look to his master for leadership. This pup is easy to train, reliable with kids, and, though he lacks self-confidence, makes a high-quality family pet. He is usually less outgoing than a pup scoring in the 3's, but his demeanor is gentle and affectionate.
- *Mostly 5's* This is a pup who is extremely submissive and lacking in self-confidence. He bonds very closely with his owner and requires regular companionship and encouragement to bring him out of himself. If handled incorrectly, this pup will grow up very shy and fearful. For this reason, he will do best in a predictable, structured lifestyle with owners who are patient and not overly demanding, such as an elderly couple.
- *Mostly 6's* A puppy that scores 6 consistently is independent and uninterested in people. He will mature into a dog who is not demonstrably affectionate and

who has a low need for human companionship. In general, it is rare to see properly socialized pups test this way; however there are several breeds that have been bred for specific tasks (such as basenjis, hounds, and some northern breeds) which can exhibit this level of independence. To perform as intended, these dogs require a singularity of purpose that is not compromised by strong attachments to their owner.

The remainder of the puppy test is an evaluation of obedience aptitude and working ability and provides a general picture of a pup's intelligence, spirit, and willingness to work with a human being. For most owners, a good companion dog will score in the 3 to 4 range in this section of the test. Puppies scoring a combination of 1's and 2's require experienced handlers who will be able to draw the best aspects of their potential from them.

Bibliography

Allen, Durward L. *The Wolves of Minong: Their Vital Role in a Wildlife Community.* Boston: Houghton Mifflin, 1979.

American Kennel Club. *The Complete Dog Book.* New York: Howell Book House, 1989.

Aslett, Don. *Pet Clean-Up Made Easy.* Cincinnati: Writer's Digest Books, 1988.

Bauman, Diane. *Beyond Basic Dog Training.* New York: Howell Book House, 1987.

Beck, Alan, and Aaron Katcher. *Between Pets and People: The Importance of Animal Companionship.* New York: Putnam Publishing Group, 1983.

Benjamin, Carol Lea. *Dog Problems.* Garden City: Doubleday, 1981.

———. *Mother Knows Best: The Natural Way to Train Your Dog.* New York: Howell Book House, 1985.

Bergman, Goran. *Why Does Your Dog Do That?* New York: Howell Book House, 1971.

Burnham, Patricia. *Playtraining Your Dog.* New York: St. Martin's Press, 1980.

Buytendijk, F. C. *The Mind of the Dog.* New York: Arno Press, 1973.

Campbell, William. *Behavior Problems in Dogs.* Santa Barbara: American Veterinary Publications, 1975.

Caras, Roger. *The Roger Caras Dog Book.* New York: Holt, Rinehart and Winston, 1980.

Cree, John. *Training the Alsatian.* London: Pelham, 1977.

Dunbar, Ian. *Dog Behavior.* Neptune, New Jersey: T. F. H. Publications, 1979.

Evans, Job Michael. *The Evans Guide for Counseling Dog Owners.* New York: Howell Book House, 1985.

Fiennes, Richard and Alice. *The Natural History of Dogs.* New York: Bonanza Books, 1968.

Fox, Michael W., D.V.M. *Understanding Your Dog.* New York: Coward, McCann and Geoghegan, 1974.

———. *Integrative Development of Brain and Behavior in the Dog.* Chicago: University of Chicago Press, 1971.

———. *The Soul of the Wolf.* Boston: Little, Brown, 1980.

———. *How to Be Your Pet's Best Friend.* New York: Coward, McCann and Geoghegan, 1981.

George, Jean Craighead. *How to Talk to Your Dog.* New York: Warner Books, 1985.

Hancock, Judith M. *Friendship: You and Your Dog.* New York: Dutton, 1986.

Hart, Benjamin. *The Behavior of Domestic Animals.* New York: W. H. Freeman, 1985.

Hart, Benjamin L., and Lynette A. *The Perfect Puppy: How to Choose Your Dog by Its Behavior.* New York: W. C. Freeman, 1988.

Hearne, Vicki. *Adam's Task: Calling Animals by Name.* New York: Alfred A. Knopf, 1986.

Holst, Phyllis. *Canine Reproduction: A Breeder's Guide.* Loveland, Colorado: Alpine Publications, 1985.

Lopez, Barry Holstun. *Of Wolves and Men.* New York: Charles Scribner's Sons, 1978.

Lorenz, Konrad. *Man Meets Dog.* Baltimore: Penguin Books, 1971.

McSoley, Ray. *Dog Tales.* New York: Warner Books, 1988.

Mech, L. David. *The Wolf: The Ecology and Behavior of an Endangered Species.* Garden City: Doubleday, 1970.

Monks of New Skete. *How to Be Your Dog's Best Friend.* Boston: Little, Brown, 1978.

Morris, Mark L., and Lon D. Lewis. *Feeding Dogs and Cats.* Topeka, Kansas: Mark Morris Associates, 1985.

Pinkwater, Jill, and Manus D. *Superpuppy: How to Choose, Raise and Train the Best Possible Dog for You.* New York: Seabury, 1977.

Pfaffenberger, Clarence. *The New Knowledge of Dog Behavior.* New York: Howell Book House, 1963.

Randolph, Elizabeth. *How to Help Your Puppy Grow Up to Be a Wonderful Dog.* New York: Fawcett Crest, 1987.

Riddle, Maxwell. *Dogs Through History.* Fairfax, Virginia: Denlinger's, 1987.

Rutherford, Clarice, and David H. Neil. *How to Raise a Puppy You*

Can Live With. Loveland, Colorado: Alpine Publications, 1981.

Sautter, Frederic J., and John A. Glover. *Behavior, Development and Training of the Dog.* New York: Arco, 1978.

Scott, John Paul. *Animal Behavior.* Chicago: University of Chicago Press, 1958.

———. *Early Experience and Organization of Behavior.* New York: Brooks/Cole, 1968.

Scott, John Paul, and John L. Fuller. *Genetics and the Social Behavior of the Dog.* Chicago: University of Chicago Press, 1965.

Sendak, Maurice, and M. Margolis. *Some Swell Pup, or, Are You Sure You Want a Dog?* New York: Farrar, Straus and Giroux, 1976.

Siegal, Mordecai. *A Dog for the Kids.* Boston: Little, Brown, 1984.

———. *The Good Dog Book.* New York: MacMillan, 1977.

Smith, M. L. *Eliminate on Command.* Friday Harbor, Washington: Smith-Sager Publications, 1984.

Tortora, Daniel F. *Help! This Dog Is Driving Me Crazy.* New York: Playboy Press, 1977.

———. *The Right Dog for You: Choosing a Breed That Matches Your Personality, Family and Lifestyle.* New York: Simon and Schuster, 1980.

Trumler, Eberhard. *Understanding Your Dog.* London: Faber & Faber, 1973.

Tucker, Michael. *Dog Training Made Easy.* Adelaide, Australia: Rigby, 1980.

Volhard, Joachim, and Gail Tamases Fisher. *Training Your Dog: The Step-by-Step Manual.* New York: Howell Book House, 1983.

Walkowicz, Chris, and Bonnie Wilcox. *The Complete Question and Answer Book on Dogs.* New York: Dutton, 1988.

Index

269